John Hillaby's London

By John Hillaby

Journey to the Jade Sea
Journey through Britain
Journey through Europe
Journey through love
Journey home
John Hillaby's Yorkshire

John Hillaby's London

Constable   London

First published in Great Britain 1987
by Constable and Company Limited
10 Orange Street London WC2H 7EG
Copyright © 1987 John Hillaby
Set in Linotron Bembo 11pt by
Rowland Phototypesetting Limited
Bury St Edmunds, Suffolk
Printed in Great Britain by
St Edmundsbury Press Limited
Bury St Edmunds, Suffolk

British Library CIP data
Hillaby, John
   John Hillaby's London
   1. London (England) – Description – 1981–
   I. Title
   914.21′04858   DA684.25

ISBN 0 09 465520 0

For Katie.
Daily help.
Good references.

Contents

	page
Foreword	11
Matins	15
The primrose path	30
The royal architect	50
Bob and his brethren	60
Into the maelstrom	69
Within the walls	94
The crucible	130
Upstream with Essex	150
Down to the Borough	183
City for all seasons	214
When the living is easy	252
The Iceman cometh	271
Evensong	289

Foreword

Good fortune enabled me to explore strange lands from the fringe of the Arctic to equatorial Africa. But age and ambition have frontiers of their own. Where would I now travel if I were younger, fancy-free and passports and other national restrictions were unknown? The evasive answer is not as far as I have done in the past. Experience teaches the traveller that people are the living elements of geography and the fascination of learning more about what less well-travelled people do and dream about is irresistible.

A suggestion from Ben Glazebrook, my publisher, that I might consider exploring the build and shape of London, its inhabitants and what they have meant to me professionally put a brake on romantic notions about going back to the Barrens around Lake Athabaska or that most theatrical of tropical rivers, the Ishango which meanders round the Mountains of the Moon – especially since I knew that the Redmen I had seen spearing salmon and driving caribou over cliffs no longer exist as self-sufficient tribes, and Zaire is a no-man's-land for whites. By contrast, although I have walked the streets and open spaces of this enormous city for well over forty years, what did I know of the tidal restlessness of its teeming millions, its prehistoric past buried under the West End, and its architectural splendour which has been chopped about and overshadowed by vast blocks, overpowering at close quarters and looking downright disorderly at a distance? There were other inducements to stay at home.

My wife Katie and I have often talked about leaving our top floor viewing-platform on the fringe of Hampstead and pushing off somewhere else. But we have never got around to it; Katie because she's a relative newcomer to the city nobody really knows in its totality and I because London has become as important to me as the skin of an old bear.

It will soon become apparent that this is a lightly disguised slice of urban autobiography, a foray into an estuarine swamp below two ridges of hills where world history has been made and, some of us think, undone. Middlesex has almost disappeared. That lifelong and discriminating pedestrian, Sir Ralph Wedgwood drew attention to the persistent and independent, if often forgotten existence of the county of which London is not even the county town; he cited a number of villages, such as Cranford, still hanging on with an indestructible air of good breeding in reduced and jostled circumstances. Others are doomed to nominal extinction. They are being slowly buried alive beneath loads of red-taped reports tied by intolerant bureaucrats who plan without regard for coherent architecture and the wants of strollers, loungers, fugitives from exhaust fumes, shoppers and their children. Then why, you may wonder, am I so enthusiastic about the Great Wen of William Cobbett?

Because no other city in the world known to me has such an extravagance of tree-lined streets, palatial parks, breath-catching vistas and huge skies where the celestial scene-shifters are forever at work. The complexities of contours and convection currents are such that London's weather abides by no rules, something I've looked into with help from one of those droll sprites who parade their depressions after the nine o'clock news. It is almost impossible to revise and broaden London's cramped thoroughfares in the manner of Georges Eugène Haussmann but the inquisitive pedestrian, provincial born as I am, can avoid the main drains and take to the tributaries, the narrow streets drawn by Doré and sketched in detail by Dickens.

You may pore over their history from a hundred or more books but none, as far as I know, tells you much about the earliest known Londoners, those flint-knappers who, a quarter of a million years ago, poled their way across a sluggish estuary whose successive mudbanks are now marked by the Strand and Oxford Street. My business for long has been with natural history, history and prehistory, and if I go on overmuch about the ancient hippos and enormous cats found under Landseer's lions in Trafalgar Square, then turn the page over to where, in a nearby street, you may be surprised as I was to encounter eighteen grossly desecrated statues hewn from Derbyshire limestone by that creator of sombre mysteries, Jacob Epstein. Like A. E. Housman I have tried to pluck some flowers in season before desire shall fail. Honest attribution of sources is not the least of my problems. I owe so much to so many.

For fundamental data about buildings I am hugely indebted to the man I have called the Master, the incomparable, the late Sir Nikolaus Pevsner and his learned and attractive successor, Bridget Cherry who never failed to answer enquiries and put me on to all sorts of little-known architectural treasures. My neighbour and friend of long standing, Otto Koenigsberger, definer and designer of human habitats, an architect and teacher of architects in the grand sense of the word, introduced me first to Leslie Ginsberg, the distinguished planning consultant and then to Sir John Summerson, historian and former Curator of the Soane Museum in London, a man who breathes scholarship. On several occasions Sir John invited me to his fine home in Georgian St John's Wood where I'm pretty sure I fatigued him with questions about John Nash and those giants of late Classicism. Eric Robinson of University College, London put life into building-stone by taking me out on geological walks, showing me, as he has shown so many of his students, the fascination and practical value of the stratigraphic table. Others I'm much obliged to include my former neighbour, Rabbi Dr Norman Soloman; Arthur Bell, Director of the Royal Botanic Gardens at Kew; Bernard Moore, former Head of External News in what used to be the BBC Overseas Service; Douglas Matthews and his staff of the London Library; Bernard Kaukas; Leslie Randall; John Wade; Frank Allen

'The Apothecary'; and those valued companions of my youth, Philip Hartley and David Wood. Prudence Fay of Constable has been quick to weed out many of my inconsistencies in the manner of her father-in-law, my friend and mentor, the late Gerard Fay, London Editor of the *Guardian*. Those frailties that remain are entirely my own and for once I am at a loss to say what I really think about my wife.

Katie has been at me since this work began nearly three years ago. In addition to supplying innumerable ideas she helped me with the photography, although all the processing was done by our highly professional colleague, Corry Bevington who supplemented our efforts with some shots beyond our competence and supplied the colour illustrations for the jacket. Reproduction of the material quoted from Benny Green's enviably good book, *The Streets of London*, is by permission of the publishers, Pavilion (Michael Joseph). The pictures on pages 68 and 133 which appeared in that book are by kind permission of the London Transport Museum. For the works quoted from *London Lines*, edited by Kenneth Baker and published by Methuen, I am grateful to Jonathan Cape for permission to reproduce Adrian Mitchell's poems on pages 119 and 162; to Methuen for Elizabeth Bartlett's lines on page 42; and to Peterloo Poets for the extract from U. A. Fanthorpe's poem on page 173, which originally appeared in *Standing To* (1982). The picture on page 272 is by Michael J. Stead. David Piper's admirable *Companion Guide to London* (Collins) is too set about with shrewd opinions to be opened often by an author in search of his own definitions.

Were there no limits to the length of this book I should have introduced some amiable villains from the East End, especially my old comrades at arms who sometimes led me astray and those neighbours we meet regularly on our early morning walks across Hampstead Heath. They include sweepers up, caretakers, postmen, and Colin Rudd and Frank Yates, two cheerful cops.

J. H.
1987

Matins

The notebooks on which much of this narrative is based are cross-referenced to a filing system and a host of works which at the time I regarded as quotably authoritative. In stationery quality they range from an elegant calf-bound affair, a birthday gift from an indulgent aunt, to thick cloth-boarded diaries of the kind used by game wardens to record what they see in the field. They have been brought back from various parts of the world. Their contents differ widely, too, but essentially they all stem from the first entry in Aunt Violet's almost forgotten birthday present. It is dated 14 September 1944.

An exhilarating, an anxious time. We had but recently taken up humble lodgings, our first in Hampstead. The war seemed all but won. Charles de Gaulle had entered Paris. The US First and the British Second Armies were thrusting into German soil. Nobody seemed to know where George Patton had got to, not even Eisenhower. But people were whistling 'Don't Fence Me In' and reading *Forever Amber*. Yet there was still much to be done. We knew that, since enormous rockets were falling on London.

I awoke that morning to hear on the radio that the Second Belorussian Army under Konstatin Rokossovsky had entered the eastern suburbs of Warsaw. The fact is notebooked. It also says it was a marvellous morning. On the doormat I noticed a letter and opened it with some trepidation. From the hand-writing I knew it had been shoved through the letter box by a woman rudely referred to by a few of us as Mouldy Maudie, a little moppet who, though young in years, combined the zealotry of an Ayatollah with the command of an RSM. I feared her, I liked her because of her zealotry which lay in finding things, mostly weird things: insectivorous plants, poisonous fungi, carrion beetles, slime moulds. She was a considerable naturalist and a considerable nuisance since on short acquaintanceship she occasionally turned up late at night, once with a little owl in her pocket which shrieked and gave our resident landlord, a Mr George Reynolds, the impression that all three of us were engaged in unnatural commerce. Her name, I should explain, arose from the fact that she had about her the odour of very old and rather damp newspapers. The note said briefly: 'Have found *the* lily. Will see you at Hampstead Gate, Kenwood, at 8.30 a.m. M.'

To handle a woman with a bee in her bonnet requires an apiarist far more nimble than I am and, within minutes, shorn of all initiative, I was climbing over Parliament Hill on the Heath, the better to collect my wits. Maybe it saved my life since otherwise I should have gone straight to Kenwood.

When I came within sight of the Highgate open-air swimming pond which – fortunately – was unpopulated, the sky was split open, first with a blood-red splash and then with a huge blob of smoke. There followed a pause, can it have been two, three or four seconds? I can't remember. I was terrified by an ear-splitting bang. It seemed like the end of the world. Some hardware hurtled down into the pond, raising a water spout as high as the high-diving board. Something else crashed into Kenwood.

Maudie was waiting there, somewhat impatiently I thought. Before I had time to recover my breath, she almost shouted, 'I've found 'em! Three plants. You know. The May Lily. It's a three-star rarity.'

'B-b-but what about that bang?' I spluttered. Maudie looked up contemptuously.

'Oh, it's one of those bloody rockets. A good job it went off in the air.'

Together we inspected *Maianthemum bifolium*, a rather in-conspicuous lily with two heart-shaped leaves on the stem and spikes of little white flowers. We agreed to photograph it, which it's unfortunate we never did since the lily has not been seen in the south of England again. Nowadays I have the feeling that someone in search of botanical notoriety planted it there. But that morning we talked of this and that and parted, she in search of badger droppings and I to the village for a newspaper with my mind more on man-made thunderbolts than *Maianthemum*.

It is possible, though unlikely, that if I hadn't found another rarity on the way home, Aunt Violet's notebook would have remained in Harrods' gift box to this day but with the sort of coincidence which I regard as a sign from on high I looked, fascinated, at one of the most beautiful beetles in this country, an entomological treasure. In those days I knew only a bit about botany, and birds too. But insects were a different matter, especially beetles. I had first collected them in short pants. And there on a neighbour's bush clambered the Rose chafer, *Cemtonia aurata*, an exquisite insect with a golden gloss over its shiny iridescent body, a beetle which, set in a pendant of Nubian gold, might have graced Nefertiti's bosom. I had never seen the species outside museum collections. I took the creature home in a matchbox. That night I filled in page one of Notebook One, the first of many.

Since the lower end of the Heath, that portion known as Parliament Hill, lay immediately beyond our landlord's garden, it was no difficult matter for a jobbing journalist to quarter some 500 acres below what I still refer to as Mouldy Maudie's Wood. I carried corked tubes and sweeping nets. I sank jam-jar traps into carefully selected and meticulously mapped out-of-the-way places where courting couples often fondled each other. But not at seven o'clock in the morning. I had become an ardent coleopterist. It gave point and purpose to pre-breakfast walks hitherto devoted to sombre reflections on the inability of Fleet Street editors and the Controllers of the BBC to recognize latent genius. But I was living the life of exalted errancy. And rather enjoying it.

You will find no mention of insect hunting in Urquhart's

List of Game Manuals (1893). The physical hardships in urban habitats are slight. A risk perhaps of anosmia, the impairment of the sense of smell provoked by the injudicious employment of formaldehyde. I suffer from it still. But that ranks small among those whose lives have been devoted to the pursuit of ubiquitous locust and tsetse fly. Beetle-hunters get off lightly.

What threw a spanner into the creaking machinery of my marital relationship was the purchase of an expensive low-power binocular microscope and a second-hand copy of Gangelbauer's *Die Kafer von Mittleuropa*, the Handbook of European Beetles, from funds which should have been devoted entirely to mutual enjoyment including that of a six-month-old breastling. In vain I protested that without that four-inch-thick volume I couldn't distinguish between the speciation of *Halipus*, a rare genus of lentil-sized water beetles. And there was, I discovered, a colony of those creatures in a pond scarcely a hundred yards from the source of the Fleet, the streamlet which led down to the street of newspaper offices. In brief, my wife had no love for the Coleoptera, that Order of insects which fascinated Darwin both before and after the publication of his best-seller.

A year later this impoverished naturalist had captured, named and mounted 280 species within a mile of his lonely bedroom. Notebook One was impressively spattered with scientific names, and the paper he read to the Hampstead Scientific Society on 'Some Observations on the Carabidae of Hampstead Heath' received polite applause and a five-line mention in the *Hampstead and Highgate Express*.

About that time Mouldy Maudie lost her job at the laundry. It might have been that owl but, resourceful girl that she was, she eloped, to put it politely, with a US serviceman who admired the way she pressed his pants. Her departure to some point south of the river deprived us, temporarily of the services of an entomologist, a post subsequently filled superbly well by a typographer from the East End called Freddie Buck and an elderly lady who stalked dragonflies with a pair of field-glasses. We thought something might be done together, a resolution fortified by a kindly and influential man

who opened magic casements on my extremely narrow view of the world.

Hampstead Heath is roughly bisected by a high road with a famous pub at each end, Jack Straw's Castle and the Spaniards. Below the Castle lies a patch of sandy heath and an infamous wood which I'll come to later. On one early morning foray I noticed a man swatting at something with a collecting net. I had met him several times before a friend told me that Sir Christopher Andrewes, the distinguished virologist and a much-travelled man, spent time on the Heath on his way to and from the nearby laboratories of the Medical Research Council. When we began to meet fairly regularly, exchanging notes, he admitted that collecting insects was a distinct relief from the long hours he spent peering into an electron microscope. In addition to the work that brought him fame throughout the world, he was an outstanding entomologist, studying various groups because his children were interested. He had a large family.

'Children tend to be over-awed by a father who knows too much,' he said, 'so when the first youngster began to look around for himself I dropped my interest in gall wasps and got him going on beetles which at the time I didn't know much about. We studied them together for a year or two but he turned to postage stamps. By this time my second child had taken up butterflies and moths. Much the same thing happened. He switched off for soccer.' This apparently happened three or four times, leaving their father, as he put it, 'to peg away at all sorts of things on my own'.

Sir Christopher suggested I should join the London Natural History Society and go further afield with specialists. Without lapsing into the jargon of ecology he continued to point out what he called the most interesting places on the Heath, explaining how they got to be that way. One of them was the infamous wood where figures were to be seen flitting through the trees at dusk. Many years elapsed before I discovered it was a brothel for weather-proof homosexuals.

The society affectionately referred to as 'the London Nats'

was as much part and parcel of that decade of optimism as the flamboyant architecture of the South Bank with its exhibitions and Royal Festival Hall. The Society's membership grew so rapidly that the botanists and bird-watchers, the geologists and entomologists broke up into inter-related sections which surveyed not only the heaths, commons and parks around the capital but also the inhabitants of water-filled bomb-holes and prostrate buildings, especially in the vicinity of St Paul's. Far more than the mere names and local addresses of beetles began to appear in my notebooks. With, occasionally, a geologist as a companion I took to walking down to Fleet Street by way of Langham Place, noticing how the Portland stone differed in its content of fossils of oysters and cockleshells, sea urchins and starfish. And the colour varied, too, ranging from purplish to ochreous tones even among that which had been cleaned of its patina of soot.

Not that any insects went unnoticed. One bright morning I recall seeing a tattered-looking butterfly, the Comma, a relative of the Red Admiral, dancing round the window-boxes of a big insurance office in Fleet Street. It's curious how the usurers like to put out a folksy front. But how had it got there? Its larvae, I knew, fed on nettles and much searching disclosed a large patch in the adjacent ruins of Middle Temple Yard. With some difficulty I sweated out 200 words in the somewhat archaic style of what was then the *Manchester Guardian* and submitted it to their London editor. No words of mine had ever before appeared in that paper and I'm pretty sure the suggested title did it. With immoderate pride the next morning I stuck down a cutting into my notebook headed 'Commas in Fleet Street'.

Others followed. I had struck a small but unworked seam. By that time we had moved from our apartment on the edge of the Heath to a more spacious place in a less fashionable quarter of Hampstead where, with a remarkable view across London, I have lived ever since. Each day at dusk almost uncountable numbers of starlings begin to assemble in Kenwood and fly down to night roosts in St James's Park and the adjacent squares. And at dawn they return, flying within sight of our windows. They keep to rigidly determined flight lines and the height at which they fly is related to the barometric pressure. We followed them on bicycles to determine their route and the *Guardian* dropped me a polite note saying that for the time being they would not require anything more about starlings.

I switched to the fauna of the City and the West End. There were owls in Covent Garden which fed on rodents among the refuse. Large numbers of semi-wild cats began to appear in areas flattened by the raids. The news that they were being trapped and put down provoked indignant Letters to the Editor. I was commissioned to report meetings of the Field Sports Society ('Tallyhosis') and Guppy Clubs and importers of tortoises and goldfish which were in short supply after the war. The *Guardian* paid badly but when, eventually, I pupated and emerged as Our Zoological Correspondent I wore the byline like an honorary doctorate.

The change in status meant that one could seek opinions from the directors and staff of learned societies, institutions and museums. The *Guardian* had its own table at the back of El Vino, that wine and spirit shop in Fleet Street where editors drank, assistant editors plotted and thoughtful lawyers looked on. They were years of wonder and seemingly endless opportunity. I felt charged with the responsibility of recording minutiae which brought life to the dull thoroughfares of the capital. But A. P. Wadsworth, the editor in Manchester, sent me another polite note saying he felt sure there was more to be said about the Zoo than the fact that at dusk on cold nights the howling of wolves could be heard in Camden Town.

A problem here, since I didn't much like the look of pinioned flamingos nor the sight of large animals in small cages. I tried to get into the vaults of the Natural History Museum where somebody assured me there were still unopened boxes marked 'C. Darwin. Return to HMS *Beagle*'. A rebellious janitor leaked the fact that London's much loved but overwhelming pigeons were being enticed into the quadrangle of Somerset House after dusk and quietly knocked off with doped grain. Some interesting details about investigations into what turned out to be the archaeological hoax of all time came by a very devious route. It concerned the Piltdown skull, my first big story.

If he is any good at his business the correspondent who specializes soon becomes an expert in one broad field. He becomes an expert in experts. For the inestimable benefits of the quotable or off-the-record opinion he gains the confidence of those who he thinks know more about a particular subject than anyone else. My list of approachable authorities slowly increased as my enthusiasm for beetles diminished. It virtually came to an end after I had captured and classified between 600 and 700 specimens which could then be found on the Heath.

There is a class of newspapermen called science correspondents prepared to tackle any subject from astrophysics to zoology and, for ten years, I did what I could to practise their craft in Europe for both the *Guardian* and the *New York Times*. At the National Physical Laboratory in Teddington I even managed to examine with some difficulty a huge rocket captured in Holland, about which more later. But as I see from entries in my notebooks, there were areas, large areas, about which I knew little and wasn't really competent to pass much in the way of an opinion, received or otherwise. There were even larger areas in which I was interested but for which space can rarely be found in the ephemeral columns of a newspaper. They have to do with getting to know more and more about living in the heart of London.

This is a clumsy way of expressing something which I shall try to clarify by recollections of two people. The first is Eric Warmington, a classicist who, like Christopher Andrewes, refreshed a high degree of professionalism with what he knew about and loved out of doors, mostly while walking around London. His knowledge lay in plants and birdlife. He taught me about both. He had a phenomenal ear for bird song and calls and could sense where both plants and birds were likely to be found.

I recall the occasion when we attended a soirée of the Linnaean Society, that resort of distinguished botanists behind the iron gates of Burlington House in Piccadilly. We had paid our respects to the President and his lady. We had stayed so late that we felt it best to support each other on our way back to the tube station beyond Leicester Square. In that bedlam of entertainment on a cold November night neon lights flashed,

hot-chestnut sellers cried their wares, cab drivers honked. The noise was terrific.

Eric unlinked himself and peered upwards into the night. 'Listen!' he said. 'Listen!' And with great difficulty above that uproar I could just make out a faint but continuous '*Seep . . . seep . . . seep*'. 'Redwings,' he said rapturously. 'They've come back!' It must have been a large flock since we heard it for several minutes. After launching their families on the Russian border the migratory thrushes were flying in to where the living was easier.

In quite a different way Francis Hemming broadened my view of all that was meant by the words 'natural history', that is without the naturalists' besetting obsession with collecting things. Like Christopher Andrewes, Hemming had an all-round knowledge of biology. But he will be remembered as the central figure, the Secretary, during a difficult period of the International Commission on Zoological Nomenclature.

All living things from the lowliest of plants and animals to the largest of vertebrates have to be named precisely, often in a mixture of Latin and Greek. Without internationally recognized scientific names they cannot be exactly defined and identified. This is not merely a matter of vanity to someone who discovers a new species and wants to perpetuate his name, although I got to know a prominent zoologist who lost both his wife and an associate professorship when it was discovered that three marine worms he discovered bore the lightly disguised names of laboratory assistants with whom he had been on intimate terms.

In the case of a carrier of a disease which could reach plague proportions, say a flea or a liver fluke, the precise name and a precise description of that carrier is of enormous medical importance. To someone unacquainted with the anatomy of fleas there would appear to be very little in the matter of structural differences between the homely species (*Pulex irritans*) which bites and tickles but is otherwise harmless and *Xenopsylla Cheopis* which is the carrier of bubonic plague.

Nomenclature, the method of assigning scientific names to organisms, stands four-square on an elaborate Code of eighty Articles and innumerable clauses which, since it has to be revised periodically, has provoked as many international disputes as current wrangles over the European Common Market. At these congresses of categorizers I listened, fascinated, to delegates shouting at each other over such points as the gender of protozoa and family connections between giant pandas and racoons. And yet, essentially, the Code is a logical structure in which everything throughout the whole animal kingdom, including the relationship of Man to the great apes, can be related to something else.

Except for one congress where a copy of the Code was chucked at an Australian delegate who was unduly insistent about what should be done about the Scyphozoa (jellyfish) there was usually little that could be telexed to Manchester and New York about these meetings. But for me it put much into perspective. Beetles became even less important: they were just an Order within a Super Order. It was good to be able to recognize the general structure of all insects, of course. But no more than that. Here was a definable philosophy related to the Doctrine of Categories. I took it far beyond the boundaries of biology. Could it, I wondered, be applied to human populations, to communities, to the boroughs of London, that collection of villages, Eliot's unreal city?

In this I was encouraged by the *New York Times*. There was occasional space in its supplements for 'sketches' of different quarters of the capital many of which can be seen from this window where the view spans an arc of almost 180 degrees, with the Surrey Hills to the south some twenty-five miles away. And yet it's far from easy to grasp the dimensions of the 'dear, damned distracting town' that moved the blind Milton to exclaim, 'What would I now give but for one more look at the sun, and the waters and the gardens of this fair City?' There is first the consideration of popular epithets.

Contemporary London, we are told, 'is too big, too mixed, too loud and too lovable for circumscription'. It is a bad habit one hates to lose since 'no Londoner and nobody else really knows the place'. A more cynical view is that Greater London is a collection of peripheral villages which, since they can't expand inwards, have become shabby townships of dubious identity, overlapping each other, threatening the continued existence of the protective Green Belt. Paris is more compact by far and Manhattan has been obliged to expand skywards because of the absence of any other places in which to grow. We might therefore consider how it came to be called London.

I cannot go along with the guidebooks that say the Romans adapted the Celtic name of *Lyn-din* (the river place) since, as far as I can make out, there is no evidence for any pre-Roman habitation in the vicinity of the Wall and the Tower although there is an old flint arsenal – older by nearly half a million years than the coming of Claudius and his elephants – much further downstream. Eilert Ekwall, that learned student of place-names, is probably nearer the mark with his tentative suggestion that the *Londinium* of Tacitus is derived from an Old Irish stem *Londo* meaning wild or bold. But why Irish? James Bone, the 'London Perambulator' of the *Guardian*, had a nicer notion. He turned the word over in his mind. He said it aloud, dwelling on that equipoise of syllables. To some it sounds like a warning, to some like applause. In his opinion only one other great capital has its might resounding in its name and that is Rome or Roma, for, say it how you will, it puts you in mind of the shout of legions or long waves breaking on the shore. But not better than London which has about it the sound of distant thunder.

As with its names so with its inhabitants. In my Doctrine of Categories there were three kinds of Londoners. There were those who were born here. They accept the size, the noise, the variety, for London has more of everything than other cities. They have grown used to it. Next come the commuters who work but don't sleep here, and I suppose they have got used to being pulled and shoved around twice a day. To them Charing Cross and Piccadilly are places where they change trains without coming to the surface. Their London is an office and a pub or an eating-place within walking distance of where they work. Then come those Londoners who, like myself, were born somewhere else and came here in search of something. 'Commuters,' says E. B. White, 'give a city its tidal restlessness, natives give it solidity and continuity, but the settlers give it passion.'

I brought next to nothing to the intellectual life of where I quickly settled down but through friends, neighbours and professional contacts London offered me more than could be easily absorbed. There were scientists, especially zoologists and prehistorians, who were not averse to being consulted; architects put me in touch with City planners and those who advise the planners and arbitrate at public enquiries. There were medical men, particularly pharmacologists and researchers in foundations, trusts and teaching hospitals, who were sympathetically disposed towards my *naïf* enquiries often, I suspect, because it must have been apparent that I knew so little. I was constantly surprised by what to others seemed obvious.

Among those discoveries was one so simple but to me so important that I have never been able to set it to paper to my entire satisfaction. It is that whilst walking is a recognized way of enjoying the country, it is also one of the best, the most pleasurable and by no means the slowest ways of moving across the constantly changing face of a large city. The proposition is set about with a number of qualifications. You must, of course, enjoy the physical pleasure of walking and have feet capable of withstanding the pounding of pavements. But given curiosity, a little knowledge and a reasonable sense of direction, it is usually possible to walk to a place in only a little more time – say half as much again – than it would take to reach the destination by public transport, without all the hassle, the waiting, the getting on and off buses and underground trains.

We shall therefore take some walks across London from north to south and from east to west. Several other quarters will be considered, not least the river, that street paved with water where Gloriana incessantly queened it up and down. 'Traitorous river,' said James Bone since, during two wars, she signalled London to the enemy.

The foggy town that Doré engraved and Dickens and Eliot wrote about is no longer with us. With the exception of those arch-polluters of the atmosphere, the big power-stations, relatively little smog-producing coal is burnt. But fogs have been replaced by violent storms due, I suspect, to a ceiling of oil and petrol vapour that hangs over the estuarine swamp. At night the sky glows a weird orange colour from mercury-vapour lamps. There is a huge half-subdued roar almost everywhere from circular roads and penetrative motorways. But there is still much to be seen in certain half-deserted streets so, in the manner of J. Alfred Prufrock, let us go then, you and I, first looking down on this great city.

The primrose path

From the City to Westminster and beyond, most of Central London can be seen best from the top of seven hills below which the sluggish Thames crawls into its saline estuary some fifteen miles to the east of Gallions Reach. The hills lie across ridges of high ground bounded by an equilateral triangle with a base line from Richmond east to Blackheath above Woolwich and an apex on the northern heights of Alexandra Palace in the Haringey district. The sides of that triangle are close to twelve miles in length. They are not to be recommended as routes for a walk of any kind. I have done it once and never intend to do it again. But when you reach them the vistas vary enormously in variety. Some, such as views from Alexandra Palace, are vast in extent but distinctly dull. With the exception of the huge Palace and its gardens there is scarcely a memorable feature. Others are intimate in the extreme. There is, for example, a narrow glade in an overgrown wood just inside the Star and Garter entrance to Richmond Park through which one and only one building can be seen on the most distant skyline and that building is St Paul's.

The views of London from Highgate and Hampstead Heath are probably the best known. The Spaniards Road which pulls them together like a turn-buckle affords fascinating glimpses of the whole City through gaps in a screen of trees above a leafy rise. Far-distant buildings appear and disappear momentarily. I often wonder whether that's how the world appears to an over-groomed Old English sheepdog. Other vistas may demand attention later but our first perambulation down to the Strand and the Thames will start from Primrose Hill in North London. The vista is not only intimate. It is almost tangible. The foreground is literally at your feet. For me it has enormous familiarity since I walked that way many hundreds of times en route for Fleet Street. It usually takes about an hour and a half and the going is downhill all the way.

The hill is of no great height, only a little more than 200 feet. The northern slopes are prim but prosaic. Scattered clumps of thorn trees and intersecting paths leave you wholly unprepared for the panorama which appears on the crest. By day on nearly any sort of day it is almost impossible not to stare around from east to west, up the river and down. What is the essence of it? There are cities more beautiful by far. Seen from any high point such as the Palisades, New York is an essay in verticals. In Paris the Sacred Heart looks down on an orderliness of streets. There is no apparent order about London. Its size, its heavyweight strength is the remnant legacy of wealth accumulated from the greatest modern empire in the world. Viewed in the round it is simply bigger than anywhere else and has more of most things, including ugliness. But not from Primrose Hill at dusk when high-rise filing cabinets begin to dissolve like the Cheshire Cat and leave in their place scores and scores of neon-lit jewellery boxes.

Over a period of forty years I have seen the gradual high rise of London correspond with a monumental fall in the quality of what can be seen from the floor of the capital. To me the curious thing is that Richard Seifert, perhaps Britain's best known post-war architect, the man who spoilt the view by building no fewer than 500 shove-'em-up-quick office blocks and released a herd of touristic leviathans during the hotel-building boom in the mid-'seventies, protests that he has no wish whatever to see our great cities submerged into skylines that can only be viewed from the street. He wants them to be seen from panoramic points of vantage. I wish I could see it that way. In fact I wish I knew what he meant.

Seifert's 'Beirut Baroque' has drawn more critical fire than the work of any architect since John Nash began to burden Regent's Park with something close to palaces which were to be the terminal point of the great street that now carries the Prince Regent's name. Seifert, the tweediest of our architectural knights, seems to relish all that is said about him. He blinks behind his pebbly glasses; he calls himself a post-modernist and appears wholly unmoved by the fact that Deyan Sudjic, one of the most vociferous of his critics, says that his works are 'not uniformly dreadful; rather they are conventional, third-rate reflections of the prevailing norm of contemporary design'. They range, says Sudjic, 'from reach-me-down imitations of Marcel Breuer in the case of Centre Point to cut-price post-modernism and crude Victorian pastiche for his most recent efforts'.

Could this be the envy and intense irritation of members of the profession who lack the irrepressible Colonel's considerable skills? It could be. Sudjic talks of Seifert's 'legendary skill for creative interpretations of the rules of the planning system', implying that he knows more about municipal legislation than the classical Orders.

When I first walked over Primrose Hill some two or three times a week not long after the end of the Second War-to-end-all-wars I greeted St Paul's and Big Ben and the even taller Victoria Tower as one might old friends. They were the outstanding symbols of the City and Westminster which had miraculously survived the bombing. A glance to the east assured me that at least the tower of the Caledonian Road market had survived and Pentonville Prison too. St Pancras Station, that Grimms' fairy-tale castle, still raised its pinnacles and turrets to the sky. And was that sabre-like flash to the south-east London's river at Limehouse Reach or tomato sheds on the flanks of Blackheath? Behind them all stand the hills of Surrey, not in a great wall but in a great heave like an advancing wave though not as high as they appear from my study window. The south-west used to be marked by the Roman Catholic Cathedral and that other power-house at Lots Road, its four chimneys like an upturned table. Used to be I said. They are largely point-blocked out nowadays.

Despite everything the orchestra stalls of Primrose Hill haven't changed much over the years. Although the old thorns are, of course, more gaunt in the autumn than they used to be they still house flocks of berry-seeking goldfinches. At the foot of that great slope are the gates, the walls of London Zoo with its moon-range, the Mantegna-like mountains of the Mappin Terraces from which, as I reported to the *Guardian*, the yowling of wolves and coyotes, the hoink-hoink of sea-lions, whooping of gibbons and the shriek of fish eagles can be heard a mile away. Today many of the animal houses are new and the net-like aviary on aluminium stilts, designed by Lord Snowdon, is no longer flawed. To start with many of the exotic birds escaped into neighbouring gardens.

All this I saw recently as through new spectacles since I had a most excellent guide, a member of the Primrose Hill Society. The kite-flyers stared up at their colourful tadpoles in the sky and old folk walked up the hill in the sweaty wake of joggers. Several small dogs on short leads all but strangled themselves when boisterously beset and barked at by free-ranging hounds. Few were called to heel. Dogs have a whale of a time as they race up and down those grassy slopes.

My informant lived nearby and said that after a busy day's work there was something almost sacramental in being able to walk up to the summit and look around. Such a simple statement that, but how many city-dwellers can claim as many central parks as Londoners enjoy? Close to my old landmark, the Market Tower, he pointed out something I had never been able to identify before, a sprawl of buildings which were, he said, the warehouses where goods brought to London on the old horse-drawn barges were switched to puffing billies at the rail junction. By a trick of perspective, intimate little churches seemed to be peering out shyly from behind point-blocks a mile or more away. Likewise, the Post Office Tower appeared to be standing on the roof of the Zoo's new Elephant House, and the Shell Buildings, perhaps the ugliest block in London, reduced Big Ben to the size of a child's crayon. If I seem to have it in for those blocks, I'm hanged if I can see how they can ever inspire affection or be distinguished one from another. My guide hoped that the children in prams would grow up to find primroses growing on the hill again. Saplings have been planted to nurture those shade-lovers which, together with buttercups, daisies and bluebells, are among the most-loved flowers in Britain.

Nobody knows when the last wild primroses were seen there. Eton College which owned the land until about a hundred years ago was persuaded to hand it over to the public in return for a piece of Crown property near Windsor. The top of the hill on which the Prince Regent thought of building a palace (he had many thoughts on this subject) had been crowned by a battery of ack-ack guns during the war. I strode down to Regent's Park on a steep path on which a fit man feels obliged to walk fast. A sharp turn to the right and you are on St Mark's Bridge and the fairest stretch of the canal in North London.

In addition to the geologist who told me how Portland stone, like the plane tree, became the essence of the streets of London, I recall walking down that steep slope in the company of other memorable characters. The first that comes to mind is Tom Stephenson, creator of the Pennine Way, that grand old man of the Ramblers' Association who did so much to establish rights of way in the period between the wars when walkers were ranked by gamekeepers as vermin. He had business in town and I was training for the first of my long-distance walks.

What he told me about gear, gait and pack-load distribution has long since become part of my pedestrian capital. It is less easy to describe his views on organized walks, especially those on newly blazed trails, since he foresaw, as John Ruskin did, that thousands would eventually set out to savour the solitude which their coming destroyed.

Another companion of several occasions was the late Philip Hope-Wallace, the *Guardian*'s distinguished music critic and an old friend of mine who lived in nearby St John's Wood. He frequently walked through the park on his way to the BBC. It temporarily cleared his head of what he delicately referred to as latent crapulence or 'the primrose path to the everlasting bonfire'. On one spring morning he wanted to know something about bird song, the subject of a broadcast he was giving on composers who imitated their calls instrumentally. Perhaps Respighi and Vivaldi. The heavily scented hawthorn flowered. He mused on Proust, on the hedges of Combray and the persistence of memory. Not that he liked the scent himself. Too heavy. Like privet, he said.

The lower slopes of Primrose Hill are far from rich in bird song. They are too open. After much quartering about I managed to get fairly close to an insistent wren, a hedge sparrow, the stammer of a chaffinch and a distant blackbird. Philip seemed rather disappointed. Suddenly a cuckoo flew overhead, loudly proclaiming its name. Philip looked up, smiled and imitated the call. 'Almost a major third,' he said, 'but Daquin and Delius did it better.' The notion is note-booked.

On the canal, barges with washing flying were snugly moored under an aquatic avenue of chestnuts. Several long-boats chugged along, one of them with a narrow dog in the cockpit, an immense Borzoi. Do barge-owners go in for two-dimensional breeds? This is a good place to watch for barges heading for Camden Town since there's always the chance they will foul the sharp bend just beyond the bridge. Within my experience young boys used to dive from the bridge for pennies thrown into the water. But the residents objected to the bare bums on the bridge-rail and spoil-sport police were brought in to deter the divers.

Immediately across Prince Albert Road from the head-quarters of the Zoological Society stands the gate of the Broad Walk of Regent's Park. As that walk extends in one dead straight mile towards the glorious Ionic colonnades of Park Crescent, the gate with its notice printed in twenty languages invoking visitors to use the litter bins is virtually the back door to the only part of the London of John Nash which remains almost wholly undisturbed. His architecture surrounds the whole of the Park.

In a sense the Broad Walk is a ghost walk. It might have become the Royal Mile of the capital, connecting in one broad sweep everything associated with the Court, Parliament and Law around Westminster and St James's with the palace that was never built on Primrose Hill. Today it is a leisurely parade ground for nannies and their charges and lovers and countless numbers of visitors, and since it is within sound but not within sight of the traffic that swirls around the Park who shall say it is not better the way it is? But since it is a ghost walk and a very beautiful one at that, we might profitably call up some of its contemporary familiars.

The year is 1811, a portentous year in view of what followed. The Russians have seized Belgrade. With victories at Fuentes de Onoro and Albuera, the Iron Duke is pursuing his relentless way towards Madrid. At home John Rennie has built Waterloo Bridge and Jane Austen is launching a book called *Sense and Sensibility*. George III, completely mad, has been confined to Windsor Castle and the Prince of Wales with a marked interest in women and architecture has taken over as the Prince Regent.

After years of shilly-shallying it had become quite clear that something had to be done about extensive Crown land on the very fringe of north London, an area known as Mary by the Bourne Park alongside a stream, the Bourne, with a notorious piece of furniture on its lower reaches, the Tyburn tree. The land had been leased to farmers and in 1811 the leases were due to fall in. One remarkable man foresaw that 'on the return of Peace, the Town may be extended there'. The words are those of John Fordyce who in 1793 had been appointed Surveyor-General of His Majesty's Land Revenue. A very shrewd man and one little recognized as a town-planner. What was wanted first and foremost, he knew, was an overall plan and a central highway, the much talked about New Street that would link the enormous possibilities of the new and unbuilt with the old and congested property around St James's. A new Wren had arisen and without his foresight we might have heard less about Nash, that ambitious and rather ugly little man with an attractive wife. Unfortunately, after inviting competitive architects to submit plans for what Fordyce foresaw in astonishing detail – from fine homesteads, a church and accessible markets right down to sewers, stands for hackney coaches and fire-stations – Fordyce died.

There is still much of a mystery about how Nash contrived to grab the coveted opportunity. And about much else concerning him too. It is not even known where he was born. He did not wish it to be known. He went bankrupt early in his career and yet suddenly this moderately successful architect acquired a fortune. Could it have been his shadowy association with the Prince Regent who was not averse to borrowing his friends' wives? Usually they were casual affairs. It is possible that Mrs Nash, née Mary Anne Bradley, was among them, but the friendship persisted and she adopted five children said to have been 'remotely related to her'. On this as on other matters her husband was understandably reticent. But it didn't matter much. The new Prince Regent was said to have been 'very impressed' by Nash's designs for what became Regent's Park. He thought it would 'quite eclipse' what they were doing in Paris in honour of Napoleon who at the time was at the gates of Oldenburg and thinking about how to reach Moscow.

Nash worked hard. He worked incessantly. He was involved in intrigues and stern parliamentary enquiries. He made a fortune and lost it. There is a bizarre story about how his debtors tried to snatch his body for ransom on its way to the grave. Although what he left behind in stucco-fronted brick can scarcely be disregarded on this perambulation we must leave him awhile and say something about the Park and the adjacent Zoo.

My attitude to a thick file of dated cuttings about what went on in that huge menagerie may be likened to that of a lover who flicks through a bundle of turbulent letters when the affairs is long over and done with. The *Guardian* was at the bottom of it. In addition to its self-conscious liberalism, the paper's attitude towards caged animals became subjectively coloured, I discovered, by a somewhat irascible assistant editor who had been bitten by an ape in his boyhood. He told me so, and no story of mine about the arrival or behaviour of some exotic animal stood much chance of appearing in print unless I justified its incarceration on the grounds that it might otherwise have perished in the wild. Until the World Wildlife Fund turned the phrase 'Man's irreplaceable possessions' into something close to a cliché, I kept to variations of the line that not a few endangered species such as the Javan rhinoceros and the Arabian oryx had no future whatever unless they were bred in captivity and released under surveillance.

It followed that stories about escapes from the Garden went down rather well with that zoophobic editor. There was Goldie the golden eagle who achieved world coverage as a cage-buster. It got out three times. On the one occasion when I saw the bird on the loose it had taken to swooping on small dogs on the playing-fields around the Broad Walk whilst anxious keepers with nets hid below. But it never carried one off. A small dog I mean.

Because the Zoo tried to keep the affair quiet, a less well-known but potentially more dangerous escapee was an old male chimpanzee so ugly, even by anthropoidal standards, that he was called Mr Cholmondeley. Efforts to allay his restlessness by providing him with females came to nothing when potential mates fled screaming at his appearance. Otherwise he was docile but infinitely cunning in his efforts to get out. He was dextrous too. He stole keys. He lay on his cage floor, feigning illness in the hope that the gate would be left open. And he had one other curious characteristic. He became enraged at the sight of black visitors.

He broke out three or four times. On the last occasion he climbed over the boundary wall and boarded the bus to Baker Street. Not, it is thought, with any particular desire for a ride. The bus conductor was a black man. In the ensuing panic the ape literally fell off the bus platform and I have forgotten how he was eventually recaptured. The last I heard of that resourceful animal was how he tried to disrupt a minor surgical operation. He had swallowed something, perhaps another key. The pathologist administering the anaesthetic could not understand why he failed to lose consciousness. The gas pressure remained high. It took him some time to realize that, furtively, Mr Cholmondeley was squeezing the tube that led to his face mask.

The zoo is both a learned Society and a vast public menagerie occupying thirty-six acres of Crown property for a peppercorn rental. About once a month at the gentlemanly hour of half-past four the learned Fellows file into the Great Hall to listen to three or four scientific papers. These

occasionally provoked scenes not easy to report. Above un-gentlemanly shouting there was much calling to order and the Categorists, those who sought for order and precedence in the animal kingdom, were usually at the bottom of it.

In the days of Mr Cholmondeley the Fellowship was far from wholly scientific. Lay Fellows who fancied a good lunch in the Zoo restaurant and the right to put FZS after their name swarmed in for a few quid a year. This came to the ears of Nemesis in the guise of the Charity Commissioners, those probers into tax-free funds. There were threats of huge rents and retrospective taxation amounting to a crippling figure. More heated meetings and resolutions followed in what became a divided Fellowship. Enter Solly the Fixer.

Sir Solly, now Lord, Zuckerman made his name as an anatomist and an animal behaviourist, concentrating on the hierarchy of baboons in the Transvaal. This, I suggested in print, must have been of considerable value when he took over as principal scientific adviser to the government and boss of the Zoo. My comments provoked a degree of coldness be-tween us bordering on glacial frigidity since he made it abundantly clear to the staff – and to me – that *he* ran the place. Much went on behind the scenes in Council before he man-aged to straighten out the Society's affairs by defrocking the unscientific Fellows and calling them Associates. For quite different reasons, the sheer cost of running and rebuilding the place, the Zoo is again in deep financial trouble which has been averted, temporarily at least, by a massive government grant.

Although Solly the Fixer and I later became as intimate as a professional heel-biter can be with the chief scientific adviser to the government, our friendship, if such it can be called, began with stormy exchanges in his office and culminated in a flaming row in the appropriately named Smoke Room of the Athenaeum to which, I told him, I had been beguiled under downright false pretences. The voice of the Fixer rose to a gravelly roar as he concluded a homily with the threat that if I persisted in criticizing the policy and structure of the Council in general and his own attitude in particular, he'd have me chucked out of the menagerie where I was technically a

Katie with friends

Scientific Fellow. As Ed Murrow used to say: I can hear it now.

At heart I felt damn sorry for many of the Zoo's internees, especially the apes confined to cages about half of the size of one of their royal patron's spare lavatories. The public blew raspberries and pelted them with unshelled Brazil nuts and worse. Were we back to the days of the bear-pits I asked?

> Soft fur, bare arses, hair styles
> like rock groups, the apes look intelligent,
> but bare teeth in sudden warning.
> The people bare theirs in quick smiles
> or laugh aloud to see themselves gibber
> on the other side. So far I have not
> seen men beating hairy chests,
> but it will come. Meanwhile they make
> bombs and grunt at love.[1]

By far the biggest and most magnificent-looking anthropoid in the menagerie was Guy the gorilla whose Highland cousins I had seen in the wild. Knowing that the Great Apes hate to be stared at, a sign of aggression within their ritualized behaviour, I tried to glance at him through finger-screened eyes.

Guy arrived at the Zoo in traumatic circumstances on Guy Fawkes Day 1947 and whimpered and finally screamed in terror as rockets zipped and bangers banged around Regent's Park until far into the night. But comforted by that remarkable woman, Mrs Pinto-Leite – who spoke French to him – and Head Keeper Smithy who had a way with apes, Guy just managed to get through a bad bout of pneumonia by hastily swallowing a doctored ice-cream which Smithy cunningly allowed him to steal. For years he pined and underwent the psychological torture of a million stares, eventually scaling over 400 lbs. Unhappily, in that time, his balls shrank for if

---

[1] Elizabeth Bartlett, *London Lines, The Places and Faces of London in Poetry*, selected by Kenneth Baker, Methuen, 1982.

there was one thing Guy wanted only a little short of freedom it was a doll.

Now had the Fixer – who always kept his cards close to his chest – told me that two efforts to import spritely young she-gorillas had come to a dead stop in France where, missing the ever-warm wet air of the French Cameroons, the females quietly expired, our *détente* might not have been so long delayed. Nor did I know that Solly had a very rich, compassionate philanthropoid in tow, Sir Michael Sobell who gave the Zoo a small fortune to build six primate pavilions which are probably among the best in Europe. They were equipped with gardens and Guy was at last given a doll, a saucy little piece from Chessington called Lomie, one-third of his weight and age but quite capable of giving her massive overlord a clout if he got over-uppish.

Lomie could climb quickly, but Guy couldn't. So that she would know how to get out of the way among the overhead gymnastic apparatus if anything went wrong, Keeper Callard, Smithy's successor, gave her the run of the bridal suite for a month before, lightly doped, the two animals were introduced. At the first musty-sweet sniff of a female, Guy blinked like a schoolboy at a nude show. But Lomie never hesitated. She started to wrestle with him, nibbling his neck, and they were at each other from the start. Guy still stared, but with his huge arm round his beloved's shoulders, he stared with what looked like pride.

If I had one criticism of their new quarters, it was that, as far as I could see, they hadn't a place for a bit on the quiet, and the tragedy was that the most magnificent animal in the Zoo died in 1978 after only relatively few years with Lomie. The news went round the world on the agency wires. No great ape ever had more fulsome obituary notices. But it's high time we returned to the Broad Walk.

The playing-fields narrow, the trees thicken, flanking the flowerbeds and, if you should chance to raise your eyes you become aware of three high and mighty figures peering down through the thick screen of trees. They are death-white statues or acroteria on top of the spectacular pediment of Nash's Cumberland Terrace, one of the five blocks of imposing mansions that overlook the eastern side of the Park. In winter, when the London planes shed their immense leaves, a dozen squat ornamental vases can be seen below the pediment which has recently been done up in Wedgwood blue the better to show off the imperial ladies cavorting about within the flattened triangle of brick and stucco.

To me those vases have always borne some resemblance to a coconut-shy and I was immoderately pleased to discover that James Elmes Esq, a contemporary of John Nash, wrote that 'Lord Byron scarcely hated a dumpy woman more than I hate those dumpy jars of the apothecary'. But whatever sharp-tongued critics say about the terraces they attract the tourists in their thousands.

Nash clearly knew what he was doing when he named them after the seven sons of the mad King George. In order of precedence they were the Regent, who gave notoriety to the park itself, and then his brothers: York, Clarence, Cumberland, Kent, Sussex and Cambridge, a squalid crew who 'brought the title of gentlemen into disrepute throughout Europe'. Lytton Strachey described them as 'nasty old men, debauched and selfish, pig-headed and ridiculous, with their perpetual burden of debts, confusions and disreputabilities . . .' Cumberland, in his view, 'was probably the most unpopular man in England. Hideously ugly, with a distorted eye, he was bad-tempered and vindictive in private, a violent reactionary in politics and was subsequently suspected of murdering his valet.' What did he think of the terrace which bore his name? He probably admired it enormously. He admired himself. He said so.

The other day, as fine a day as you could have wished for, gardeners on the Broad Walk were exchanging stiff daffodils and tulips for a rash of geraniums and small silvery-leaved plants to which I can't put a name. The beds were being dressed for summer. Down the central path a little black chap with a huge Mum in a flowing turquoise robe bowled a hoop, the first hoop I had seen in years, come to think about it. She nodded and grinned expansively at my greeting. Young white

children with nannies shrieked cheerfully as they turned cart-wheels on the soft grass. Noticing my binoculars, a fellow in City togs with a brolly said it was a damn fine morning and stopped for a chat about nothing in particular. People rarely pass without at least a smile on that suburban esplanade. But there are exceptions.

In twos and threes a small procession of black-veiled, almost faceless Muslim women drifted past with what looked like minders discreetly in the rear. Were they young or old? Impossible to say, but in openly public places there is always something slightly ominous about these hermetic groups. To quell some uncharitable thoughts I scanned the trees, especially the conifers, the spruce and the pines. All planted originally by Nash who made good use of know-how acquired from his brief but lucrative association with Humphry Repton, the leading professor of landscape-gardening, a phrase he coined himself in one of many books he wrote on the subject.

In addition to a pocket notebook which in recent years has been replaced by a tape recorder the size of a pack of cards, I usually carry midget binoculars on all but the most formal of perambulations. Countless numbers of young starlings, a species I dislike, screeched and foraged half-seen in the uncut grass like lice in a tramp's clothing. Chiff-chaffs chiffed and their half-cousin, the Willow-warbler, poured cascades of song from among the gently swaying tresses of *Salix pendula*, the Weeping willow. There are I don't know how many species of willow on both sides of the Walk. Perhaps a dozen. Maybe fewer, since they are much given to hybridization. As a family they are second only to the birch in my affection. But a squirrel not a bird tempted me off the path that morning.

Not one of the Grey squirrels, those rattish-looking pests with a tail like a bottle brush. They are all too commonplace, even in suburban streets and gardens. In Regent's Park they are so tame that they have taken to begging. They follow strollers cautiously, and if any interest is taken in them they sit up with forepaws folded, hoping to be fed. It is less well known that they are inveterate nest-robbers and fledgling-killers. What I thought I saw was a Red squirrel, a slightly smaller animal with ear tufts and a very bushy tail. They are now extinct throughout most of their southern haunts but, as I knew, there is more than a chance that one or two can be spotted around the Broad Walk these days since half a dozen pairs were released from the Zoo a year or two ago. This is an experimental exercise in reintroducing an animal to an abandoned habitat. The operative word is abandoned. They were not driven out by the alien Greys as most people believe. But had I seen a Red or merely a reddish-looking Grey which are not uncommon?

It squatted almost hidden in the fork of a larch. I followed with field-glasses at the ready. In a small clearing near the Park fence I all but stumbled over the robed and veiled Muslim women. Two minders immediately rose to their feet. The squirrel fled and I slunk off, somewhat indignantly. This has happened before.

On that occasion I came across what from a distance looked like a quartet of white-robed druids, but not behind trees. Their sumptuous-looking chairs were arranged around a low table in a corner of the playing-fields. Feeling that the Park was as much mine as theirs I strolled over until, through glasses, I saw four bearded Arab chiefs in full fig, that is with flowing robes and head-dresses with gold fillets. The heads of Trucial States or a breakaway group from the Arab League? I shall never know.

Around them at a discreet distance stood seven or eight bare-headed fellows with ominous-looking bulges under their armpits and one of them, I noticed, was looking at me through field-glasses. In a wild flight of imagination I strode towards them, brushing aside the guards, and bowed gravely to Their Eminences, trusting that their state of health did not belie their appearance. In fact, I shuffled past, slowly, whistling breathily.

Some days later I described this to a Park keeper I had known for years. He nodded sympathetically. A friend of his, he said, had been a caretaker in one of the nearby blocks of renovated mansions. Luxurious places rented out to 'proper gents. Never wanted nothing done that might change the place,' as he put it. 'But when them Arabs come they had proper difficulties.' Several wouldn't sign leases until the

47

windows were shielded with bullet-proof glass. One brought in a security man who worked out a field of fire for 300 yards and crept about outside whilst an assistant watched him. There were big trees nearby 'and he tried to get the bloody things chopped down, he did'.

Were the Arabs a nuisance? I put the question squarely to David Caselton, the Park Superintendent who has an office on the Inner Circle. He looked a trifle disconcerted. He drummed with his fingers. Mr Caselton is a civil servant responsible to the Department of the Environment who run the Park on behalf of the Crown. The Arabs used the Park a great deal, he admitted, particularly the Queen Mary's Garden which, with its little bowers and waterfalls, is his especial pride. On some days they came there in droves, he said. But a nuisance? I repeated. After another pause he said that some of his men thought so. In what way? He temporized. Some of the Muslims, he conceded, 'didn't always respect public gardens in the way to which most of us are accustomed'. And that was that. I felt that at all times I could rely on his most distinguished sentiments.

There is nothing obviously earthy about Mr Caselton. Trim-suited with a discreet shirt and matching tie, he is the very model of a modern superintendent. You could see him in the role of Discretioner of the Grace and Favour Apartments at Hampton Court. He came to the Park nine years ago by way of college and the National Trust. There are half a dozen subjects I had hoped to talk to him about, such as hybrid vigour or the rather curious reproductive life of his Ginkgos, those trees which have remained virtually unchanged since the age of dinosaurs. But his mind, I felt, was more on his automated glasshouses where each year about 150,000 plantlings are heated, ventilated and watered by his masterly touch on the buttons of micro-processors. He likes colour and variety but confessed, almost off the record, that he wasn't *personally* impressed by all the bedded-out stuff. His staff has been ruthlessly pruned down from 200 to seventy of which only about half are gardeners, since the Gardens have to be watched and warded by day and through the night.

His staff – including Mr Tony Ducket who looks after the

ducks – work under the stern eyes and beetling brows of Doug Richardson, his Foreman, who has uninhibited views about almost everything including his own inclination to talk too much. Born under Leo, he says. His tongue had 'let him down more than a few times'. The subjects which cause his blood pressure to rise like a lift are litter louts, cyclists – who shouldn't be cycling there at all – the fouling of his paths and grass by dogs. And irresponsible Muslims. 'I've seen them Arabs get out of their bloody Rolls Royces and pick the flowers, watched by their English chauffeurs. They are our people, them car drivers. They should know better.'

The temptation here at the bottom of the Primrose Path, that is to say at the junction of Chester Road with the Inner Circle, is to swing back north into the heart of the Park and then west to get the feel of what John Nash would have liked to do if only he could have sold more mansions and hadn't been so preoccupied with at least half a dozen other schemes such as the canal which flanks the Zoo at the foot of Primrose Hill. The temptation must be resisted. What with the heronry and the Boating Lake, the formal and the almost wild gardens around tinkling waterfalls, it's easy to devote at least a day to Regent's Park and even then miss the acres of roses where on a warm summer's morning, says David Piper, you are likely to find old ladies and lovers almost afloat on the fragrance. Better by far at this point to take a closer look at what John Nash, that designer of architectural scenery did – among much else – for the great Park that still bears his patron's name.

The royal architect

It now looks as if Nash had at least a hand in the plans of John Fordyce to develop what a contemporary called 'that dreary waste of dank pasturage' which today is Regent's Park. Knowing what was afoot, Nash quickly put up a scheme of his own which for sheer grandiosity made the plans of his rivals look trivial. How much of it was his own and how much had been put to paper by Fordyce unaided by anyone else will never be known. It scarcely matters. Nash foresaw in masterly fashion that the projected New Street from St James's north to the foot of Primrose Hill would have to be constructed as economically as possible to stand the best chance of being accepted by the Commissioners for high rents and expensive freeholds to swell royal coffers depleted by the protracted war with France. What better, therefore, than to drive a grand boulevard, a Royal Mile, between the congested squalor, the criminal rookeries and harlotry of Soho and the great squares and mansions to the west of the New Street? The poverty-stricken could be bought out cheaply; the highborn and the new rich were being offered easy access to town and country. Two social classes would be satisfied. Perhaps three, since Nash and his fellow designers, speculators, builders and sub-contractors foresaw an enormous amount of business in and around the Park. An ethical affair too, since the town would become more of an integrated whole with at least one longitudinal axis.

Meanwhile the Prince Regent with his vagaries, his insatiable appetite for women and noble architecture, might be compared to Samuel Taylor Coleridge in the throes of an opium dream.

> In Xanadu did Kubla Khan
> A stately pleasure-dome decree:

Not just Brighton Pavilion which Nash put up for his royal master. In the very centre of the Park, he sketched out in terms of brick and stucco a regal *guinguette* on the French pattern, a huge house for refreshment in whatever form it was desired. But Nash had less of a Park and more of an aristocratic garden suburb in mind. What are now the great terraces on all sides but one were to be the mansions of a noble enclosure. All facing inwards for coveted glimpses of HRH about his play. All very desirable property. Unfortunately a Hamlet without the Prince. In his capricious fashion, HRH never got there.

Today, of all those terraces, Cumberland between the seclusion of the Inner Circle and the cheerful squalor, the homely pubs of Euston and Mornington Crescent less than half a mile to the east is by far the most spectacular. The painted pediment is not functional except as a stage platform for James Bubb's blanched statuary but the projecting centre block upheld by fluted Ionic columns is unquestionably theatrical, the subject of much rhetoric by the couriers of tourists in *Dieselomnibussen* and flag-decked Italian *Torpedoni*. Cameras are forever clicking. But the palazzo lacks a palatial forecourt. As you may discover for yourself, a mere fifty paces separates the elevation from the outer hedge of the Park. Through chinks in the brocade curtains there are glimpses of opulent emptiness. The mansions on either side of the towering centre block have a breadth of only eighteen paces.

Critics of the great scenery designer – he contributed nothing to the interiors of the houses in Regent's Park – have not been slow to point out that Nash broke the rules of taste and scholarship in many directions. But the weightiest words are those of Sir John Summerson, the historian of three centuries of architecture (1530–1830). He described Cumberland Terrace as 'the most ornamented, the most ostentatious and spectacular building in the Park'. Yet, he goes on to say, 'The terrace is a composition of great energy and brilliance. To complain of the poverty of detail, insensitive profiles and ill-considered junctions would be to say again what has often enough been said: the thing is the work of men in a hurry and looks it.'

At this point I cannot overstate my indebtedness to Sir John for the talks I have had with him in the comfort of his nearby Georgian home. As a scholar and trained architect he recently retired after nearly forty years as the curator of that treasure-house in Lincoln's Inn Fields, the Soane Museum. Sir John Soane (1753–1837), a contemporary of Nash, designed the building and lived there surrounded by a glorious confusion of all the objects he had collected, objects as diverse as Hogarth's paintings and Napoleon's engraved pistol, books, busts, bronzes, Greek vases, Christopher Wren's watch and, wholly unexpectedly, an open sarcophagus of the Pharaoh Seti II in the basement. 'To work there,' said Sir John, the curator, 'was to work in the totality of a pre-eminently cultured and gifted man.' Soane and Nash, he added 'were the two great figures in the last phase of English classicism'. By suggesting what I should look at and how it should be looked at, Sir John opened my eyes to highly formative periods in the build and shape of London.

As a youth raised in Victorian Leeds I learned next to nothing of the aesthetics of architecture because Leeds – which caters for communists and conservatives – has little use for aesthetics. Its inhabitants were too busy staving off starvation or amassing a fortune. Probably the best building in town is Cuthbert Broderick's Town Hall surrounded by a brickopolis of Gothic churches and chapels and the endless terraced houses, tram-sheds and waterworks of the hilly suburbs. In London, largely inspired by James Bone's *Perambulations*, I became aware of Portland stone and the great quarries south of Weymouth where it came from. Bone called that peninsula the matrix of London's grandeur. A visit to Athens and

Delphi coincided with my preoccupation with Categories and there amongst hosts of columns and their entablature I managed to pick up some knowledge of the classical Orders. But what lay behind English classicism? At least one very shrewd man.

Nash was nothing much to look at. Though dedicated to his work and conceited professionally, he had no illusions about his appearance, describing himself as a 'thick, squat, dwarf figure with a round head, snub nose and little eyes'. Summerson, his biographer, adds that he was 'bullet-headed with a facetious Cockney mouth and impudently tilted eyebrows'. But on the other hand, Sir John says, 'he must have been amusing and full of vitality. And portraits are deceptive.'

No matter whether he was thinking in terms of getting rid of his first wife, a very inconvenient woman, or entering the innermost circle of the Carlton House set or planning what the great New Street would lead to, John Nash invariably saw things in broad perspective. And he was undeterred by setbacks that would have broken less self-assured men. To take just one example, it needed considerable nerve to overlook the fact that the bridge he built at Stanford in Worcestershire collapsed but he offered – and succeeded in getting the contract – to build it again, successfully.

It was over the border, in Wales, among his relatives, that we first hear of the hectic goings on of J. Nash Esquire, Architect. He put out several of the stories himself, possibly to cover up what was going on in London about that time. Before his early bankruptcy he had been apprenticed to Sir John Taylor, a considerable architect who did well among patrons with thick purses and artistically unencumbered minds.

In Wales the irrepressible Nash fared better. Buildings from notable church renovations to castles and gaols in the vicinity stood to his credit. But not the iron bridge over the Teme for Sir Edward Winnington. It fell down only two hours after Sir Edward's children danced over it in glee.

The way in which the great scenery designer is believed to have got rid of the first Mrs Nash is relevant primarily, one feels, to how he first began to appear in Court circles with his second wife, the Royal temptress. It is in the appearance and disappearance of Jane Elizabeth, his first espoused, that Nash – who had been on the stage, briefly – played one of his most intriguing roles. Jane Elizabeth was hugely extravagant, especially in matters of dress, at a time when her husband owed a great deal of money – he was twice arrested for her debts. He packed her off to Aberavon in Wales 'where she remained sulking in her fine London clothes'.

The next we hear is that her thoughtful husband sent down Charles Charles, an unmarried boyhood acquaintance of his, a clerk, later, in a coal yard, to brighten the hours of Mrs Nash in exile. In this enterprise he was, it seems, successful since in (almost) no time at all she became pregnant, admitting that the baby girl had been sired by a Mr C. Charles. It looked like a case of collusion from the start.

The mystery is not so much how nor, indeed, why all this came about. The question is how a man saddled with debt and on the verge of bankruptcy could even contemplate divorce which in those days meant petitioning the House of Lords to bring in a special Bill, a rare and expensive process. The Bill failed but, providentially for Nash, Charles Charles died and Mrs Nash too, since in 1798 her husband had married again. Nash became an opulent lackey, a big-wig of back-stairs intrigue at Court and one who consequently and suddenly acquired a princely house in Regent Street and an estate around a castle in the Isle of Wight. But we are straying from his work in the Park.

On the same side as the road which is now the Outer Circle are other terraces in that pageantry of stucco which is the great hallmark of Nash. To the south of Cumberland in Chester Terrace which was to be 'nearly as long as the Tuileries' and beyond it Cambridge Terrace with huge statues above the gates. They are trinities of Roman ladies in a curious stance. They are standing bottom to bottom. Mr Bubb again, one presumes. He had yards full of them, ready for instant delivery.

The next building, a very modern one (1960) is the head-quarters of the Royal College of Physicians by Denys Lasdun, an architectural showpiece and one perhaps more praised than

any other modern building in London. Unpretentious, it is a model of grace and conformity.

Across the thundering traffic of the Euston Road no student of Nash nor, indeed, any other architect can fail to look at the great curve, the symmetry of the twin-colonnaded arms of Park Crescent without an intake of breath. It dates from 1812, the very beginning of Nash's triumphant progress up to the Park by way of the New Street. But to start with nobody would buy the houses. They faced farmland. Some collapsed and so did the fortunes of Charles Mayor who took out the original lease. He went bust. It was left to others to restore their classical dignity.

When Goering's airmen poured fire on London much of their Ionian splendour – with respect to T. S. Eliot – was laid low. But again they were restored, scrupulously, and it was during that period I recall first approaching them by way of Cumberland Terrace where some minor repairs to the roof were being effected.

A misty morning in May. The great trees which Nash had planted in the Park became as silhouettes, black and motionless against the water vapour that reduced the traffic in the Euston Road to a murmur as from a distant waterfall. Suddenly from afar came the clip-clop of horses' hooves. And out of the mist came three brewer's drays drawn by as finely paired Clydesdales as ever I have seen. They were, I knew, heading for the annual show parade in the Park. But in my mind's eye I saw them as carts bearing loads of bricks and barrels of Mr Parker's patent stucco from his wharves in Southwark.

The year is 1827 and the materials have been ordered to Cumberland Terrace by an entrepreneur, William Mountford Nurse, who has bought the site at so much a foot-frontage after much bargaining with the Crown agent, a bullet-headed fellow with a snub nose and little eyes. The two are standing together, talking intently but always with an eye on the labourers who are unloading the bricks and prizing open barrels with jack-staves. The agent is impatient and, strangely for him, more than a little nervous. Things are far from what he had hoped for at the age of seventy-four. There is as yet no crest on his fine carriage. And within an hour he has to be back at another site which eventually became the most notorious failure of its time: that sprawl of Portland stone facing St James's Park: Buckingham Palace.

Before we leave the terrace to the labourers, the bricklayers, the carpenters, joiners, masons, plasterers, glaziers, plumbers, painters, carvers and paviors employed by the entrepreneur's sub-contractors and his promising young architect, James Thompson and, of course, the Great Designer himself who has supplied them with an elevation (that is, a vertical projection together with a block plan) a word must be said about what had gone on before William Mountford Nurse put his houses up for sale after they had been approved of by the Crown's agents.

As Sir John Summerson put it with his usual precision: 'The size and shape of the London house have been conditioned from the first by the economic need to get as many houses as possible into one street . . . Georgian London was a city made up almost entirely of these long narrow plots with their tall narrow houses and long narrow gardens or courts.' The French saw it differently 'and learnt at an early date to live horizontally and most, if not all continental capitals followed the French lead.'

Until it became clear that, between them, Nelson and Wellington had nailed the French, domestic building in Britain had been at a virtual standstill for over two decades. Moreover architects, as we understand the word today, were wholly unknown until the middle of the preceding century. Sir John says, 'The title was adopted by anyone who could get away with it.' Buildings were put up by master-builders and surveyors who might come from professions and crafts as diverse as adventurers and playwrights (Vanbrugh), mathematics and astronomy (Wren), coach-painters and joiners (William Kent and Henry Flitcroft).

John Nash was different. From the start he was quick to capitalize on what he learnt from the drawing-boards of William Taylor in an era of enormous social change and the rise of a new class with aristocratic tastes. As we have seen,

Nash sought to bridge the gap. He tended to smudge those portions of his life which he thought might diminish his social and professional stature. We know so little about his origins. There was the unfortunate case of the first Mrs Nash, the bankruptcy and his accounts of roistering in Wales at the same time as he appears to have been building some very considerable houses in London when he was twenty-five. He designed numerous miniature castles in Cornwall, Ireland and Wales. But he was sixty-three before he gained royal favour. Thereafter we have him building in Regent's Park amidst a whirl of activities elsewhere.

We may imagine him again outside the almost completed shell of Cumberland Terrace. The ground has been levelled, trees planted and roads built. An inch-thick layer of stucco is being applied to an enormous carcase of brick. Remarkable stuff, that stucco. It was new but not wholly new as a building material. Inigo Jones had used it and so had the Adam brothers. But it was Nash who plastered the west of London with paste made to look like stone which was very expensive. Parker's patent, one of several, was, essentially fired nodules of clay from the Isle of Sheppey in north Kent. It was produced by the ton.

> Augustus at Rome was for building renown'd,
> And of marble he left what of brick he had found;
> But is not our Nash, too, a very great master?
> He finds us all brick and he leaves us all plaster.

The clay arrived on the site in the form of fine powder. Nash waited until it had been lightly watered and made into a pile of paste as high as a man. He had to make sure it was good paste. There had been trouble at Brighton, trouble at the Palace and trouble in the Park where this particular site was to be his show-piece, the one facing the *guinguette*. He snapped his fingers and motioned a workman bearing a hod to his carriage. He rolled a small pellet of the stuff between his fingers, critically, as an apothecary might. He nodded and called for two bricks. They were mere place bricks costing about a guinea a thousand, perhaps of clay from Hampstead Heath.

But they had to be uniform in texture. He weighed them up, one in each hand and then scratched the surface with his thumb nail. They seemed pretty fair. He nodded again.

The last we see of the great scenery designer is of him shaking hands with Mr Nurse. He bows his head, slightly, in the direction of the architect and enters his carriage. The horses are as impatient to be off as he is. Very soon the fine equipage with its gilded swags and attendant grooms is bowling down Langham Place towards the New Street, where we might follow them.

Bob and his brethren

South of the Great Park and the terraces named after the nasty old men we enter what the man in a hurry described as 'the most magnificent street in London'. On the face of it a generous statement, since Nash had little to do with Portland Place. It was conceived in the early 1770s by Robert, who was by far the most famous of the Adam brothers. He foresaw those groups of fine town houses – not as a thoroughfare, but as an isolated *grande place* on the continental pattern, an urbane place fit for the Quality with their neo-classical villas in the country. Unfortunately, as a result of Paul Revere's ride and that battle at Lexington which triggered off the American War of Independence, the project had to be set aside for a few years. Potential buyers were not going to risk their loose capital on bricks and stucco when a steady income from the Colonies looked precarious.

Nash, of course, was shrewd. He praised the stately *place* which, like an expensive brooch, would clasp together handsomely his own plans for a New Street north of St James's and, beyond that enclave of the well-off, the regal drive through the Park. Portland Place is now a thoroughfare, still one of the widest in London. Viewed from one end or the other, particularly at dusk or dawn, it retains some of the grandeur the Adam brothers gave it. But it is a street devoid of coherence, an architectural hotch-potch grossly mishandled by the Victorians and rebuilt from war ruins in many places to house minor embassies, institutions and charitable organizations. Noticing *Société d'Anonyme d'Anvers* on the gilded plate of a doorway which looked like the Adams got up in fancy dress, I asked an immaculately dressed fellow, politely, what the society did. 'We are minding our own business,' he said, and closed the door, briskly.

With his head slightly on one side as if ashamed at what he's looking at, stands the statue to Prince Edward, Duke of Kent at the north end of Portland Place. He is looking down from a pedestal among a thicket of holly bushes in a padlocked garden. Possibly the least nasty of the five sons of George III – which wasn't all that difficult – he hoped to be remembered. With that sense of duty acquired in the army he sacrificed a mistress of twenty-five years' devotion to marry a Saxe-Coburg and sire a legitimate heir to the throne at a time when it was clear his brothers had gone off the boil. Alexandra became Queen Victoria who, as a young girl, vowed she would try to be good and, perhaps with her uncles in mind, she kept to her vow.

For me in those early days Portland Place became a quiet frontier between the serenity of the Park and the maelstrom of traffic at Oxford Circus, one of the noisiest and most ill-designed junctions in Central London. All that I enjoyed on the suburban part of the walk faded perceptibly outside the padlocked garden reserved for residents within the two embracing arms marked by the Ionic columns of Park Crescent. Ignoring threats of prosecution I managed to get in. Forgive us our trespasses. My eyes were on the truly enormous plane trees, the flowering shrubbery and dancing Holly Blue butterflies that once provided an ill-deserved halo for the bald head of the Duke and a few laboured paragraphs for the *Guardian*.

In the eyes of those who walk down them almost daily, streets, especially historic streets, acquire character from familiarity with their inhabitants, or some understanding of how the buildings got to be the way they are or, more often perhaps, from incidents that set them apart from all other thorough-fares. The only inhabitants of Portland Place I got to know at all intimately on my way down to the BBC and Fleet Street were the gardener of the Crescent who passed me off as his consultant, a large and affectionate marmalade-coloured cat and an old street-cleaner, a West Indian called Joe. I forget the cat's name but Joe – who fed him regularly with scraps from his cart – had been christened Juan de Humancao which, he explained about once a month, was the name of a mountain in Haiti. Unless hurrying for a studio booking I had long talks with Joe, particularly about curious aspects of voodoo and the merits of rum which he swigged at regular intervals from a Pepsi-Cola bottle.

Many years elapsed before Sir John Summerson and walks in the company of that keen-eyed town-planning consultant, Leslie Ginsburg, convinced me how little I really knew in my search for London's architectural history. The discovery on the sooty face of an old Victorian building of some Regency swags or flourishes, a few formalized acanthus leaves or a fragment of an egg-and-dart border, the symbols of birth and death, might be likened to quarrying the face of a cliff for critical fossils or trying to decipher what was left on a school blackboard after the different lessons of the day had been chalked up and then partly rubbed off. With the outstanding exception of Regent Street there are few streets anywhere in London more difficult to envisage in their prime than the street of the marmalade cat which in the early nineteenth century had been a monument of European importance. One might for-give the monotonous blocks of Paris-style apartments built in the age of Art Deco. It is less easy to overlook one building, the headquarters of the Royal Institute of British Architects, which, I suspect, historians of architecture write about with contrived respect as Old Boys might conclude there was at least something to be said for the Old School despite the fact that the staff didn't really know what they were about. Two free-standing pillars and some obscure statues on a bleak façade emphasize the rather awful *ordinariness* of that artefact of the early 'thirties.

But what of the Adam brothers who created the Adelphi (the word means brothers in Greek), the men who gave their name to a style which is now a household word, a style *par excellence* in the Age of Sensibility from 1750 onwards? It spread from Britain to the Gulf of Finland under the Tsarina Catherine and to the USA. To many it still suggests exquisitely moulded fireplaces, door knobs, and nymphs and charioteers in stucco.

Undeterred by this I first became a dedicated Adam-watcher just beyond the ill-favoured home of the British architects where above the curiously recessed doorways of two houses (numbers 46–48 Portland Place) Bridget Cherry told me what to look for. As the woman who is completing the work of the late great Nikolaus Pevsner[1] I count her among the greatest of our analysts of building fabric. She said, 'Note that the design was for groups of houses treated as a single block with the central house or pair of houses emphasized in some way, although the detail of the design varied from block to block.'

Attic storeys have been added to these and all other buildings in the street but, originally, the graceful elevation was topped by a pediment, now a pleasing salmon-pink in colour, picked out with a few delicate medallions, symbolic motifs and mythical animals which are the hallmarks of the Adam style of decoration everywhere. The full repertory used in scores of their buildings includes bosomy sphinxes, griffins, cherubic putti all carefully bordered and wrapped about with floral arabesques. Robert Adam used them in one of his best-known buildings, Kenwood House on Hampstead Heath, where I stared at the swags and borders for years without recognizing the *anthemion*, the formalized flower of the honeysuckle that resembles hands in prayer with the fingers almost touching. The marvel is that so many interiors have been preserved, but with a room by Adam to attract sightseers their impoverished owners need provide little else. Whatever the brothers touched they made completely their own.

---

[1] The twenty-six volumes of *The Buildings of England*.

How Robert became the greatest British architect of the late eighteenth century within a few years of starting to practise on his return from his great European tour must wait until we walk to the Adelphi on the Thames. It was a triumph that brought him to the verge of bankruptcy ten years before John Nash tumbled into the financial pit which, through lack of credit in London, forced him to scurry back to Wales. After effectively smudging what really happened he returned to receive royal patronage and public ridicule and, as we have seen, became an outstanding town-planner.

What stood in the way of his triumphal entry into the Park was that ugly wall-like barrier across Portland Place which, before the BBC took it over, was the Langham Hotel of some 300 bedrooms. On that site originally stood Foley House built for Lord Foley in 1758 on the strict understanding that nothing whatever should interrupt his view northwards. Hence the width of Portland Place. Never one to baulk at risking a few thousands if he thought he could double his outlay, Nash outbid the Duke of Portland for the site, pulled down Foley House and nearby built what is today, architecturally speaking, one of the most endearing churches in London: All Souls, Langham Place. Since 1931 it has been brutishly overpowered by the BBC building on one side and obscured by the gaunt wall of the Langham on the other.

Here there is a vast conflict of styles scarcely harmonized by the towering King George Hotel and it stretches the imagination to its outermost frontiers to realize that on 3 February 1601 the Russian ambassador and his party of sporty Muscovites arrived within a bowshot of the Langham to hunt 'heorts and hynde, doe and bocke' in what was then the chase of Mary-le-Bourne.

The sight of Broadcasting House today puts you in mind of an obsolete super-tanker which for want of use has been laid up in a backwater. The house that Reith built for sound radio in all senses of the word has been completely eclipsed by that galaxy of activity within the huge television centre in faraway Shepherds Bush. The feeling of change and decay is never more evident than late at night when the ghostly façade is punctuated by two or three feebly lit windows. What's going on in that warren of empty workshops? A skiffle group perhaps? Or an interviewer with a portable recorder in an otherwise deserted studio? Or an engineer-producer with a disc or a few tapes? *Eheu fugaces.*

As for the external fabric, Sir Uvedale Price, the nineteenth-century critic, said that 'mere unmixed ugliness does not arise from sharp angles or from any sudden variation, but rather from that want of form, that unshapen lumpish appearance which, perhaps, no one word exactly expresses'. Nikolaus Pevsner drily observed that 'Broadcasting House is an example of this.' 'A pudding-like monument to good intentions,' in the opinion of David Piper.

The famous sculptured figures on the building are by Eric Gill which is somewhat ironic since he deeply disliked the whole business of broadcasting but, as he said at the time, 'It is well-paid for and we are in luck.' To most people the huge ten-foot-high figures of a patriarchal Prospero and Ariel over the doorway more resemble God and the youthful Jesus than the characters from *The Tempest*, and perhaps with his tongue in his cheek Gill thought so too. He had a great deal of trouble over the size of Ariel's penis. At the preview the startled BBC governors invited a number of people including the head-master of a famous public school to pass judgement on that truly hypertrophic organ. The headmaster charitably con-ceded that the lad was 'uncommonly well hung'. The outcome was that, like Michelangelo before him, Gill was asked to remount his ladder and cut things down to size.

The last we hear of him on that particular job is from the top of an exposed platform where, chiselling away in his crimson petticoat-bodice bereft of either underpants or breeches, 'the man of flesh and spirit' shouted down to a passing friend, 'You know this is all balls.'

I find it extremely difficult to write objectively about the BBC. They paid me when, God knows, I needed the money; they offered me an obscure staff job and realized almost as quickly as I did that I wasn't cut out for rewriting agency tape into a form that could be read out over the air. They sent me abroad at a time when, in my imagination, Geneva was as far away as Tierra del Fuego is today. If I feel that many present-day programmes are unutterably trivial I try to persuade myself it may well have something to do with the increasing youthfulness of policemen.

Thinking I might have been rather harsh about the exterior trappings of what its inmates call The Beeb I nodded respectfully in the direction of Father Prospero and his lad and walked a little way down the street towards Oxford Circus and then, turning round, looked back towards All Souls and the BBC. Were they in any sense complementary? Yes, as the clown on stilts at the circus is to Columbine.

Nash was mercilessly lampooned for putting a curious, sharp conical spire on a circular portico of giant columns, but that solution of how to turn the corner into Portland Place was little short of miraculous. The rounded effect, the modulation almost subconsciously turns the eye from whatever quarter it is viewed. But this wouldn't do for the subjects of the hugely unpopular prince whose friend and architect was the man in a hurry. Under the caption 'Nashional Taste', a contemporary cartoon shows Nash impaled, fundamentally, like a weathercock on his own spire. And yet . . .

There seemed something odd about that spire. Is the whole building devoid of entasis, that very slight concave curve used on Greek and later columns to correct the optical illusion that their buildings were falling in which would result if the sides were straight? There is no authority for this that I can find. A friend put it to me, and to try and find out more I took a strongly recommended cup of tea from where you can look down on the top of the spire. This is from the restaurant and bar open to all on the fourteenth floor of the King George Hotel less than twenty paces from the sadly weathered Bath stone of All Souls.

Up there, as if seen from a moored airship, the whole of central London is wonderfully displayed in Lilliputian detail: Primrose Hill, the Zoological Gardens and the Hampstead escarpment to the north-west; the Surrey ridge to the south with a skylark's view of the line that Nash drew, shrewdly, to and from the *place* the Brothers built nearly half a century earlier. Even when you are level with its lightning conductor All Souls doesn't disclose what Nash may have overlooked, that is in this matter of entasis. But it is a striking fact that from on high the spire is seen to plunge right through the circular drum like a projecting ham-bone in a crinkled paper collar. The pillars above the vestibule are free-standing. They support only the parapet. The effect, which is what really matters, is intimate and enchanting.

As a person of a wholly different persuasion, I find it difficult to describe All Souls objectively. It is an evangelical establishment in the tradition of Billy Graham and extremely popular, especially among the young. The rituals and the vernacular responses at the services I attended were of a kind in which I felt excommunicated. To me there seemed no awe in the Presence especially in the vicinity of the altar. It would be improper if not impertinent for a person who clings to Christianity by the skin of his teeth to say more about the piety of those youthful congregations, especially as I was reared in ritualism.

My father was a Roman Catholic, a convert; my mother nominally C of E. Through no fault of theirs I was badly educated at a school for the sons of indigent Methodist ministers. My late wife was a gentle Jewish girl, a child therapist, and I was confirmed 'in mature years' amid votive pongs and gongs in that temple of the Tractarians, All Saints in nearby Margaret Street. Katie and I worship there together, regularly.

Into the maelstrom

Nothing at Oxford Circus bedevils the senses more than the stench of burnt oil and the noise, the roar, the squeal of traffic struggling to escape like pigs from a slaughter pen. At other famous roundabouts there is something to catch the eye, the poised agility of Eros at Piccadilly Circus, the glimpse of St Paul's and Blackfriars Bridge as seen from the foot of Fleet Street. But here nothing, nothing except truly demonic din, amplified as it bounces off a dissected circle of distinctly dull architecture. No human voices, not even the crackle from portable radios can be distinguished.

After the peace of the Park, the curious sense of leisureliness in Langham Place I invariably approach the maelstrom with misgivings, scurrying round the pedestrian barriers with a nervous glance up and down Oxford Street. A scamper across the road and thence down Regent Street, once 'the most fashionable street in the world'. Today when fancy takes me there, rarely – since I know the ins and outs of half a dozen small alternative streets – I hug the huge shop windows thinking, occasionally, of wartime days with the BBC Overseas (now World) Service which used to be lodged in Peter Robinson's store on the corner of the Circus, and how a bomb which nearly did us in laid bare a length of what had been the great Watling Street of the Romans.

69

Oxford Street in the 1920s

By far the best way for visitors to see Regent Street is from the top of south-bound buses which like a herd of ambling elephants, head to tail, stop and start again so frequently that details above a height of twenty-five feet can be seen as roosting starlings see them. Alternatively, the Sunday viewer, especially before Matins, can see what generations of architects have done and undone to the intention of John Nash to connect the Park and its purlieus to the liberties of St James's. With a few outstanding exceptions the wall of featureless buildings carries the Imperial style of Blomfield and his colleagues, whose façades are as flat as those of middle-class Parisian apartments.

In early forays that way for the London Letter of the *Guardian* I duly recorded such matters as the availability of sardines and whale steaks without coupons, the reopening of the goldfish market after the defeat of Japan, the weeks and weeks of writing that emerged from one cylinder of that entirely new discovery, the ballpoint pen, and the appearance almost overnight of virtually indestructible stockings made of stuff called nylon from Texan oil. I was encouraged by mean paymasters to be constantly surprised by the obvious.

Striding down there recently I noticed that the window-dressers of what Mother called the haberdashers have adopted the styles, the attitudes of embarrassingly importunate young females, the pace-makers who, in places where they are most conspicuous, such as in bus queues and shop doorways, grab and embrace their boy friends. In the windows the short-cropped dummies with their erotically slashed skirts and open shirts draw attention to their erotogenic zones. With their hands on forward-thrust hips their legs are mostly apart. In his translation of Juvenal's sixth satire, Dryden says:

> Behold the strutting Amazonian whore!
> She stands on guard with her right foot before;
> Her coat tucked up and all her motions just,
> She stamps and then cries 'Hah!' at every thrust.
> But laugh to see her, tired from many a bout,
> Call for the pot, and like a man piss out.

If a note of irritation has crept into this account of a walk down to Piccadilly Circus and beyond, it is that I am intolerant of noise and deeply dislike being jostled in a thoroughfare that lacks style. No matter how many of his ideas he may have borrowed or stolen from his predecessors, Nash, in his multiple role of surveyor, architect, agent, developer, lessee and resident, masterminded the notion of a great boulevard that both incorporated and bettered the lot of the Quality in the great squares to the west of the Street with the mean streets on the opposite side where today Carnaby Street, the resort of the young, is by far its most colourful and noisy descendant.

Hermione Hobhouse concludes her meticulous account of the rise and fall of this neighbourhood with a paragraph about the sad fate of Piccadilly Circus, that shrine of tourists and venue for national rejoicing. It is, she says, 'a living example of urban decay, unattractive to the average pedestrian and an inconvenient form of roundabout for the car-driver'. Oxford Circus is even more unattractive and a downright dangerous place from which to look up at the carved heads of lions that look down on the public lavatories below from balustrades dwarfed by the addition of attic storeys. Dozens more from similar litters – since they all look alike – decorate ledges, parapets and bald corners on both sides of the street. What had Norman Shaw, Henry·Tanner and Reginald Blomfield in mind when they ordered them to be cut or cast and craned up aloft?

One can see what the pot-bellied Buddhas represent on the north-east side. They date from the late 1860s when Arthur Liberty with his taste for all things Japanese was destined to become 'the best-known Oriental warehouseman of all time'. And there, renowned throughout the world, what was until recently his family's business stands firm today, a stately incurved building of pilasters with a striking frieze up to the skyline with figures peering over the top as if about to jump. Just around the corner, in Great Marlborough Street, Captain Liberty ordered a four-storey example of Tudor to be built out of timber from two old wooden battleships. The blast from the flying bomb that scraped it, seared the length of Argyll

Street and knocked us about in the BBC News Room in Peter Robinson's.

From Liberty's store which in 1901 offered 'every requisite for a complete outfit of mourning . . . at a moment's notice' down to Swan and Edgar's who were silk mercers in 1848 and famed until they were demolished two years ago, Regent Street's great stores were the resort of the well-off. They were recommended by Baedeker and patronized by royalty. Who hadn't heard of the Goldsmith and Silversmith's Company, Aquascutum and Burberry for rain gear, Lillywhite's for sports goods and Dr Gustav Jaeger's Sanitary System of Woollen Clothing? Nansen had taken the latter to the Arctic, and Scott less successfully to the South Pole.

Between 1926 and 1936 when I developed a youthful passion for an older cousin, a nurse-trainee at Guy's, I visited London perhaps half a dozen times at the invitation of a thoughtful uncle known as the Buccaneer. For six months in each year, in pursuit of whale oil for Lever Brothers, he drank his way from Trondheim to Oslo, a capital city which he always referred to as Christiania. In his company I went to the opera for the first time, nodded briefly, bravely, to G. K. Chesterton and Belloc and gained a fair knowledge of Regent Street dominated, as far as I was concerned, by that incomparable treasure-house, Hamleys toy shop, the Mecca of generations of schoolboys. They first opened their doors in the 1890s. Open-mouthed and wide-eyed I stared at Eiffel Towers, Forth Bridges and giant Ferris wheels made out of Meccano. Clockwork submarines buzzed as they dived under models of trans-Atlantic liners in a huge tank of water dyed marine blue. Squadrons of fighter planes in balsa wood hung from the ceiling, and all around and through Lilliputian landscapes of woods, ravines and stations, each with a network of points flashing green and red, little trains hauling freight and passengers narrowly missed each other. And today? An old friend said, 'Take a look.'

An entirely different shop. Through the first window I stared as if into a maternity ward on a busy day. Dozens of naked newborns peered through eyes half closed and misted over from the womb-dark, each with a wrist-tag and strip of gauze over their unhealed tummy buttons. Some looked positively foetal. The psychos have moved into the doll business. The child confronted with the awful prospect of a rival sibling can now have its own newborn to care for. Or drown in the bath. Later on, when it comes to terms with its extended family, it can play with an electronically controlled poppet 'that both walks and talks' and, for all I know, can be toilet trained.

Teddy bears cover some hundreds of feet of shelf space. In size range from little Koalas to almost lifesize Kodiaks that look as fierce as hell, they grunt, growl, beat drums, blow whistles or just sprawl in huge piles of Fluppets, Muppets, Puppets, Paddingtons and recently discovered Pongo-Bongos. Rupert in the old *Daily Express* would be astonished by his descendants.

You don't have to be a zoological correspondent to realize that most people, especially children, are fond of upright animals. Directors of zoos and circuses make much of the Law of the Angle. Attractiveness can be directly correlated with posture. The more upright the better. Vertical creatures pull the crowds in. Penguins, parrots and owls are good examples. Bears are even better ones although in the wild they are often more dangerous than the big cats. Psychologists have shown that many small children prefer teddy bears to human dolls of the same size. They are less competitive. They are cuddlesome and they come in all sizes and colours from pale fluorescent blue to ice cream pink. It occurs to me that the Law of the Angle applies to fish. The sea-horse *(Hippocampus)*, an upright creature, is both a three-star exhibit in zoo aquaria and, among women, one of the most popular emblems and ornaments in the Western world.

Foubert Street, a narrow gully alongside Hamleys, commemorates the activities of Major Henry Foubert who at the beginning of the eighteenth century ran a fencing and riding establishment in Swallow Street, then one of the most ill-famed rookeries in London. He seems to have been a man of probity. Less could be said of his successors who leased out premises to pawnbrokers, dram shops and whorehouse-keepers. In the words of George Augustus Sala, one of the founders of the Savage Club, to be found there 'were more than equivocal livery stables said to be extensively patronized by professional highwaymen'.

Foubert Street is signposted, boldly, *'To Carnaby Street'* below which lies the old Marylebone Stream. The neighbourhood can be heard long before you get there. The pubs with their sawdusted floors, especially the Shakespeare's Head, are relatively quiet. The Niagara Falls of noise comes from the clothes shops where the latest in pop music has the penetrating quality of pneumatic drills. Most of them sell what for the young is distinctly fashionable gear but I can't make out why such a perceptive critic as David Piper can justly claim that 'overnight in the 1960s Carnaby Street usurped the glamour of Savile Row . . .' He admits this was only for the young but what youngster would look twice at the reserved styles of tailors in the Row? From a two-foot-high pile of lettered white T-shirts I picked up one which was realistically bloodstained and inscribed *'Piss off you Bastard'*. I still think Mr Piper has got it wrong.

Back I went to Hamleys homunculi, trying to remember how the shop looked when the management had youngsters rather than their parents in mind, especially on frosty nights shortly before Christmas when their windows danced with lights and kerbside pedlars sold trays full of tinsel and trinkets and released clockwork mice around the feet of passers-by. I recall a very old beribboned man who played carols out of tune on a tin whistle and a clandestine Father Christmas who did a roaring trade just out of sight of the watchful doorkeeper.

I saw him at six o'clock at night when I found it more profitable, certainly quicker to get off the crawling bus and walk down to Fleet Street. I saw him two hours later on my way back home. But it wasn't the same benevolent scene. Two policemen were trying to separate and carry off two beardless fighting Father Christmases who were locked together like all-in wrestlers. As a bystander related the matter, the first pitch-holder, the one I had seen earlier, a jolly fellow, had been provoked by an interloper with a loud voice and somewhat unsteady stance. He had ventured too close. There were oaths; they came to blows. The spectacle must

have strained the fond illusions of children clutching gifts from yet another Father Christmas downstairs in the store. As for myself it was too late for a laconic telephone call to that paper printed in Manchester.

Regent Street's resistance to the frightful wounds of wars and fashions and economics has looped the loop since Nash dandified the whole grand sweep. It may be likened to the marvels of human skin which until the blood thins constantly regenerates itself. The texture may be rougher, the need for emollients and cosmetics greater, but the pattern largely remains the same. Many of the great stores are still there. The Café Royal too, brightened up no end. The resort today of ad-men and business lunchers, a light year away from the gilded caryatids and huge mirrors of the 'nineties which reflected Oscar Wilde, Lord Alfred Douglas, Marie Lloyd and later, after the second bombing, Constant Lambert, Cyril Connolly and the raffish friends of Dylan Thomas. If you hug the left bank to that point opposite Austin Reed where the street, like the blade of a scimitar, cuts between the County Fire Office and the ruins of the creation of Mr George Swan and Mr William Edgar, Eros is revealed but in strange company.

A house, said Le Corbusier, is a machine for living in. Storekeepers face more complicated problems. In addition to using every available square yard of space for display purposes, the building must look attractive both outside and in. In a village street there is latitude for variety. In a boulevard of potential magnificence, conformity is of overriding importance and this is what, primarily, bedevilled the building of so much that lies between Park Crescent and St James's. It took ten years (1910–1921) for another set of planners, architects and their clients to iron out most of their fierce disagreements. They finished up with what the late Sir John Betjeman castigated as 'the pseudo-Renaissance efforts of a benighted architecture as affected and "naice" as a refeened accent'.

The reference is to the late Sir Reginald Blomfield, the favourite architect of George the Peace-maker. He would have nothing to do with Modernism. He had a poor opinion of Nash and poured scorn on Epstein and James Joyce. After the First

World War the emphasis was on Imperialism in bold blocks lightly decorated with lions, those symbols of dominance. No matter that in Germany, Bauhaus, the most important school of architecture in the early part of the twentieth century, was flourishing under Gropius who, in fact, couldn't get a job here. It proclaimed the need for craft schools and for all artists and architects to work together towards the goal of the 'building of the future'. Blomfield didn't think that way. Among much else he was busy in Flanders designing Silent Cities, those vast war cemeteries with their porticos in the style of New Delhi.

Unless they pulled down the whole of Regent Street it's difficult to imagine what else Blomfield, Tanner and Norman Shaw could have done with it. In his criticism of Shaw, Betjeman is both downright unfair and perverse. In *Ghastly Good Taste* he describes him as 'a facile, expensive and pretentious architect who, like many of his followers, had facility for catching rich clients'. In a revised edition published thirty years later, the 'sham classicist', the designer of New Scotland Yard, many houses and the Piccadilly Hotel, has become 'our greatest architect since Wren . . .'

Notwithstanding his perversity, his impishness, his capacity to stir things up, I write of Betjeman with huge affection. He taught me to see style in the buildings I grew up with, the Victorian bricks and stones of Leeds. In London it happened, quite fortuitously, that we shared the same priest at All Saints, Margaret Street. Later I sought his help for my young brother, an historian and conservationist who was trying to preserve some fine old buildings in an otherwise unrewarding quarter of one of the Five Towns. Sir John rose like a trout. He travelled up to see them. He blasted the town council in a broadcast and assured me he was always glad to do what he could. He became vice-president of an hermetic organization unknown outside Fleet Street, the MGOCA, the Manchester Guardian Old Comrades' Association, the founder of which was the late Gerard Fay, the London Editor who was more or less born on the stage of the Abbey Theatre in Dublin.

Eros, that *genius loci* of Piccadilly Circus throughout the world, has been to the cleaners. Not just a *nettoyage général*. A metallurgical clinic of radiographers and corrosion specialists have probed, scoured, polished and written highly technical reports on every inch of the god's inner and outer anatomy. A technician assured me of this as, somewhat diffidently, he allowed me to peer through a squint in the strawboard pyramid which had hidden the reinstallation of the statue from vulgar gaze for weeks. Despite more than ninety years of light maltreatment, that is of being clambered over, swung on and daubed by revellers at times of rejoicing, the almost pure aluminium is still in excellent order.

A few points still puzzle me a little. Eros is not the God of Love. In 1893, the sculptor Alfred Gilbert designed and put together the fifteen parts by an unknown wax process in memory of that truly noble Victorian philanthropist, the Seventh Earl of Shaftesbury. In Art Nouveau it represents the Angel of Christian Charity. Should the little statue, therefore, fire towards Shaftesbury Avenue and not Lower Regent Street?

The point is perhaps trivial and, in light rain, I walked down that street to look for numbers 14 and 16 where John Nash built for himself and his cousin Edward a palazzo that might have served for the town house of a duke. A contemporary print depicts tall pillared wings that come forward to the pavement occupied on the ground floor, Paris fashion, by shopkeepers. The man in a hurry wanted to show the Quality how, by shrewd designs, ostentation could be made to pay for itself. As far as I could make out, the site is now occupied by a branch of Credit Lyonnais and a hamburger dispensary called Big 'Uns. So much for what was to be the rump end of the Georgian Triumphal Way.

Opposite, on the corner of Jermyn Street, stands the Plaza cinema where garish billboards are topped by a stately pleasure dome done up in striped tiles and surmounted by a lantern under a diminutive cupola. Rather fine in its way. This, together with the neo-Georgian swags that provide pigeons and sparrows with nests and starlings with nightly kips before they fly off each morning to the suburbs, are the best things in a dead deep channel for one-way traffic attacking Piccadilly Circus.

Let us praise Portland stone though in the hands of an ill-paid architect or neglected it weeps and the square-cut stone facing can look like the front of a top-security gaol. This is what has happened to the Post Office building further down Lower Regent Street. Sad ruminations on this point were relieved by the sight of an old friend, Stanley Green, the most famous sandwich-boardman in London.

'’Mornin',’ he said. 'Dampish. But it'll fine up in half an hour.’

Stanley never uses strong language. His philosophy is proclaimed on his large black board (see overleaf). He sells little booklets for precisely eleven pence each though most customers would pay more to discover he is not wholly against protein. It's merely that, in his opinion, everyone should eat less of it. Nor are the lusts he deplores simply of the flesh. They include anger, alcohol, violence and covetousness. There is nice simplicity in this man. He exists on a rather frugal diet of home-made bread, porridge, steamed vegetables, fruit and just one egg each day. He is rising seventy-three, lives in Haringey and rarely strays beyond his pitch around Oxford Circus. What was he doing in St James's?

He looked a bit owlish. It's difficult not to like Stanley. 'Got a friend down here,' he said and left me to turn over the possibilities.

A glimpse of the Athenaeum and Pall Mall brought to mind what E. V. Lucas called the material monasteries of clubland, those hallowed halls of horsehair and the snoring forties, particularly since my own stood hard by. Yes? No? No, I had a pilot to pick up in the Strand. The rain had stopped and the wind stood fair for the South Bank. I coasted along Charles II Street.

'What a bounteous banquet of costly viands is spread before an ardent-minded, grateful-spirited Perambulator.'[1] Charles II Street, behind the truly enormous New Zealand House, demands the sampling of an exquisite left-over, the Royal Opera Arcade (Covent Garden used to be called 'the Italian place') with its small groined vaults by Nash and Repton

---

[1] *Old Humphrey's Walks in London*, George Mogridge, London, 1843.

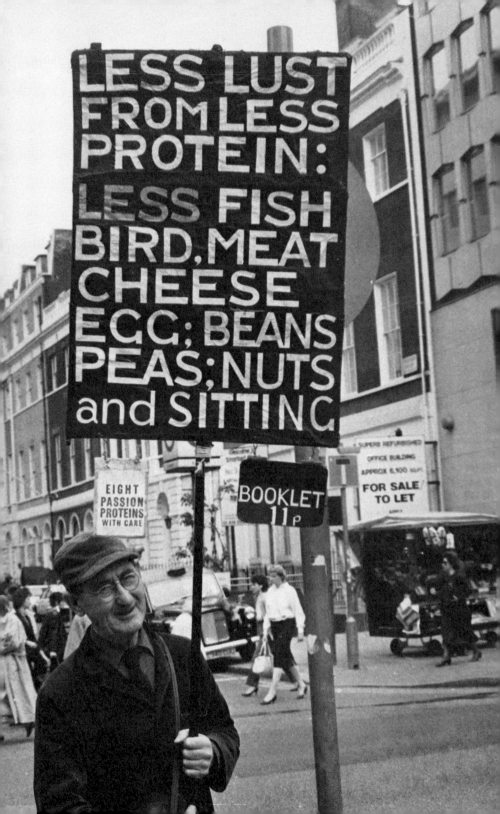

(1816), its lanterns and miscellany of shops that sell leather-bound books, maps, stamps, armour and very expensive fishing tackle.

Another cataract of traffic pours down Haymarket from the Circus, but make a run for it. Look first at the Corinthian-pillared façade of the Theatre Royal (more Nash) and nip round to the back, to the stage door where, in Suffolk Street and Suffolk Place, Prinny's favourite architect comes into his own. A hugely quiet oasis before you brave Trafalgar Square at the end of where they used to play some ball game called *palle maile*.

In geometric fact the Square is not a square but a subtle pentagon created by enlarging the old Charing Cross which nowadays lies around the corner in the Strand. It is dominated, as everyone knows, by Britain's most famous Lord Admiral, 'that one-armed, one-eyed, double-dyed adulterer' on top of his truly enormous column. Seen from a certain point in Carlton House Terrace, known to some guides, the top of his scabbard appears priapic. He looks down on milling tourists, soiled pigeons and, at predictable intervals, on chanting, speech-making political partisans.

Although less talked about and written about than Piccadilly Circus and Hyde Park Corner, the Square is London's only real political forum, big enough for thousands to gather there and shout their heads off. Standing as it does where six streets coalesce not far from the river, it is the carto-graphic centre from which all distances to and from the metropolis are measured. 'London 25 miles' it says on the signboards as we coast down the A1 on the way back from the moors, and we know we are only twenty miles from home.

The Square houses one of the world's greatest art collec-tions; the architecture ranges from the glorious to the grotesque. For children there are pigeons to be fed and fountain-gushing pools to be looked at enviously. I have actually fished in them.

During months of drought the fountains' circulatory water system is turned off. Green algae and sub-aquatic insects flourish. Accompanied by that good soul who helped us with our Heath survey by stalking dragonflies with a pair of field-glasses, I fished for water beetles before the crowds were out and about one Sunday morning. I was successful. She too, but in a lunge for an interesting larva far down in the water she all but went in head first and, in saving herself, disclosed underwear I last saw on my grandmother's washing-line.

Years later a learned prehistorian at the Natural History Museum, with the instincts of a hyena in knowing where to dig up bones, phoned up to say they were on to something good in the newly excavated cellars of Uganda House on the rim of the Square. They were hippo bones, and modern dating techniques have established that they were about 130,000 years old, that is they were from a warm period during the last Ice Age. More discoveries followed: Cave lion, Straight-tusked elephant, Giant oxen and Narrow-nosed rhinoceros. This may be reckoned a prehistoric bonanza as good as anything recovered from British soil anywhere. The snag was that the sites lay below enormous buildings and monuments including Landseer's lions and the impatient delvers had to wait until pubs and the like at the top end of Whitehall enlarged their vaults.

The Trafalgar Sequence is now an internationally recognized term among students of the Quarternary, a geological period which takes us back two million years. What brought the animals there was lush vegetation on the terraces and flood plains of the prehistoric Thames, of which St James's Park is one of the type-examples.

There had been an important football match at Wembley and more trouble in South Africa when I arrived in the Square by way of Pall Mall. The Communist Party of Great Britain was about to stage a demonstration march. Whether to assuage disturbed passions I cannot say, but the Salvation Army, headed by blue- and red-clad bandsmen, swept down from the Charing Cross Road with a spirited rendering of 'Onward Christian Soldiers'. With the possibility of riot and police standing shoulder to shoulder outside South Africa House, they swung into the relative quiet of the Strand. The alarmed pigeons flew back to be fed – do pigeon-feeders know, I wonder, that they are transmitters of psittacosis and a rather nasty species of flea? No sound except a mild cheer from a motley of skinheads as three of their heavily tattooed companions waded into the pool of water-gushing mermaids where, by clambering up on each other's backs, two clad only in fluorescent shorts managed to get up on to the uppermost basin of the fountain. Another pause before a column of police-flanked Communists marched into the Square from Whitehall with drummers ahead of the banner-bearers. *Tumpity-tumpity-tump-tump-*TUMP.

On they marched, skirting Admiralty Arch and up towards the giant portico of Canada House. Only at times like this can it be seen that the Square has been dug out of a hill. *Tumpity-tumpity-tump-tump-*TUMP. A slight scuffle outside the National Gallery where a few spectators were shoved back as they tried to join the guarded column: London cops are particularly good at disguising the strength of pub bouncers with assumed gentility fortified by a hammerlock. An odd building, that Gallery. It was erected on Dunghill Mews which are the demolished stables of the King's horses. The dome and turrets above the portico of the Gallery were likened by Sir John Summerson to 'the clock and vases on a mantelpiece, only less useful'. The columns are actually old stock from the demolition of Carlton House which were thrust on the unfortunate architect, William Wilkins, for reasons of economy. A pity this since, with his designs for Downing College, Cambridge, he was one of the pioneers of the Greek revival in England. He might have presented London with a building that truly dominated Trafalgar Square but, as events turned out, he muffed it and ruined his reputation.

As for the over-flowing art within the Gallery we may see it, as somebody said, constantly in our mind's eye but how rarely do we go there in the flesh? I am more fortunately placed since this glory lies within 150 paces or so of my publisher's office where, if the advance proves favourable, I can at least consider buying a sweeping ulster at Burberry's and thence home by way of the Venetian Rooms of the Gallery, masked and caparisoned as an Author. I dearly love Tiepolo.

More scuffles outside the bewitching church of St Martin-in-the-Fields. More serious this time. Apparently a marcher seems to have threatened a mounted policeman or, worse, his patient horse and the Comrades, to their credit, restrained him forcibly. The procession halted whilst the matter was sorted out. Did nobody spare so much as a glance up at James Gibbs's masterpiece? I have called it bewitching because the pediment supported by six giant Corinthian columns gives one the impression of a Greek temple surmounted incongruously by a Gothic spire, like the hat of a witch.

Tumpity-tumpity . . . Even the drummers seemed a bit dispirited when the rankers broke step and it was a small mob that drifted down to South Africa House for a strictly timed five minutes of ritual bawling.

Once around the south-east corner of that building you are within sight of Charing Cross, the last but one resting-place of Eleanor, the dear queen (*chère reine*) of Edward I. The present Cross and the adjacent hotel are of Victorian vintage. They have been the subject of much comment. Samuel Pepys lived nearby for several years and wrote: 'Went out to the Cross to see Major-General Harrison hanged, drawn and quartered; which was done there, he looking as cheerful as any man could in that condition.'

My original intention had been to cross the Strand diagonally and make for the river at the foot of Villiers Street but my good friend Leslie Ginsberg, that diligent consultant about almost everything relating to town-planning, insisted that I should look up at the walls of Zimbabwe House where Agar Street joins the Strand. I did so and came across an astonishing spectacle: eighteen grossly mutilated statues by the late great Sir Jacob Epstein. Heads, limbs and genitals had been hammered off. Some figures had been reduced to the mere suggestion of a torso. Who could have climbed up there to carry out what must have taken hours? Before relating what I subsequently learnt I must go back nearly half a century to the occasion when two of us were nearly thrown out of our digs when I injudiciously copied one of that sculptor's most famous panels.

We were in lodgings together in Mexborough in South Yorkshire, that is David Wood, who subsequently became political editor for *The Times*, and I. We both worked for the local paper and I learnt a great deal from him. Our landlady, a Mrs Rose, corsetière, an elderly puritanical widow, gave us to understand that we were a couple of reprobates and in that she was unquestionably right. A series of confrontations came to a head when in an effort to relieve the peeling distemper and biblical texts on my bedroom wall, I made a large copy of Epstein's 'Rima', the bird goddess, in charcoal and crayon, and hung it up. I had heard much about the sculptor from Jacob Kramer, the Leeds artist, and he had probably given me some prints.

Mother Rose blew her top. The usual arguments about art and indecency ensued and would have ended God knows where but for the broad-minded intervention of our local vicar who, unknown to us, had been called in to arbitrate. He felt that my treatment of the breasts of the Goddess was, perhaps, over-emphatic but conceded that I had some talent. Mother Rose insisted that my bedroom door should remain not only closed but locked. The spectacle within might upset her clients, she said.

The original carving of 'Rima' in an obscure corner of Hyde Park provoked a storm of protests as did almost all the public works of this genius who was hounded by the Press and self-appointed guardians of morality. But Epstein had powerful friends too, and but for them the Strand statues would not have remained unharmed for thirty years.

The figures were commissioned in 1907 by Charles Holden, the architect of the British Medical Association's new building in Agar Street who deliberately kept his façade severely plain in order to emphasize them to the utmost.

Epstein admits that the offer put him on his feet financially and publicly since his work was almost unknown except to a distinguished coterie which included Augustus John, Bernard Shaw, Muirhead Bone, Francis Dodd and other members of the New English Arts Club.

The storm broke when the scaffolding was removed from the first four figures. In his autobiography the sculptor says:

'One would have imagined that my work was in some manner outrageous. It consisted, for the most part, of nudes in such narrow niches that I was forced to give simple movements to all the figures. In symbolism I tried to represent man and woman in their various stages from birth to old age, a primitive but in no way bizarre programme.'

There were letters to *The Times*, petitions and counter-petitions, questions were asked in Parliament. 'Experts' were called in. Bishops became art critics overnight. Scotland Yard sent a policeman who wrote down the word 'rude' in his notebook. Dr Cosmo Gordon Lang, later Archbishop of Canterbury, mounted the ladder on the scaffolding and declared afterwards that he saw nothing indecent or shocking about the figures.

The Strand Statues became the subject of cartoons, music-hall jokes and songs. Buses on the way to the City slowed down to allow upstairs passengers to get a glimpse of what both the *Evening Standard* and *St James's Gazette* described as statues 'which no careful father would wish his daughter and no discriminating young man his fiancée to see . . .'. Rarely if ever has a British sculptor – actually he was born on the East Side in New York City of well-off Polish-Jewish refugees – had so much publicity in so short a time. A meeting of the Council of the British Medical Association was called to consider what ought to be done. Shrewdly, at this point, the Arts Establishment – with the exception of the Royal Academy in one of its regular tightrope-walking acts – moved in. The statues were defended in *The Times* by C. J. Holmes, Slade Professor of Fine Arts, Charles Ricketts, Charles Shannon and Lawrence Binyon. *The Times*, too, added its editorial weight.

The BMA Council tempered its awaited opinion by passing the buck to Sir Charles Holroyd, Director of the National Gallery. What did *he* think? In a dozen dignified sentences he came out solidly in favour of the sculptor. In the future, he thought, the BMA would be proud of having given him the work to do. Whether the majority of the BMA councillors really liked the statues will never be known. They were obliged to give their nominal approval and it was thought, wrongly, that no more would be heard of the matter. The same pack of rabble-rousers never forgave the sculptor. Epstein's 'Rima' was daubed; his serene and majestic 'Genesis' was likened to a pregnant gargoyle. Predictably, G. K. Chesterton considered 'Behold the Man' 'an outrage' and one of the greatest insults to religion he had ever seen. It showed on the long view what a short-sighted, bigoted fellow he was, especially on religious matters. James Bone described it as a 'caryatid of suffering . . . the most impressive of Mr Epstein's great stone figures . . .'.

In 1935, the Southern Rhodesian Government took over the BMA building and promptly announced its intention of removing the figures as the new occupants thought them 'undesirable'.

On this occasion the Establishment, with one outstanding exception, leaped to the defence of a sculptor described by one of them as 'graduating rapidly to classic rank'. The exception, Sir William Llewellyn, President of the Royal Academy, must have regretted his temerity since he was not only opposed, he was challenged by the presidents and trustees of other notable institutions. Sickert promptly resigned from the Royal Academy. The Royal Fine Arts Commissioners intervened. They approached the Southern Rhodesian authorities and were assured, they said, that the sculptures would not be removed.

It seems to have been a devious assurance because two years later, on the grounds that the Portland stone figures were decaying and were thus potentially dangerous, they were literally broken up. They were shattered before another furore could ensue. As the sculptor wrote: 'Anyone passing along the Strand can now see as on some antique building, the few mutilated fragments of my decoration.'

On the south side of the Strand immediately opposite the granite blocks of Zimbabwe House lies George Court, a narrow canyon that leads down to a clutch of streets named after the great seventeenth-century barons including that hell-rake George Villiers, Duke of Buckingham. Few relics survive but as a number of later-built houses are of good design and good stone I sought guidance from another friend, Eric Robinson, a professional geologist who can make building-stone, both ancient and modern, come wonderfully alive. By shepherding his students from University College through Westminster and the City, he has taught them in his endearing way that there's more to petrology than learning arid stratigraphic columns like multiplication tables, although they are the genealogy, the pedigrees of billions of years' prehistory of the earth. He is a fellow northerner; he dotes on walking and running and talking to people, all sorts of people with a background wider than mere academic study.

We met at the foot of the desecrated statues where he was looking at the composition of some finely polished granite through a hand lens. 'Come on then,' he said, 'and I'll show you some stone you knew as a lad.' And together we crossed the road.

At the very top of George Court, above the steps, he paused to stroke some rather nondescript grey-white rock, the facing stone of Villiers House. 'Genuine Italian marble,' he said. '*Bardiglio Fiorita* from the Apennines near Carrara.' As so often happens nowadays, the lower reaches of the cladding had been sprayed with graffiti. But as if nature were imitating the art of the daubers, the marble itself was veined with thin dark lines which turned and twisted in scores of shapes that stirred the imagination. 'The original limestone', he explained, 'has been baked by the earth's heat and subterranean pressure. A good example of metamorphism,' he added, almost apologetically.

The well-worn steps had been cut and hauled into place nobody will ever know how long ago. Possibly about that day when George Villiers, the playmate of Charles I, was assassinated. Yorkshire flags or 'coal measure sandstones', as the Geologist called them, are made of durable stuff and probably came from quarries I used to know so well in Batley and Mirfield.

A glance up John Adam Street to where the glory of the huge Adelphi by the Adam Brothers is now marked only by isolated architectural treasures such as the Royal Society of Arts building, and we cut through into Villiers Street.

Sir Humphrey Davy who 'abominated gravy and lived in the odium of having discovered sodium' took up lodgings in the basement of what used to be number 14. Peter Bushell, formerly a London guide and lecturer, tells us that, obsessed by his experiments, he seldom went out or even wasted time changing his shirts. He preferred to slip a clean one over the old. When it became too hot and too sticky to wear more than five he stripped them all off and began again. I looked down into that basement. Eric was busy on the other side of the street, examining different kinds of Portland stone for different degrees of weathering according to where the blocks had been wedged from the quarries.

Rudyard Kipling also lived in Villiers Street. Another loner, he seldom ventured out. When he wasn't putting the final touches to *The Light That Failed* he paced up and down, thinking. In his autobiography he tells us that: 'Once I faced the reflection of my own face in the jet-black mirror of the window panes for five days. When the fog thinned, I looked out and saw a man standing opposite the pub where the barmaid lived; on a sudden his breast turned dull red like a robin's and he crumpled, having cut his throat.'

The real loners spend their nights huddled up under the arches of Hungerford Bridge, the lucky ones guarding their tattered blankets. When the starlings roosting overhead are at their loudest, each one turns up with a large cardboard box, his home, and – like an impoverished squire with only a few acres – is indignant if his privacy is invaded. *Whiskas* may be on nodding terms with *Hob-Nobs* and *Chunky* but mostly they are silent, shredding their fag ends, waiting, all of them for the blue truck of the Salvation Army.

When it arrives they are (relatively) convivial. *Fairy Liquid* might recall seeing *Sony Television* at the Wandsworth kip and perhaps *Kattomeat* has a cautionary tale about that lousy new cop in the Embankment Gardens until with a mug of tea, a bowl of soup, a sandwich and a 'God bless you' from the

Army lassie, always courteous and considerate, they mooch back to their boxes. The rest is farts and snores.

In 1679, ten years after the death of his wife, Samuel Pepys came to adjacent Buckingham Street where plaques proclaim that the Prince of Diarists lived first at number 12 and then at number 14. What I can't make out is the curious ambivalence of his character. He has been rightly described as the Father of the Civil Service and the Saviour of the Navy. He was loved and respected by some of the noblest and the wisest men in England. He worked hard to keep his honour bright. After he had read some 'rogueish French books' he carefully burnt them so he should not be disgraced if they were found after his death. But it's on record that one day and, his diary tells us, not for the first time, Mrs Pepys saw him with his hands up the skirts of a serving wench and she wrote down her just complaints and wrote, moreover, in plain and very pungent English.

Pepys in an agony lest the world should come to see it, brutally seizes and destroys the tell-tale document. And then what does he do? He sets down the whole disgraceful story with no lack of detail in one of those six leather-bound diaries stamped in gold with his arms, crest and motto on the open shelves of his library.

He might have thought that posterity would care to know what he really thought about his royal master, Charles II, and his own remarkable accomplishments, but not that he broke wind immoderately, had nits in his wig and that whilst the Great Fire raged less than a quarter of a mile away, he was fondling the breasts of his wife's companion, Mary Mercer, 'they being the finest I ever saw in my life, that is the truth of it'. In what was meant to be praise, David Piper described the effusion that eventually amounted to 1,300,000 words as 'the unboringness of ordinariness'. Surely even the chatter of this compulsive diarist, the merciless self-critic who laid down the foundations of the Royal Navy – although he didn't learn his multiplication tables until a few months before his thirtieth birthday – could never be described as *ordinary*.

I hastened after Eric who was fingering the Portland stone slabs of the steps below the ancient and horribly spiked railings that lead down to the Watergate. They are inlaid with fragments of the fossils of marine algae and extinct oysters. The huge tripartite arch of the Watergate itself with its heavily rusticated pillars – 'like a clipped poodle' said Eric – is all that remains of the London mansion and estate of George Villiers, Duke of Buckingham. It stood originally on the brink of the Thames, that is before the river was dredged and deepened and the Embankment constructed.

If you can put up with the thunderous noise of the trains close to your backside, the sight of the Thames from the gangway across Hungerford Bridge is one of the finest in London, especially when the wind lifts the water into wavelets. It is Canaletto come alive. In one glorious curve the north bank is irregularly punctuated first by the rear of the Charing Cross Hotel, then the Adelphi with its starkly dressed neighbour, Shell-Mex House and, beyond, the infinitely more subtle façade of the Savoy Hotel built from artificial stone.

Gleaming white Waterloo Bridge bounds across the river: there is no other word for it. By contrast, Blackfriars Bridge wades into the water, ponderously, and between them, above the Victoria Embankment, the seemingly enormous length of Somerset House looks its best from a distance. The roofs of the Temple are too complicated to be made out as individuals but from them appears to rise the many-tiered spire of St Bride's. The figure of Justice and the copper dome of the Old Bailey add to familiarity made serene by the most familiar dome of all, that of St Paul's. It looks magnificent.

The Royal Festival Hall has been described by Master Pevsner as, aesthetically, the greatest achievement of the Festival of Britain. Inevitably critics of lesser stature have niggled. One of them likened the balcony and the irregular tiers of boxes for seating that jut out of the Concert Hall walls to drawers pulled out in a hurried burglary raid. In our brief foray into the building, Eric seized on the crinoidal limestone cladding around the main doorways with the enthusiasm of a professional horticulturist at Chelsea Flower Show.

Crinoids, popularly known as Stone-lilies, are beautiful

little creatures – primitive animals not plants which did particularly well in the bygone age of coal and lingered on although they are rare in our seas today. The smoky-grey stone, known to the trade as Derbyshire Fossil, seems to be full of their slender calcareous stems and bulbs. Inside, the equally fossiliferous oatmeal-like limestone paving came, he told me, from the famous Hopton Wood quarries in Derbyshire. It is the material out of which Henry Moore created sombre mysteries.

With the exception of this exotically dressed lady under an umbrella which can scarcely be described as useful, the contemporary sculpture, as a visitor from Dallas, Texas put it, had him 'somewhat intrigued' which, I suppose, is what all art is really about. A rather Rodin-like figure entitled *The Cellist* by Siegfried Charoux depicted a man apparently puzzled by the problem of playing a metallic instrument deprived of all except its outer framework. A third work by William Pye entitled *Zemran* could be an anagram which I have yet to work out since it portrayed an igloo cowering beneath two enormous sinuous shapes all made out of what appeared to be stainless steel.

There is a curious sequel to this superficial study of some of the sculpture in the vicinity of the Festival Hall. Katie photographed the lady with the umbrella not long after I was there in the company of the Geologist. Shortly before most of this manuscript was sent to my publisher, I hastened down to the South Bank to find out something about the intriguing woman. Not only had she disappeared but an Information Officer, the resident security guard and a sweeper up who'd worked there for years all said they'd never seen her. It came out, eventually, that she had been exhibited, briefly, by the Hayward Gallery for *Homage to Barcelona* and had been sent back home. By that time I had got to grips with some of the most enduring stone in London, the Walls and the Tower.

Within the walls

Dawn broke like an addled egg. The great walls of the Tower would soon resemble a pitted Cheshire cheese but at that hour they were dire, death-black, a silhouette or, to put it another way, a backcloth to one of the great set-pieces of London's history. Did I imagine it or could I really hear the hideous ravens croaking, hopping around for their daily gobbets of old horseflesh? I listened again. Even at half-past four in the morning London is never wholly quiet. The all-pervading hum, that bane of solitude seekers, of urban bird recordists, has no particular point of origin. It is the continuo or figured bass against which immediate sounds spring to raucous life. There on the skirts of Tower Hill I heard the fish trucks rumbling along Lower Thames Street, to and from the great market of Billingsgate.

Fifteen years have elapsed since I left Hampstead at two o'clock in the morning to arrive at the Tower at dawn. Billingsgate – where I had a pint of tea in the company of fish buyers, vendors and their attendant porters – has now been pulled down and moved to some less romantic market on the Isle of Dogs. On that occasion I had a mind to see the men at work and heard scarcely an oath amongst those polite white-coated fellows but heard much about the current price of home-water chats, kits, gibbers and jumbos which are regional varieties of haddock. I didn't stay long because I wanted to reach Hampton Court in the late afternoon which, including diversions, amounted to more than twenty-five miles on foot.

On my present walk, as upon that earlier one, I looked only at the grim exterior of the Tower for I know little more about its grim interior history, especially during Tudor times, than can be picked up from one or two guidebooks.

> The clangour of mailed footsteps sounding like a storm of hail in the passages . . . died away; and now a black frost of silence sealed the world from all life . . . The young girl with the lion-coloured hair and the great golden haunting eyes who had just entered the Tower by the Traitor's Gate sat quietly, looking at the door of her prison, as if she waited for someone . . .

That woe-draped glimpse of the girl who became Gloriana is how Edith Sitwell saw her on the first page of *The Queens and the Hive*. It inflames the imagination. But I leave it there preferring, as I did only a few days ago, to sit down quietly for a few minutes on the steps above the entrance gate and scan the walls through the keen eyes of my pocket-sized Zeiss. Sermons in stones.

Primed by what I had learnt from the Geologist I made out some details of the walls of the Tower from both Roman and Norman times onwards. They are largely of Kentish Rag or Greensand from quarries close to Maidstone in Kent, the nearest source of durable stone for building purposes. 'Rag' or 'ragged' denotes its rough qualities. As the quarries have been worked for more than 2,000 years it could be that the word Maidstone is significant.

What I find wholly remarkable is that the Romans were able to find the best source of stone almost as quickly as it was needed. Many many thousands of tons of Rag went into the building of *Londinium Augusta* with its two miles of surrounding walls originally about eight feet thick. Unlike the Normans, the Romans did not regard the area of the Tower as primarily a fortification point. With the devastating invasion of Boadicea in mind, the Romans built a fortress to the north, in Cripplegate. But the Wall ran right through the present Tower, and curled round the City, coming down to the river by way of Ludgate Circus. The ubiquitous Portland stone later replaced Norman material, but Kentish Rag with its ground-up oyster shells appears in all sorts of unexpected places from in-filling rubble to hewn blocks which are never large.

From the chance discovery of the remains of a very ancient hulk at the point where the Fleet River enters the Thames – now through a huge pipe under Blackfriars Bridge – archaeologists have unravelled a fascinating story of how the Rag reached *Londinium*. It's more than twenty years since engineers started to build an underpass around that point. They made a coffer-dam, that is they isolated a slight loop in the Thames with watertight palisades and pumped it dry. Fascinating things – for archaeologists – came up with every scoop of the mechanical grabs: old coins, pottery, shreds of eel traps and woodwork including the ribs of a ship, flat-bottomed with a cradle for mast and sail, not unlike the Thames barges of more recent times. She had been at sea. The fact is indisputable. There were marine worms in her timbers.

This ship and two others are referred to in the technical literature as under Roman domination and commission no doubt. But the fact is that the Celts from which large numbers of us are descended, if only through those damned so-called Anglo-Saxons, have an ancestry and tradition older by far than the bellicose road-builders and plumbers from that imperial headquarters on the Tiber. Celts had been carrying stone in boats for 5,000 years. Stonehenge attests the fact. The great blue stones from the Prescelly mountains of Pembrokeshire, weighing over four tons apiece, must have come at least part way by sea, around the dangerous Gower Peninsular.

The Ragstone quarries lie below the North Downs. Some Celtic barge-captain, probably from the subjugated but honoured tribe of Batavi from the Low Countries renowned as watermen and bridge-builders and maybe a seafaring member of the Kentish Cantiaci, had inched his craft down the Medway to Rochester and through a mesh of marsh channels.

After such a voyage, breasting the treacherous tide-rips and mud banks of the estuary, it must have been humiliating to feel her sinking, her planks rotting in the mouth of the slow-flowing Fleet that rises on Hampstead Heath. Her holds were half full of Rag. Let us cast our minds back.

Those huge holes in the hill, the *Magnae Lapicidinae* lay within a league of where today stands Maidstone. The new Governor, Octavius Scapula, had ordered a good road to be built from the quarries to a port on the Medway where now you may find some of the finest orchards in Kent.

For day after day, for month after month, from sunrise to light-fall, the Ragstone was hauled to the estuary on heavy-wheeled carts pulled by teams of broad-shouldered Celtic oxen which had to be thrashed until their flanks ran red. Their agonized roars could be heard 'way back in the quarries. The centurion transferred from the Twentieth supervised the loading at *Lapicidinae* to where another centurion, Decimus Bolanus who had fought with him when they first landed under the Eagles of Plautius five years earlier, stood on the quayside with arms folded over his breast-plate, looking with undisguised contempt at the ship, her crew and the owner. The pilot stood a little aside.

Bolanus swayed in that great wind, the Eiger, which for days had blown from the north-east of the world and had in it at once the vigour of the Arctic and the southern things which it was seeking. The wind stood against the rotting scow which meant that it could only be rowed and this had provoked much argument between the owner, a creepy little man who ran the biggest whore-shop in North Kent where profits from the legionaries had made him rich. He invested his sesterces in old Roman ships which, when converted, could be used for carrying Ragstone under contract.

He was all for pulling out that afternoon but the pilot, a Batavian, a client tribesman of the Romans and therefore a Gaul with authority, shook his head. If the Eiger backed and blew south as he feared it might, they would need more rowers. Otherwise they would be blown south into the Roman Channel between Britannia and Gaul.

The centurion, not understanding the *patois*, the heavy

Germanic vowels of the Batavian and the clipped consonants of the Kentish Celts, called the pilot to him. He saluted him. Rome respected her clients. 'What's all this about?' he asked in the pigeon Latin of the conquerers. The pilot, a thoughtful man, paused a moment. He wished to be as exact as he could. '*Gubernator sum*,' he said: he was both pilot and Master. He needed more oarsmen. Otherwise . . . he shrugged his shoulders. But the boat-owner, the whore-keeper started to argue. It would cost more money. The centurion hit him in the face. 'Let oarsmen be brought here,' he said. '*Praesens!*' At once.

Thus it was that the rotting old scow known to her crew as the *Valfischmager*, the Whale's Belly, was rowed out of the Medway, into the very teeth of the Eiger with twelve extra oarsmen aboard. As a small form of insurance for his own safety, the Batavian asked to be accompanied by one of the centurion's young boy-friends.

Just as he feared the Eiger backed and it became necessary to lessen her burden. The Master ordered the crew to jettison half or more of their cargo. After that he rarely spoke. But he stood aft with a long skein of flax over his shoulder at the end of which he had tied a copper cylinder of grease. From time to time he threw it overboard and smelt the mud to know precisely where he stood.

The Horned God was on his side. When he stood to the lee of what today is Barrows Deep in the German Ocean the wind freshed and blew from the east. 'Right up our arse,' he said to a fellow-Batavian. They turned the *Whale* about and raised the huge thread-bare sails. The oarsmen, with nothing to do, massaged their stiffening biceps. Some diced out of a carved horn. Others went for'ard under the half-deck and wrestled with the slaves who, being slaves, allowed them the throw.

The Master stared ahead as the *Whale* buried her bows deep and yawed so wildly that the helm kicked and two oarsmen had to be set to lean against it. After being at sea for two days the Master just managed to inch her into the estuary of the Thames and up to the mouth of the Fleet where, ignominiously, she sank.

★

When the coach-parties began to roll in and the crowds dutifully queued at the Tower turnstiles, I thought of the miles ahead and struck west, along Great Tower Street. All Hallows, Barking is capped by a pretty copper-green spire with much treasure below, right down to the tessellated Roman pavements in the undercroft, but it's the skin of buildings I'm concerned with. The railed-off road around All Hallows – which probably marks the eastern limit of the Great Fire – must be crossed with extreme caution but it's worth the risk both to see and feel what architects can do by cladding their relatively modern buildings with inch-thick plates of rock originally spewed out of the earth's interior, especially granite and marble in all their gleaming colour and varieties.

There on the corner of Seething Lane where Samuel Pepys lived and worked stands Knollys' House faced by Sardinian beige granite with its high proportion of feldspar, glittering mica and amethysthine quartz. Perhaps one of the cheapest of the granites, there is a warmth about it but it ought to be washed down as often as the ground-floor windows.

I paused, briefly, outside Wheelers where you can get a more than tolerable lunch for about fifty quid and struck up Mincing Lane. Plantation House is a sprawling Colossus flanked by columns of Portland stone on a base of grey Cornish granite. The panels of Colonial House on the opposite side of the road are made up of one of the best known igneous rocks used in ornamental frontages. This is wonderfully patterned blue-green Larvikite from a small region on the Oslo fjord. The iridescence from the large crystals should be seen on a light-flashing day. The rock is so much used on the fronts of pubs and the innumerable branches of a well-known tailoring firm that the trade sometimes refers to it as Montagu-Burtonite.

Mincing Lane has a long association with the wholesale of tea and spices. My wife, Katie, the widow of a Ceylon tea-planter, recalls Plantation House as that mysterious place through which their product was marketed. As David Piper nicely puts it: 'Mincing Lane should be the cosy home of the mother of teashops,' for, despite the espresso bars, 'tea is to the Londoner as petrol is to a car. But Plantation House is bleak beyond endurance.' The massive Imperial style of the façade has been vulgarized by gilt paint splashed on to the medallions.

Eastcheap is the extension of Great Tower Street. A glance up Rood Lane makes it clear that, in their desperate search for an originality so few of them possess most modern architects don't care a hoot about conformity or regional planning. Within the Rood, literally the Cross of Christ, is a plain church by Wren with a beautiful but most un-Wrennish spire. Beyond is a group of Georgian town houses which echo Ruskin and Venice but, towering above all to the north, is the new Lloyds building on the pattern of the Pompidou Centre in Paris, a blue and red monster laced about with its own entrails, its pipes and shafts all exposed.

Eastcheap, so-called from the market (*ceap*) held there in the Middle Ages, used to swarm with merchants who sold things you could actually see. The merchants are still there but today they sell oil from distant places or represent banks and insurance offices where they go in for usury on the grand scale. From Elizabethan times onwards piety and commerce went hand in hand. The merchants who built the churches were the true lords of London. Neither the Crown nor the ecclesiastical authorities could exert authority over the City without the consent of its most affluent citizens. It followed that, after the Great Fire, Wren had much rebuilding to do hereabouts.

Five of his churches, each unique in different ways, lift proudly near St Margaret Pattens which, some think, had to do with those who made clogs in Rood Lane. To the west lies St Clements with fine woodwork but which otherwise is rather bread-and-butter Wren; to the south the blitzed but still glorious shell of St Dunstan-in-the-East. Immediately to the west in Lovat Lane is St Mary-at-Hill which used to be called the Fishermen's Church since it lies within smelling distance of Billingsgate. The belief is that a clergyman who went a long way, Thomas Becket, served his time there. In the ghastly, ghostly tunnel of Lower Thames Street stands St Magnus Martyr with what Tom Eliot called its 'inexplicable splendour of Ionian white and gold'.

I made for the flying buttresses of St Dunstan's with keen anticipation since on that earlier walk the rubble below the tower – which is all that remains of the church – was thickly overgrown with fleabane, thistles, ragwort, Rosebay willow-herb and a riot of Red campion. Painted Lady butterflies darted among the blossoms and, wonder of wonders, a solitary specimen of that rarity, the Hummingbird hawk moth sampled the nectaries of a cascade of honeysuckle planted, perhaps, by some soul saddened by the ruins. A naturalist whose name I can't remember said this rare species 'is an ambassador among moths, flitting across the Channel from France, taking the hospitality of our gardens for granted with his lovely presence'.

On this occasion I found the wasteland transformed into a formal garden with a trim lawn and seats among clambering clematis and bushy ceanothus with its powdery blue flowers. As a centrepiece there are exotic oaks which have been carefully chosen since, like the Lombardy poplar, their branches are fastigiate; they grow upwards not outwards where they would have shielded this small enclosure from the sun. There were no butterflies but bees bumbled among the blossom and on the grass I teased an old friend, a click beetle which when overturned has the good sense to turn a somersault, not just once but time and time again until it lands on its feet. A lesson for us all. A blackbird sang from the slender spire.

Most of Wren's City spires are thin. They carry the line of the tower, and in more congested times his masons had no room to build except upwards, towards the sky.

From Mary-at-Hill it's but a minute's walk down to Monument Street and Pudding Lane where the Great Fire started. When the Lord Mayor, Sir Thomas Bludworth, was called to the scene early in the morning he said, 'Pshaw! a woman might piss it out.' Within a day and a half when the holocaust 'altogether vanquished all human counsel and resource,' they saw him scurrying about, wringing his hands and crying, 'Lord, Lord, what can I do?' He had the good advice and comfort of Samuel Pepys who had already been to see the King for permission to pull houses down ahead of the wall of flame. John Evelyn was in despair.

Oh the miserable and calamitous spectacle [he wrote] such

as haply the world had not seen the like since the foundation
of it, nor will be outdone till the universal conflagration. All
the sky was of fiery aspect, like the top of a burning oven,
and the light seen above forty miles. God grant mine eyes
may never behold the like, who now saw 10,000 houses all
in one flame, the noise and crackling and thunder of impetuous flames, the shrieking of women and children, the
hurry of people, the fall of towers, houses and churches was
like an hideous storm, and the air all about so hot and
inflamed that at last one was not able to approach it . . . the
clouds also of smoke were dismal and reached upon com-
putation near fifty-six miles in length . . .

The original inscription at the foot of the Monument ascribed
the fire to the work of Papists. Royalists obliterated it at the
Restoration. A plate in the stone now records how, during five
days, the fire consumed some 436 acres of the City's fabric,
including about 13,000 houses and 89 churches. The story of
its 'diabolical consumption' has been vividly documented
both by Evelyn and Pepys who had the good sense to bury his
valuables in the garden of his house in Seething Lane. But, to
his consternation, his wife, entrusted with the task of burying
a large sum in gold, couldn't recall the exact site and it took
them several days to find it. By that time there was 'naught but
the reek of blackened timber' in what, a week earlier, had been
the most populous and prosperous City in Europe. The fire
started in a bake-house and not so long ago the Worshipful
Company of Bakers offered a formal apology.

It might well be called the Second Great Fire. The one
started by the Celts under Boadicea or Boudicca of the Iceni in
AD 60 left a two-foot layer of charred buildings which is still
encountered in deep excavations. The Monument itself, sixty-
one metres in height, is almost twice the height of Trajan's
Column in Rome. The degree of erosion of the Portland stone
can be appreciated from the rain-pocked surface of the base
and the angles around the suicide-proof platform at the top of
those breathtaking 311 steps within a cramped spiral. Up there
you can all but see the sea.

★

In May 1940, I cowered in a pub among an imperturbable company when I thought Goering's airmen were about to incinerate us on the same scale as had happened twice before. As field gunners we had been sent home on embarkation leave from a camp in Kent. I reached London Bridge station after dark, anxious to catch a connection to Yorkshire from Kings Cross. The sirens had sounded. All hell of a noise on all sides. With no experience of air-raids I dodged the military police and decided to make a run for it across the bridge. Carrying full pack, including a kit bag, I soon regretted the decision. Bombs were falling pretty close, I reckoned.

No shelter on the bridge and brisk fires were burning around what I now know to have been St Magnus Martyr. 'Down there, chum,' shouted a warden from a doorway on the north bank. He pointed to an almost concealed opening lit by the glare. I stumbled down stairs that led into the cosiest pub you can imagine, an underground place. From their quiet chatter a dozen or more elderly people, mostly women, gave the impression they were merely having rather a noisy night out.

They greeted me warmly. Drinks appeared unasked for. After each tremendous explosion, plaster fell from the ceiling and the bottles danced on the shelves as the company debated who'd copped it that time. Could be that boozer in such-and-such a street and a mean old sod the landlord was too. Another crash, nearer this time. More speculation and more gossip. Their comments were caustic and often hilariously funny. The possibilities of destruction and death were cauterized by dispassionate mock-indifference. These were the forced-to-stay-at-homes, the brave people of London, always helpful, deeply caring, united as perhaps they had never been united before.

Since most of the area had been bombed flat, I was lucky to find that pub again. I questioned an amiable old fellow who was sweeping the carpet under the sumptuous paintings of Moses and Aaron on the reredos of the renovated St Magnus Martyr. Did he know an underground place within a hundred yards of the Bridge? Aye, he did that. Could only be the Square Rigger, a Charrington house. Not a bad drop of beer in his opinion. No, he didn't know whether it had been bombed. Came from Hoxton himself, he said.

Within five minutes I had climbed up to King William Street and crossed the road. Traffic poured over the Bridge. 'Who could have thought death had left undone so many?' There stood the pub. All I could recognize after forty-six years were two flights of heavy wooden stairs that led into a spacious cellar. A cheerful girl looking after things during the manager's absence didn't know whether the place had ever been bombed. If so it must have been twenty years before she was born. I felt rather old.

As I regained the open air I saw in my mind's eye a street littered with broken glass and the ambulance that pulled up alongside the man lying face downward on the road. From the brewery I subsequently learnt that the Square Rigger had been built on the site of a very old pub, the Crooked Billet, which was possibly of seventeenth century origin and had been hit, date unknown, although early in the war.

Upper Thames Street is remarkable for very little except a distant view of St Paul's and nearby Cannon Street station, apparently in the process of being strangled by the tentacles of a very modern building next door, the Black Horse, function unknown. I wanted to get down to the river. Did no street, no back alley lead right down to the water? If one did I couldn't find it. The first person I asked on Dowgate Hill looked as if he worked in one of the many insurance offices there. A very British type with trim moustache and club tie. A manager perhaps. At my question he looked puzzled, apologetic. '*Pardon?*' he asked, '*qu'est-ce que vous voulez?*' I smiled, bleakly, bowed slightly and, unable to frame a subtlety in French, I thanked him and wished him an *extremely* good day. The thought occurred to me that an Englishman on the Quai d'Orsay might have looked equally puzzled when asked how one could get down to the banks of the Seine.

The old man sweeping the gutter on the corner of Cousin Lane looked equally puzzled, probably at my ignorance. I might have seen the river if I'd looked carefully. He straightened his back, wiped his nose on his knuckles and looked me up and down. Then he jerked his thumb over his left shoulder. 'Right *dahn* there, chum,' he said. 'Sixty paces and you'll walk right into the bleedin' water.'

He was right, of course. But it's not at all easy to dabble in the flood of a stream which is overhung by warehouses. In Cousin Lane you clamber, gingerly, down some slimy steps almost under Cannon Street railway bridge and there in her ignobility flows the once sweet Thames, bearing her burden of dead dogs and driftwood to the sea.

Three fellows were mud-larking, that is digging or probing the filthy pebbles with electronic metal detectors, looking for treasure. The archaeologists are very cross about this because the larkers have found some good stuff, but there is not much they can do about it. Dressed as I was in bourgeois fashion, Fellow One took me for Authority and implied, rudely, he'd as much right to be there as I had. Fellow Two was digging, not for treasure I noticed, but small, red Tubifex worms, food for exotic fish which must sell for about £1 an eggcup full these days. Here was something we might have gone into, deeply, but I felt he had left this world, temporarily I hope. At my questions he shook his head, slowly, sadly. Perhaps it was frustration. His three jam-jars were empty. Fellow Three had a face deeplined with character, a face Epstein could have made much of.

Peter Smith, or Pee-er Smiff as he pronounced it, came from Wapping. Near the Old Dock Stairs. Knew the river like the back of his hand for as long as he could remember. Dad had been a lighterman 'in the bad old days'. Didn't fancy the job himself. Joined the Merchant Navy. Ellerman Line. Had seen most of the world. Four years with the RN. Destroyers. Torpedoed twice. He held up his left hand minus three fingers. Retired ten years ago. Worst thing he ever did. Apart from a bit of fishing he didn't really know what to do with himself. He turned off his buzzing metal detector, a gift for his grandson who'd only used it twice. After more ritual pleasantries – where did I come from? what did I do? – I asked what I really

wanted to know: had he ever found anything really worthwhile? He laughed. Not often, he said. 'But if you strike it,
you might be in for a couple of hundred.'

Although, as he put it, you could be nicked for it under Port
of London regulations, the most knowledgeable mud-larkers
dig deep holes under ancient outfalls and wash the black silt
from the bottom of the hole through a sieve. How deep? Up to
four or five feet, he said. Then why use a metal detector? Once
you were down to the good stuff, it saved a lot of digging and
sieving, he explained. What was 'good stuff'? 'Wherever you
find anything metallic, especially coins. There's likely to be
more there.'

It soon became apparent that Peter knew much about the
currents and the old levels of the river and about antiquities,
too. What he dreamed about was the discovery of a Celtic
coin. Metal objects from the river, such as coins and bits of
weaponry, were better preserved than those found on dry land
because of the airtight qualities of the mud. He had found
pilgrims' badges, the haft of a dagger and several valuable
coins including a 'hammered' sixteenth-century halfpenny.
Hammered meant before coins were moulded. Brought him
in a packet from a posh place in the West End. He hinted at
three figures. I asked him what he remembered most clearly of
the river when he was a youngster.

The fogs, he said. 'They licked round us in them days.' He
remembered, too, the old sailing-barges without engines. Dad
promised him a trip on one for his twelfth birthday 'providing
I did what I were told'. He never forgot it. Upstream against
the tide and tacking when the wind hit them hard and head on.
Using the handle of his detector as a mast, he showed how the
Master and a young lad ('not me') lowered everything horizontally to shoot the bridges. You needed 'a lot o' way on'.
One fouled rope and you were chucked back against a
breakwater. It was his job to haul up and lower the leeboards.
'Them boats were beauties,' he said. He nodded in the direction of a line of moored dumb barges. 'Not like them
bastards.'

★

It's not easy to walk over the slimy pebbles under the girders of Cannon Street bridge and the prospect is far from pleasing. Everything looked foul, dead. Yet not quite dead. A few clumps of wind-sown ragwort, bright yellow amongst the fronds of ferns, clung precariously to the rusted ironwork overhead. In the distance, two Pied wagtails scampered like clockwork mice at the edge of the oily stream and leaped into the air to snatch at flies. *Chissick,* they called. *Chissick, chissick.* I listened more carefully. Another bird sang. Not a call this time. A song. A short warble of about three or four seconds' duration, ending in a remarkable rattle, like a handful of ball-bearings shaken together. And at those songs I could have leaped into the air myself.

They were Black redstarts. One trilled musically from the roof of the old station. Another appeared to be raising a family on the bridge. These birds, distant relatives of the wheatears and the nightingale, used to be regarded as one of Britain's rarest breeding species. It is common on the Continent, singing from the rooftops. The Germans call it the *Hausrotschwanz*, the House redstart. Why it should come here except that, as in the case of the much cosseted ospreys of Speyside, Britain is at the extreme tip of its north-westerly range, is difficult to understand. Max Nicholson, the former head of Nature Conservancy, considers that 'being by origin a mountain and cliff dweller, the Black redstart probably views a city as a series of artificial ravines which may offer suitable precipices for breeding and finding food, undisturbed by people, their dogs, cats and rival species of birds'.

Keeping out of the way, as it does, it is not an easy bird to spot: black with a rusty tail, but if you know its signature tune it can be picked out at once. The bomb-sites provided it with a variety of homes during the war. The number of breeding pairs fluctuates and I doubt whether it is known accurately. Determined on dropping a postcard to the Bird Census people, I walked on, feeling there was quite a lot to be said for the shiny stones. In inauspicious places birds can buck me up no end.

Chissick-chissick by the water's edge and high above the trill of redstart. No sound from the traffic deep in the underpass.

Downstream a large ship, probably a Baltic freighter, moaned mournfully as she breasted the tide. By contrast with what everyone was accustomed to in centuries past, London today suffers only from mechanical noise, mostly at the traffic crossings. At every hour the City in the days of Gloriana rang with bells from half a hundred churches. Hucksters called their wares; carters threading their way through the narrow muck-laden streets shouted at one another. And in the air and on that wide, fast-flowing stream came the clamour of vast flocks of birds: gulls, cormorants and shags and raft upon raft of edible fowl.

The most agile, the most intrepid of the flesh-eaters were the hell-kites of which Shakespeare made much. In a letter to his Doge, the Venetian ambassador said he had counted more than sixty in St Paul's churchyard. Bold and daring, they snatched food from market stalls, even from baskets on people's heads and they were particularly fond of rotting human flesh.

The present London Bridge echoes faintly its sprawling predecessor, the first stone bridge designed by Peter the Chaplain, completed in 1209; for six centuries the only bridge across the river. It became one of the sights of Europe. Houses and shops and a chapel dedicated to the Blessed St Thomas of Canterbury stood high above the breakwaters. At each end was a fortified gate adorned with a dozen spikes on which were impaled the heads of traitors, like toffee apples. It was here the bird known today as the Black kite, most gregarious of the raptors, circled and swooped and settled down to peck and tear and yelp at each other. A head rarely remained intact for more than a few days.

I walked back and, recalling what the man who loved the river had said, I looked afresh at the stinking sewer that ran alongside the station wall. The Walbrook is one of those tributaries of the Thames which, like the Fleet, today go almost unnoticed, notwithstanding their historic importance from Roman times onwards. It rises in Moorfields alongside the ancient Hackney Marshes, the islet of *Hacca*. The so-called brook flows down or, rather deep below Dowgate so up that hill I went to the street that is still called Walbrook. It must have been a last-ditch defence point before the building of the Wall, a little port crammed with alien ships. They sang of it in the marvellous days of the old music-halls: 'Wiv a ladder and some glasses you could see the 'ackney marshes if it wasn't for the 'ouses in between.'

West of the Cannon Street bridge there is 'no pleasant whining of a mandoline' such as Mr Eliot claimed to have heard but there is, unfortunately, quite a lot of noise, especially during the unholy Introit at nine-thirty and the Dismissal at five. On the corner, where the street winds up to St Stephen Walbrook, the facing of Lloyd's Bank is as luminous as the upturned tail of a peacock; more Larvikite.

The church itself is not much to look at, at least not from the outside. A rather plain, box-like structure and inside not a thing to be seen beyond a phalanx of milk bottles, ladders, planks, wheelbarrows, hoists and small mountains of mortar. It has been gutted and is being done up. The curiosity if not the charm of the church lies in the walls, especially the one at the back just off Bond Court where, adequately briefed, I picked out blocks of Kentish Rag, interlaid with pieces of flint, Roman brick and some fine-grained stuff I couldn't make out.

Around the other side, in the shadow of the playful spire, one of Wren's best, is a relatively small dome, much in need of cleaning and rather hard to see since it's obscured by the tawdry rear of the Mansion House. But this dome, standing on eight arches, is an historic structure to which Wren devoted much time and thought. It may be regarded as his prototype, his working model for the great dome of St Paul's.

Christopher Wren is not so much a mystery as an intellectual Titan, a myriad-minded giant of whom it could be said, as it was of Leonardo da Vinci: *Facile cosa e farsi universale* – which may be loosely translated as: It's not a difficult matter to make oneself a master of all things. Isaac Newton went out of his way to pay him fulsome tribute. A little more than sixteen years after the death of Shakespeare, Wren was born (1632) into an England where he, his parents and all his nearest relatives were hereditary members of a new-style governing aristocracy. The 'Invisible University' at Oxford was just emerging from the turmoil of Civil War when his career there began. Within two years he was both a Master of Arts and a Fellow of All Souls. But this wasn't so much a beginning as a continuation of almost in-born scholarship begun at home and sharpened at Westminster School where his knowledge of the classics and mathematics soon outstripped that of his mentors. Thereafter there seemed nothing he couldn't turn his hand to.

He took to anatomy and produced beautifully exact drawings of brain dissections and movements during blood transfusions. He studied the mechanics of the forces between celestial objects, the ebb and flow of the world's tides. Some important inventions were to him as playthings. 'He seemed never to have been satisfied with the abstract unless he was able to exemplify it by the concrete.' He was at one with Francis Bacon and Descartes, rather than the dead hand of Aristotle. His transition from Savilian Professor of Astronomy to Surveyor-General of the Royal Works is superbly summed up by that one epitaphic word of his son: *Circumspice*. One has only to look around at his works.

St Stephen's and the Mansion House with its steps badly in need of a good scrubbing down took me to within eyeshot of Herbert Baker's prison-like parody of what until 1924 had been John Soane's masterpiece, the Bank of England. The destruction of the Bank's interior, the crude face-lift, really upset Master Pevsner who accused Baker of 'egregious diddling' when, in his biography, he tried to justify what he had done. The Art Deco seems to be wincing under the weight of the pediment.

Although it's now no more than a show place, an exhibition ground, I'm rather fond of the Royal Exchange on the other side of the road. The building, the third on the site, may well cock a snoot at the classical tradition but it looks as rich as its original founder, Sir Thomas Gresham, unquestionably was. Difficult, though to make out why a merchant prince, a man concerned about imbuing public confidence in his enterprise, should adopt the grasshopper, that symbol of improvidence, as his emblem. Both buildings of Portland stone stand on grey granite, low enough for close inspection.

St Paul's can be reached most directly by way of St Mary Aldermary, 'the earliest true Gothic Revival church in

London', and thence along some 300 yards of the Roman road that became Watling Street. Appropriate too for historic day-dreaming since on indisputable authority (funerary urns) the legionaries buried some of their fellow soldiers under what became Wren's showplace. Yet I paused. The Poultry affords a glimpse of that Florentine palace, the Guildhall, centre of the government of the City of London for over a thousand years, and full frontal exposure to St Lawrence Jewry.

The very name Poultry carries faint echoes of the fourteenth and fifteenth centuries. Just as people today living, often, in small apartments send out to the supermarket for cold cuts and a bottle of wine when the unexpected guest turns up, the Cheapsiders in the days of the Black Prince could bargain with the public cooks for a capon ready roasted, fit to be served in a pewter stay-pot, and nicely hot.

Close by Bread Street, Milk Street and not so far away Fish Street, Pudding Lane and the Vintry are of the pattern of that day when cooking meant more by far than switching on an oven. Few people owned their own. In his *London Likpenny*, John Lydgate presents a thoughtful picture of the plight of a stranger to London with only a penny or two in his pocket.

> Hot peasecods one began to crye,
> Strawberry rype and cherries in the rysse:
> One bad me come nere and by some spyce,
> Peper and sayforin, they gan me bede:
> But for lacke of monie I might not spede.
> Another cryes Rybbs of befe, and many a pye.
> Yea by cock! Nay by cock! some began crye
> But for lacke of monie I might not spede.

Down Poultry, past Grocers' Hall Court, towards Cheapside, the nearest thing to a boulevard in its day, I strode fast, seeing, high above all else, the finest tower and spire of all, the one Wren built for the Vestry of St Mary-le-Bow. No description, surely, can better that by David Piper.

> From the pinnacled top springs a rotunda of pillars, and the lines of these are drawn beautifully upwards through the

balcony above and curving into a second cluster of pillars, merging into the ejaculation of the slender obelisk spire; at the top, poised as if by magic, a little ball and still above that the vane, a splendid dragon some nine feet long.

From Cheapside you should venture north, towards the Guildhall, pausing only to marvel at the exotic cladding of the banks there: Mitsui, Banco do Brasil, Bank of Baroda and First Bank of Nigeria, mostly done up in watery greens and blues and soft purple from thin sheets of rock with colours baked by volcanic fire.

They were up to something in the spacious yard of the Guildhall, a rehearsal, I suppose. Sweating pikemen in full fig marched around the parked Daimlers whilst gentlemen with brollies and one with a stopwatch looked on. The policeman told me, politely enough, that I couldn't go into the building and with good reason, I admit, since this perambulator looked pretty scruffy after scrambling about in the mud under Cannon Street bridge.

The Church of St Lawrence Jewry stands at the centre of what was an old Jewish community thickly populated until the beginning of the thirteenth century when the inhabitants, together with those in other parts of the country, underwent a series of fearful pogroms brought about to a great extent by the stupidity, veniality and stark military incompetence of King John.

The Jews had been brought over to London from Rouen by William the Conquerer at a time when throughout Europe the words 'merchant' and 'Jew' were virtually synonymous. Certain branches of trade and manufacture were almost exclusively in their hands. They were an important source of government revenue and were treated with reluctant favour tinged with contempt. On one occasion when the Jews of London brought William Rufus a handsome gift he persuaded them to debate religious matters with his bishops and churchmen at Court. Not content with the scandal it caused he swore by the Holy Face of Lucca, presumably in jest, that if they were victorious he himself would embrace Judaism – an impiety which can hardly have enhanced their popularity in ecclesiastical circles. It reached the ears of the Pope who was horrified.

Notwithstanding the terrible massacres of the Jews at York and Norwich and charges of ritual murder brought against them in many English towns, the Jews were tolerated and encouraged to trade at considerable profit to the Exchequer enhanced by enormous levies for concessions. Despite the laws which forbade it, Jewish financiers lent money to abbeys and minsters against the security of church plate and – worst scandal of all – the relics of saints. In return they were allowed to place their womenfolk, children, business deeds and valuables in monasteries at times of disturbance. When England became more and more isolated from the Continent and the Crusaders discovered that wars in the name of Christ were an expensive business, the English Jewish communities with their overseas relationships and associates became bankers in embryo but more often than not at a fearful cost.

I have described elsewhere[1] my youthful relationship with the huge Jewish community in Leeds. Here in West Hampstead I am in the company of many Jewish neighbours and have learned much from a warm friendship with Rabbi Dr Norman Soloman who left us to become a senior lecturer at the European Centre for the study of Judaism and Jewish-Christian Relations in Birmingham.

We first met, not infrequently, at that most soul-chilling of places, the graveside of my Jewish neighbours in mid-winter; then on social terms among his former students and friends, including the Chief Rabbi, during Norman's visits to this City where I began to see something of what being a rabbi meant, especially in Hillel House, that get-together place in the Euston Road where he moved easily among many.

The title of 'Rabbi' cannot be compared with that of priest or minister. The word simply means teacher or, literally, *my* Teacher. He is not an intermediary between God and Man, a position achieved only through personal prayer. His rank, traditionally, gives him no power, no hierarchical status. He interprets the tenets of Judaism, particularly through the

[1] *John Hillaby's Yorkshire.*

114

Torah, that is the Pentateuch, the Five Books of Moses, the first Teacher, and the Talmud, to me a bewildering compilation of sacred law, ethics, ceremony, commentary upon commentaries and wisdom. 'Learning is the best merchandise.' Rabbi Norman is a man of many parts.

He walks wherever he can. That was a bond between us. He plays the piano extremely well, often accompanying his handsome, his so warm-looking wife, Devora (the *Rebbetsin*) who is a professional violinist and also a teacher. *Rebbetsins* are the spiritual leaders, the comforters, the confidantes and just about everything else to the womenfolk of their communities. The saying is – and Jewish folk have a saying for just about everything – that they are also magicians. They have to be for who else could raise a family on what their husbands earn? 'Better close to the *Rebbetsin* than the Rabbi.'

In Hillel House not so long ago they were celebrating Succoth, the Festival of Tabernacles or the Feast of Booths, the ceremony that starts the fifth day after Yom Kippur, most soul-searching of Judaic rituals. It might be compared, very loosely, with Mothering Sunday during the austerity of Christian Lent. Succoth, pronounced to rhyme with 'took us', represents that time more than 4,000 years ago when Jews set up simple dwellings as God led them out of forty years of wandering in the wilderness as related in Leviticus: 'Your generation may know that I made the Children of Israel to dwell in booths when I brought them out of bondage . . .'

An annexe to Hillel House had been left open to the sky, roofed over only lightly with branches of palm, willow, myrtle and fragrant citron, each symbolizing a particular virtue and characteristic of Man, and through that lattice it rained, steadily. I drank a glass of warm Israeli wine and ate a simple meal, sitting on a bench that wet my bottom, reflecting on what we Christian boys will do for our friends.

As a bee among flowers, Norman the Teacher hovered around, speaking to groups of lovely Israeli girls and youngsters from half a dozen local synagogues. There were two grave Hassidics there and the famous Phineas May, Honorary Custodian of that nearby treasure-house, the Jewish Museum.

How was cousin Reb getting along in the Gateshead

Yeshiva? he asked. Did young Resnick's Bar Mitzvah go down well? Such a fine lad. May God *bentsh* you, he murmured to another, a simple old man, nearly blind. No, he hadn't been to Tel Aviv that year but who knew? Perhaps in a few months' time. He spoke quietly and privately to those engaged in Talmudic studies and laughed with the tubby man, a member of the Board of Deputies who said his skull cap was small as it was meant only to cover his brain. Jewish humour is of a particular self-deprecatory kind, whetted by their forebears' persecution and the poverty, the share and share alike of the *shtetls*.

I asked Norman how his work for the betterment of Jewish-Christian relations was getting on. Very well indeed, he thought. Half a dozen bishops including our Primates were enthusiastic and regularly joined in their consultations and councils. Though some Jews . . .

Out of Norman's hearing I put the question to an elderly Rabbi who, possibly through his association with the US Bible belt, foresaw in the movement clandestine opportunities for Christian proselytism. But surely, I said *credimus in unum Deum?* He shrugged his shoulders. Unquestionably yes, he conceded. But there were many paths to Absolute Belief and the Jews were the oldest, the first chosen by God. I spent the rest of the day with Norman and wish now I could have told him what, a year later, I learnt in the precincts of St Lawrence Jewry.

That large, magnificent church commemorates the name of that Roman saint popularly believed to have been roasted on a grid for his pious levity. Ordered by Diocletian to hand over the valuables of his church, he promptly buried them and assembled all the sick and the poor of his parish. 'Here', he said, 'are the treasures of the church.' He went bravely until his blackened body blistered. A weathervane in the form of a grid-iron flies above the steeple of the present building.

The pediment of the spectacular east front is supported by four Corinthian pillars with pilasters at the corners. Very fine. First rebuilt by Wren and then in recent times by Cecil Brown

who, with the Second World War in mind, ordered the gilded vane to be upheld by the simulated shaft of an incendiary bomb. But it wasn't the Orders of architecture on the pillars and arched windows that gripped my attention half so forcibly as a clattering noise, the sort of noise I recalled from the toy windmills made of celluloid I brandished as a youth. It was coming from flower-laden window-boxes high up on the walls of the chambers of the Honourable Irish Society alongside the Guildhall. A huge insect hovered there and then darted off with me in close pursuit of *Anax imperator*, the Imperial dragonfly.

What the police thought would be interesting to discover since I scampered round the yard, staring upwards as the high-flyer with its banded body and bright blue head zoomed up to the pediment and then made off westwards along Gresham Street, clinging to the walls of the church. It alighted on some flowering rush in a splendid little pool, undoubtedly its birthplace, below the West Door.

A pause there and a pause for me, too, before it took off again to quarter the long avenue of lime trees in adjacent Aldermanbury. Ignoring the puzzled look of sightseers and young City workers munching sandwiches on the flanks of the pool, I tidied myself up a bit and went off in search of the vicar.

A friendly fellow, healthily pink-faced from twenty-seven years spent mostly at sea 'on all sorts of ships from subs to battle waggons', Father Basil Watson exchanged his job as a chaplain in the Navy to become Vicar of St Lawrence Jewry in 1970. Due to retire soon 'after sixteen glorious years' he said, repeating the words, slowly. He sighed and slid down into a comfortable chair in the vestry. And a comfortable job, too, he admitted, since his spacious white church with its banners and emblems and a fair amount of gold splashed about is *the* place of worship of the City Corporation. He has no curate, no parish; his church is not open on Sundays. He is obliged by statute to hold only five services a year for the Lord Mayor and his gorgeously got-up retinue. 'Not that I ever seem to have a moment to myself,' he added, rather hastily. He holds three masses weekly 'and umpteen lectures and music recitals' for a casual population 'that just sort of pops in'. In his time he has been chaplain to sixteen livery companies.

Father Basil and his wife are tenants of a large four-bedroomed flat with a garden above the church. 'She waters the flowers each night and talks to them. Very important and very therapeutic,' he said. He glanced at his watch and apologized. 'Good heavens, must get upstairs and change my togs. I'm due at a lunch at the Mansion House.' He smiled. 'There are those who say I spend more time in a dinner jacket than clerical garb. They could be right. They could be right.'

What would he do in retirement? He sighed again. 'God knows. But no more collar duties. Certainly not live in the country. It'd kill me. I'm gregarious. I like people milling round the whole time. Always have done.' We shook hands, warmly. He blessed me and I left for the anonymity of Gresham Street. Traffic noisy, crowded, people milling about all over the place, but nobody seemed to be talking, except to themselves.

When I am sad and weary;
When I think all hope has gone,
When I walk along High Holborn
I think of you with nothing on.[1]

Old John, my paternal grandfather, an impious ne'er-do-well and a great story-teller prefaced many a yarn with the words, 'I tell you my boy when I first rode a horse . . .' and many of those stories I still remember. One of them swung on the questionable fact of how he had mistaken the footman of some local lordling for a cab-driver and ordered him to turn the horses round and drive grandfather home. Some altercation ensued. As usual Old John ended the story with a heavy aphorism. 'The greatest change I've seen in my lifetime,' he said, 'is you can no longer be sure who a man is by the clothes he's wearing.'

This came home to me in Cheapside that morning when

[1] Adrian Mitchell, *London Lines, The Places and Faces of London in Poetry and Song,* selected by Kenneth Baker, Methuen, 1982.

there seemed to be distinction only between City togs including Chester Barrie suits and the casuals that everyone else
seemed to be wearing. Cheapside in London's early days was
by far its most important street and up till the eighteenth
century

> the daily scene there must have been a pageant of contrasting
> characters. Each man announced his calling and his place in
> life by externals. Earlier still the crowds there were some-
> thing we now see only at fancy-dress balls. Merchant,
> knight, courtier, priest, money pedlar, apothecary, scriv-
> ener, gallant, soldier, ballad-singer, beggar cut-purse,
> cripple, water-carrier, milk-maid, money-changer, all were
> there, and each had his own manner and his own drab or
> gaudy apparel.

Thus Thomas Burke, who makes the good point that
Londoners of the past were more Latin in their ways than those
of later ages in that they lived a good deal more in the street
where much of their business was transacted. They made
communal feast and carnival in the street. Kings held occasional court in the street and the princes and gallants that
accompanied them caroused and raised hell's delight there. It
was between the houses that grown men as well as children
played games. In the street men aired their grievances much as
they do in Hyde Park or Trafalgar Square today and in the
street at the cart's tail, in the pillory or on the gallows they paid
for their daring. And the streets were incredibly filthy.

Huge piles of garbage and dung, animal and human, were
allowed to accumulate in blind alleys; urine flowed through
the gutters. In districts where the Guilds were strong their
Masters ordered cartloads of refuse to be carried off and
dumped beyond the City walls, but it was a Sisyphean task.
Tradesmen and common labourers deprived of Guild support
clubbed together to buy fearfully sick and lean pigs and
allowed them to forage, tethered among the stinking laystalls.
There were problems there. If they grew fat and were left
unguarded they were usually stolen. Much scavenging was
done by crows, ravens and flocks of kites. Clusius, the great

Flemish botanist, reckoned there were more kites in London than ever in Cairo. The heart of the problem lay primarily in congestion. The City was no bigger then than Hyde Park is today. The citizens were obliged to build upwards. To venture outside the Walls except under armed escort was hazardous.

Present-day Londoners who live north of the river are as parochial as those to the south. In the purlieus of Chelsea and Putney they regard Hampstead and Highgate as rather freak-ish hill villages and Islington as some place on the borders of Essex. We in turn look down on those between Sloane Square and Hammersmith as fashionable faint-hearts without the wit to escape the mists that drift off the Thames. Greenwich and Blackheath I rarely visit except to stretch my legs. Before I essayed this foray and the one that preceded it fifteen years ago I hadn't visited the City regularly since groups of us conducted what we called the bomb-site surveys, the region blitzed almost immediately behind St Paul's. That was in 1944 and 1945 and my own enthusiasm came to an abrupt conclusion for macabre reasons.

Because of the point blocks that now tower over faceless thoroughfares and clusters of shops in the role of intruders, the area today is unrecognizable. Cripplegate and Friday Street – where before the war my father ran his London office – were almost completely flattened. Yawning cellars filled with blackened debris and pools of water, some of them converted into static water tanks for the heroic fire-fighters, were sur-rounded by the ruins of walls. It looked like a featureless archaeological site. Apart from the aftermath of previous fires, especially the one that started in Pudding Lane in 1666, there was more open ground than there had been since the Middle Ages. But the hell-made rock gardens, the pools and the sodden earth and carbonized timber provided acres of ex-ploitable habitats for invasive plants, birds and adaptable animals.

The wrongly called fireweed, the Rosebay willowherb, put in a strong bid for a take-over which is not surprising since a single young plant can produce 80,000 wind-borne seeds of which about 80 per cent are fertile. It is still the commonest plant in central London. But it was up against stern competition from Common groundsel, the bane of gardeners, the Oxford ragwort, chickweeds, campions, mallows, the cresses, vetch (various) and a hundred more. Sallows and the rank elder did their shady best. Buddleia, too. Tomato plants got into the translocation act probably from the remains of City workers' sandwiches.

As for birds it was in Cripplegate that I heard for the first time the ball-bearing-like rattle of the Black redstart and saw sandpipers and wheatears which had discovered a new type of desert from the one in which they normally breed. Overhead hovered the ubiquitous kestrel which has now taken to the verges of motorways. Mallard duck reared their chocolate and vanilla chicks in the ruins of boiler houses and wine cellars and then the semi-wild cats moved in.

Two or three outstanding naturalists such as the late Sir Edward Salisbury, former director of Kew Gardens, Ted Lousley, banker and master-botanist, and Richard Fitter, a great all-rounder decided that here was an entirely new habitat, ripe for exploration since it had a predictable lifespan. The rest of us from the London Natural History Society more or less did what we were told. Although I know most about six-legged animals they put me on to the cats.

The area swarmed with the descendants of domestic moggies and warehouse mousers. It was our job – though mine didn't last long – to count them, to find out what they were up to and how they were divided up into regional troupes under the domination of king-cats or lean old queens. We had one would-be anthropologist, a second-year student and a surly fellow. My recollection of him is that he didn't do much except use terms such as reduction, segregation and stimulus-diffusion which were of little help. Unlike government ecologists who snuffle about like pigs for truffles in the shape of a knighthood or at least an OBE, we were cheerful amateurs, prepared to devote a few hours each week to an exercise that might lead nowhere. I suspect we were inveigled into this by the bird people who were concerned about the cats' effect on the local avifauna. Couldn't we, as one of them put it to me, 'lower the population level at night'? Naturalists can be as nasty as anyone else.

We couldn't and we didn't. Our first task was to map the local kingdoms of catdom, spot the Rumpuscats and, what pleased me most, name them for identification purposes. In the latter endeavour we leaned heavily on Tom Eliot's nomenclature from *Old Possum's Book of Practical Cats*. Unfortunately there were too many Rumpuscats who, like Growltiger on his barge at Molesey, didn't last long. The fights were terrific. The principal battleground in my sector (Three), we discovered too late, was on the partly wrecked ramparts of a series of cellars where each morning at about nine o'clock, a retired caretaker shambled in and distributed fish offal from Billingsgate. He knew what he was doing. He laid it out at intervals near thick shrub cover. The cats knew this too. They were there, waiting, invisible except, as we could see through glasses, a mere twinkle, a mere twitch of Old Gumbie, Rum Tum Tugger, a Pollicle or maybe a Jellicle (black and white with next to no tail) or my friend, the Bounder ('white polo-neck sweater, white trousers and a tweed cap') my notebook records. Like Bustopher Jones he would have worn a black hat in the City.

The Bounder got his come-uppance. A fellow Catamite, as we were known to the botanists, found the *disjecta membra* in a bed of Creeping thistle which had sprung up through the rusted skeleton of a spring mattress in Sector Four. One must assume he had strayed into the wrong club. By this time I had left the congenial company of the Catamites to become Worshipful Master and sole coadjutor of the Swaddies, the Static Water Tank Delvers.

I quit because it seemed futile to study group behaviour among animals which were regularly fed. I had, moreover, found some animals in my own field: dragonflies, not the big clattering Imperial but dainty Demoiselles which 'hung like a blue thread loosed from the sky' above some introduced water-lilies in a rather filthy tank. I fished in those tanks for weeks, returning all I caught to the water after identifying them. I turned to aquatic snails brought in, I presume, on the feet of ducks which often flew down, keeping a wary eye open for marauding Pollicles and Jellicles. My enthusiasm waned, abruptly, when I fished out something small but unquestionably human. But not for the first time I find I am digressing somewhat.

From Gresham Street I turned down Foster Lane which for some reason is believed to be a corruption of one of the titles of St Vedast (Bishop of Arras) in whose name Wren rebuilt the church near Cheapside with a very fine interior, marble floor and a ceiling which flashes gold and aluminium that could pass as silver. Not surprisingly it is the Guild Church of the Actors' Church Union. With God? Vedast deserves sainthood in that he converted King Clovis, one of those terrible Salian Franks who made sport of harrying everyone from bishops downwards.

Outside, in brilliant sunshine, I looked first at the trees and then at the flying buttresses which lead the eyes upwards and ever upwards to the dome-topped majesty of St Paul's. How the cathedral that once stood on this site, the predecessor of the present one, came to be used as a right of way, a parade ground for the rich and poor, a trade centre to which resorted moneylenders, marriage-brokers, pimps, whores, even a place where, during Cromwellian times, soldiers were billeted and their horses stabled, stems from the (relatively) simple fact that the old St Paul's was an extension of Cheapside. In *Every Man Out Of His Humour,* Ben Jonson's Mr Shift sets the scene by saying: 'I have been taking an ounce of tobacco hard by here, and am come to spit private in St Paul's.' Thomas Dekker, Jonson's contemporary wrote: 'Now if you chance to be a gallant in the Mercer's books, your Paule's Walk is your only refuge; the Duke's tomb is a sanctuary, and will keep you alive from worms and land rats that long to be feeding on your carcase; there you may spread your legs in winter a whole afternoon; converse, plot, laugh and talk anything . . .'

Especially if it had to do with business. Each pillar in the middle aisle became the centre of a particular trade. Drapers and clothiers from Lombard Street sent along their barkers with rich cloaks and slashed hose, anxious for the patronage of the 'men of long rapiers'. Anything could be bought there, wine from the Vintry, spiced capons from the Poultry, corn, seed and caged finches from Soper Lane, even a fine palfrey from the copers in Smithfield who wouldn't leave a nag worth a small piece of gold tethered to a tree. They would take it inside. Here were the beginnings of a supermarket and here I once did business myself. It had to do with the infamous echo.

The history of that echo goes back to its earliest days. Wordsworth made some classical references to the nymph, vainly loved by Pan, who drove so many shepherds mad that they tore her to pieces. The echo lasted about five seconds from choir to portico, an infamous defect only slightly bettered (or worsened) by the Albert Hall before they shoved tampons in the roof. During orchestrated oratorios distinguished conductors complained that slow pizzicatos were heard *staccatissimo* at the back of the cathedral.

This I know from personal experience when I was ushered into one of the best seats by my neighbour and friend, Hope-Wallace, I listened to a staggering performance of Verdi's *Requiem* on the strength of his press ticket. He was 'doing it', as we say, for at least three broadsheets including *The Gramophone*. I had never before heard a live performance of what he lightly referred to 'as probably Joe Green's best job'. We had Caniglia, Stignani, Pinza, the lot.

The *Requiem and Kyrie* began so softly on a small staircase of minor chords that my untutored ears were wholly unprepared for the *Dies Irae* when all hell broke out from the heavy brass and tympani. The flames, God! You could hear, you could see, you could almost smell the flesh-searing tongues of fire foretold by David and the Sibyl.

Quantus tremor est futurus
Quanto judex est venturus
Cuncta stricta discussurus

The damned screamed, the vandals of religion, the robbers of men's souls, the brutes, the oppressors, the harlots and the whore-keepers, usurers, all who defied the Decalogue were swept up into God's apron.

Towards the end the flames died down to a whisper and in the awful silence that followed, Death and Nature stood

aghast *(Mors stupebit et Natura)* to await judgement proclaimed, softly at first, by a single trumpet call in E flat and
then another and then another until a quartet of trumpets,
supplemented by half a dozen more somewhere out of sight,
ejaculated cascades of sound, *fortissimo*. This, indeed, was *the*
Last Trump.

> *Tuba mirum spargens sonum*
> *Per sepulchra regionum*
> *Coget omnes ante thronum*

Philip looked straight ahead, his fingers clenched. Tears
streamed down his cheeks. We tiptoed out at the end of the
Libera me ('requiem aeterna dona eis') and left the cathedral,
making for El Vino in Fleet Street where he promptly ordered
a bottle of Bollinger.

After a glass or two I ventured a comment. As far as I
understood their function, critics were impassive auditors,
unmoved by vulgar emotion. What I actually said I can't
remember, but he took my point. He looked at me in surprise.
'Couldn't you *hear* that bloody echo?' he asked.

The scene changes. I had been charged to write commentaries on the scientific scene in Britain for the *New York Times*
and it happened that my first job, some time in 1953, was to be
in at the death of the echo in St Paul's. A young sound engineer
demonstrated to about half a dozen of us what had been done.

After a brief preamble he walked up to the high altar and
fired a shot from a starting-gun. It sounded like the climax of
High Noon. Echoes leaped out from the most unexpected
quarters with faint ones from somewhere up in the dome. He
pressed a button and fired again. Result: a single explosion that
temporarily deafened us.

The engineers had installed microphones on all the pillars.
They were wired up to a large disc in the crypt where the
recordings were successively lagged and piped back into the
nave so that, when re-transmitted, the echoes were swallowed
up. At least that's how I think it worked. I am better at the
peculiarities of beasts and plants than vulgar electronic plumb-
ing. Apparently that's now old hat. As one of the ladies behind

the postcard desk put it to me, 'We go in for those marvellous chips nowadays.' I thanked her and began the long, long climb up some 600 steps of the Golden Gallery of the cathedral built by Wren.

What did he look like? What did he do better by far than any other man of his time? As to his appearance we have in the Ashmolean the superb marble bust by Edward Pierce, one of that company of master-craftsman chosen by Wren to whom the *Archi-tect* said he owed so much. The carving is of an uncommonly handsome man with flowing locks, wide-set eyes 'like Michelangelo' and an exquisitely formed mouth, quizzical, enigmatic but of an essentially humanistic person one feels. Those he attracted about him were nearly all spiritual followers of Francis Bacon who had taught them to take nothing for granted: *hypotheses non fingo*. Flamsteed, the great astronomer, found him 'the only truly honest person I have to deal with', plain words in an age notable for moral laxity.

He was of 'shorte stature'. Interesting this since *Wrenna*, Old English, denotes a small bird with a cocked-up tail and its scientific name of *Troglodytes* means a hole or frequenter of caves, a quick-acting, restless bird.

The embers of the Great Fire provided Wren with the God- or Devil-sent opportunity to rebuild almost the whole of the City and spiritualize the metropolis of commerce with fifty new churches. The overall plans were before his monarch within a week. As for St Paul's his prime problem was how to join an aisled nave to a domed space carried on eight equal arches. With some sleight of hand, as Sir John Summerson puts it, cautiously, he solved it by building domes within domes supported on screen walls upheld by flying buttresses.

Here we come to the profound matter of arches which provide strength between two weaknesses; the domes themselves may be regarded as arches in rotation.

Like a brilliant general, Sir Christopher had the capacity to temper bursts of furious activity with spells of rest and con-templation. When the last stone had been laid and Wren had survived his seventy-sixth year, the story is told how he inspected his masterpiece, minutely, from a basket slung from

a giant crane. Wren, the sole survivor of those who had witnessed the laying of the foundation stone thirty-three years earlier. That night, it is said, he went down into the mean streets of the City, heavily cloaked, to eavesdrop, to listen to what common people were saying about the great dome that towered above his galaxy of spires and steeples. When the early morning sun appeared to fire the Golden Cross would some recall the awful years of Bloody Mary? Did they regard it as *the* great house of prayer? We shall never know.

Arches in rotation

The crucible

From the top of the black diorite steps of St Paul's it's just possible to see the buildings around Ludgate Circus some twenty-five feet lower. Today those gates, Ludgate, Aldersgate, Cripplegate, Bishopsgate, Aldgate and The Tower are mostly the sites of Underground stations, but for centuries they guarded the portals of the old walled City of London.

Ludgate Hill together with Fleet Street which rises from the western rim of the Circus shows how steeply the land dropped down into the basin of the Fleet Ditch, now a sewer below the cellars of a pub, the King Lud. Lud connotes noise. The newspapers for which The Street is remembered with affection are fast moving east, to Wapping and south of the Thames. But the noise is still tremendous.

> From north and south, from east and west,
> Here in one shrieking vortex meet
> These streams of life, made manifest
> Along the shaking quivering street;
> Its pulse and heart both throbs and glows
> As if in strife were its repose.[1]

[1] Isaac Rosenberg, 1906.

Within its medieval walls the City of London grew over-big and started to expand beyond them, especially westward to Temple Bar where the jurisdiction of the City ended and that of Westminster began. A curious anomaly and one which might have ended in a no-man's-land between the Bar and Ludgate had not the lawyers, as astutely as ever, stepped in. Standing as they did between the centres of politics and commerce and knowing that both sides had need of their services, they created a legal sanctuary in the shape of their four great Inns of Court.

What the old Bar was like before Wren rebuilt it – it was banished to Waltham Cross in 1876 – nobody seems to know, but we may imagine a barrier as carefully warded as Checkpoint Charlie especially when, enriched by flourishing trade from overseas, the City began to get uppity.

Let us take the end of the seventeenth century. William and Mary on the throne. The Bank of England and the permanent National Debt had just been invented by the fertile brain of a Scot, William Peterson. England's population was about five million. Most of London's dirty work was done 'by a turbulent population of Cockney roughs': porters, dockers, day labourers, watermen and a fair sprinkling of professional criminals, living uncared-for and almost unpoliced in rookeries of tottering, insanitary houses, many of them in liberties outside the City walls, especially to the north of Fleet Street. The locals slipped in and out of the labyrinth around the Inns of Court at will. But strangers, incomers, impoverished countrymen in search of work were grilled at Temple Bar.

They were obliged to lift up their smocks. Any signs of the clap or spots on the chest that might betoken the dreaded plague? Had they any means of identification? Many of them didn't know what the question meant. Had they a trade or skill? Could they raise the price of at least a week's lodging which usually amounted to about fourpence? If not they were sent back until such times as they might earn or steal enough money to bribe their way in.

Most of those narrow alleyways between the side entrance of that ancient pub the Cheshire Cheese and the less respectable purlieus of Fetter Lane were still standing more or less as

Johnson and Boswell knew them when, during my infrequent visits to London, I was conducted by that benevolent uncle who bought whale oil for Lever Brothers. From the old Central News offices on the other side of The Street, he pointed out G. K. Chesterton waddling up and down the pavement outside the Cheese, looking at his watch. And he had seen him hauled out of the pub, often, by Mrs G.K.C. who arrived, indignantly, in a cab.

Goering's airmen plastered the place but there was enough left of adjacent Wine Office Court for two of us, myself and an old and famous racing tipster, Larry Lynx of the *People*, to hire a room there for twenty-five shillings a week. With a family to support, life wasn't easy even when a pint of beer cost about a bob and, during flush weeks, a cab could be hooked from Holborn to Hampstead for six or seven shillings with a tanner for the driver.

Since there were stories to be picked up on the way, mostly I walked. Even by provincial standards, the *Manchester Guardian* paid badly and argued, cynically, that it was a privilege to represent the Voice of the North. With their own jobs in mind, the London Editors realized that the future of the paper lay in The Street and paid a little extra, about a guinea for anonymous short, self-contained paragraphs in the 'London Letter' on the leader page. Easier money this by far than features, then known as Specials where the going rate for an outsider rarely worked out more than £3 or £4.

With hindsight the occasional byline, with its opportunities for more lucrative work outside the London office, justified two or three years of sheer sweat and it was at such times I thanked God for Larry Lynx whose real name was Arthur J. Sarl and what that generous man taught me. We met in a pub, the White Swan in Bouverie Street, better known as the Mucky Duck.

Tall and thin as an eel, he had worked successively in his younger days as a scene-shifter at Covent Garden and a member of a touring repertory company where, to authenticate the role he had to play in a gangland drama by Edgar Wallace, he mingled a bit, as he put it, 'with the villains', the members of the infamous South London gang. Whether he

132

just happened to be what actors call 'resting' at the time or actually worked for them as a minder I never discovered. He had certainly mastered judo. The expurgated story of that transition is related in the first piece he ever wrote for a newspaper, the *News of The World*. The yellowed cutting was headlined 'From the Boards to the Broads'.

The upshot was that from his association with bookmakers, 'dips' (pick-pockets), thimble riggers, ace-crackers and the whole racecourse mob, he collected tips and sold them, at first retail. Afterwards through a chance meeting with a racing correspondent in the 'thirties, he received a small private income for helping to make that man famous. When his employer died, Arthur applied for his job and got it. Thanks to his trusted association with the Mob and his astonishing memory for the genealogy of famous gee-gees he became the best-known tipster in the business.

Our association honourably sealed over several pints of Fullers Best, we went into partnership. He found the office. Arthur always knew somebody who knew somebody. In the understatement of the year he thought he might be able to introduce me to some newspaper people whilst I, in return, could perhaps help him with his writing which he admitted he wasn't much good at. Within a few months I had become a zoological correspondent and a ghost-writer, and I look back on Arthur and that sleazy office high above the Cheese with enormous warmth.

I never knew how old he was but guessed he was over seventy. When asked he invariably replied he was just over six foot two and intended to remain that way, a device which I make much of myself nowadays. It became clear from the start that with ever-increasing sciatica and rheumatism, the screws as he called it, his active days on the courses were limited to two or three meetings a year with, perhaps, a look-in at the yearling sales and the like. Our arrangement was that, in addition to our own fields, we should split what we could do together, an over-generous arrangement when I look back on it since some of his commissions, based on proposals I wrote from his knowledge, occasionally brought in cheques for £30 or £40 which to me was really big money.

In the course of rewriting or ghosting his features, I learnt, superficially about many of the great jockeys from Fred Archer to Steve Donoghue who had been a friend of his. I knew even less about the bewildering dynasty of classic horses and much homework had to be done before I grasped the fact that all the thoroughbreds in that equine Debrett, *The General Studbook*, were the descendants of three great stallions of the eighteenth century, the Darley Arabian, the Byerley Turk and the Godolphin Barb. Arthur could quote chunks of their ancestry in the manner of that chapter of Genesis which records that:

> . . . the sons of Ham were Cush and Mizraim and Phut and Canaan. And the sons of Cush: Seba and Havilah and Sabtah and Ra-a-man, Sheba and Dedan. And Cush begat Nimrod who began to be a mighty one upon the earth. He was a mighty hunter before the Lord . . .

Arthur referred to the few people, mostly from the *Guardian* who were usually to be found in El Vino at lunchtime as 'your classy chums' but he introduced me to the news editors of popular Sunday papers and I could be certain that he was always trying to give me a shove in the direction of profitable markets. The screws plagued him more and more; he also tried to suppress a dry hacking cough but he kept up with his old cronies and he was still uncommonly tough as I discovered.

Through the intervention of a big bookmaker we managed to get a phone installed in our office at a time when worthier citizens had to wait months. We left a somewhat shifty-looking character fiddling about with wires whilst we went off to the Rainbow, a dark place at the end of a passage alongside Middle Temple Lane. Now demolished, it was considered the oldest pub on the site of the oldest coffee-house in London. As the electrician had almost finished we told him to slam the door when he left.

After about a quarter of an hour in the taproom, a little man, a retired jockey, handed Arthur a slip of paper. Not a betting tip. It was the current state of health of a horse fancied for The Guineas. A drink and a note changed hands and Arthur said he'd better get back to the office to use the new phone. There was much at stake. Knowing I could walk much faster I said I'd follow in a few minutes.

Half-way up the last flight of stairs I met that electrician coming down in a somewhat unorthodox fashion, almost head first in a series of somersaults and followed by a canvas bag and a shower of tools. Arthur who walked slowly and very quietly had surprised him with his hands in our petty cash box. The fellow tried to bluster and followed it up with heavy threats. To me Arthur demonstrated how he turned his back on the man as if resigned to the situation and then stamped on his foot, hard, and threw him over his head, through the open door. We went back to the Rainbow for a stiff one. 'I wouldn't like to be in that fellow's shoes when Charlie hears about this,' said Arthur.

The man who seemed to know just about everything in the less respectable echelons of London's sporting world had more tips to offer than those the *People* paid him for. One of them concerned field-glasses, which I knew something about. His own pair of war-battered Zeiss looked as if they weren't new when the Kaiser's fleet was scuttled off Scapa Flow. But they were important to him. They had viewed every major race-track in Britain and they were called Blinkers after a notorious thoroughbred of that name. But they were heavy and Arthur, practical as ever, had taken to hiring glasses on the course, knowing that the £5 deposit would assure him the means of graceful retreat if his calculations went amiss.

But towards the end of our cheerful association, he took Blinkers off to Goodwood. I have forgotten why and I have forgotten how they came to be (literally) nicked except that wide-boys can sever a strap with a razor blade. An indignant Arthur took to the telephone the next morning. The master-fence, if such he was, told him that within forty-eight hours they would be hanging up in a certain cellar not a biscuit toss from Blackfriars Bridge.

Arthur went down there where, as he related it, there were more glasses hanging up – amidst other 'hot' material – than could be seen in a shop. He was directed towards the latest intake from what was referred to as the Southern Circuit.

Blinkers had been cleaned and polished up almost beyond recognition. 'Sorry, Arthur,' said the man-in-charge. 'They must have been swiped by some little bleeder who didn't know who you was. Our lot wouldn't ha' done it.' Refusing to take a far more expensive pair 'almost new', Arthur brought back Blinkers with an assurance that the careless nicker would, like the electrician, be given something he would remember.

The sands were fast running out for Arthur. There were days and then weeks when he couldn't make the journey up to town. I asked him if we should close the office down since I had acquired a much larger apartment in Hampstead and could work from home. A frail voice on the phone said he thought it might be for the best. When, inevitably, he went off to join the majority there were about fifty of us at the graveside. We told stories about him afterwards, over drinks. I wish I had told him how much I liked him.

After the first year of our association we celebrated by a round table conference in the Rainbow where, among several others, I met Ian Mackay, the literary knight of the old *News Chronicle*, and Cassandra (Bill Connor) of the *Daily Mirror*, perhaps the best-known columnist in The Street. We subsequently became friends; both influenced me hugely and both, I can now see, enabled me to take up an apprenticeship lost when Arthur died. Bill, who employed me on his own short-lived weekly, *Public Opinion*, advised me to take up Saturday work as a rewrite man for the popular Sundays, a raffish exercise which drove me back to the columns of the *Guardian*. I was beginning to learn that you can't have it both ways.

Ian Mackay seemed never beset by doubts. From the trenches in the 1914 war he wrote sketches for the *John o' Groats Journal* and when the throat of the *Chronicle* was cut by the Quakers, grief-filled letters poured in from readers who said that the first thing they read each morning – after glancing at the front-page spread – was his Diary and later his essays. They overflowed with images, memories, comic notions, scraps of poetry and quotes from an encyclopaedia of scholarly information. His reading ranged from the classics, especially Homer, to Ruff's *Guide to the Turf* and the *Board of Trade*

Journal. Truc, he often stretched points but, as a colleague wrote: 'To use a form of phrasing that Ian himself was fond of – not since Rudolph Erich Raspe wrote the *Travels of Baron Munchausen* has a writer so plausibly and engagingly enlarged on life.'

'It doesn't seem like 26,729,280 minutes,' was the opening sentence of a piece he wrote on his fiftieth birthday, a date which he claimed to share with 'Shakespeare, Cervantes, Turner, Hardy, Anson, Allenby, Lord Haw-Haw, Cripps, Simone Simon, Charlie Brooks of the Manchester Press Club, Ethelred the Unready and Shirley Temple.' Somebody pointed out that he was, in fact, born not on St George's Day, but on 24 April. 'What sort of man would I be,' he asked, 'to let a mere twenty-four hours stand between me and Shakespeare?'

He was born in Wick 'within smelling distance of the kippering sheds'. There were three if not four Mackays who, if we are to believe him, all had different fathers. Readers were well acquainted with Grandmother Hughina who had such a high opinion of the Devil – whom she called Sahtan – that she wouldn't even strike a match on the Sabbath and used to give Ian a skelpin' every morning on the principle that 'I would surely earn it by night'. They were told, too, of 'Aunt Magersfontein; his father, Angus Mackay, the engine-driver who once sneezed his top plate straight from the footplate into Loch Shinn' and died of a strange encounter with a haystack.

Jester though he could be and often was, the executives of the Labour Party trusted the man who had been his paper's Industrial Correspondent and could always be relied on to put their case fairly, albeit with a wry twist. In the twenty or more taverns in the Street there was always an honoured place at the ale bench for the master-anecdotalist who once cleared the bar in the Codgers by setting fire to his hair, wilfully, and eating a bunch of daffodils for a bet. A common appreciation for Glenmorangie and natural history brought us together.

A tattered cutting reminds me that he'd been asking me about the habits of bluebottles and why, at the onset of cold nights, they flew about as if drunk. It seems that he felt guilty about knocking down with a rolled-up copy of the *New*

Statesman a fly which had disturbed him at his writing-desk. He likened his act to that of Marcus, the brother of Titus Andronicus whom Titus rebukes for killing a fly. 'But how', asks Titus, 'if that fly had a father and mother? How would he hang his slender gilded wings, and buzz lamenting doings in the air!' All Marcus could say in reply was that it was 'a black, ill-favoured fly like to the Empress Moor'. Not even a bluebottle.

'Shakespeare had a great weakness for flies and beetles,' Ian wrote. 'There is that overwhelming passage in *Measure for Measure*, perhaps the most stupendous statement in the whole of Shakespeare, where Isabella cries, "The poor beetle that we tread upon, in corporal sufferance finds a pang as great as when a giant dies." It must have been the memory of that that made me throw the *Statesman* in the grate. But the great world kept turning and I had to get ready for the road. And as is the way of all humanitarians, I soon forgot all about my friend the bluebottle.'

On another occasion, familiar to late-night tipplers in the newspaper business, we had been discussing whether or not, in view of the fact that all phosphorus should be returned to the soil, cremation ought to be made illegal. Ian said that, although he wasn't a morbid man, he sometimes wondered what he should want done with his remains when the time came. At one time he thought he would have his ashes scattered among the spruce trees on Morven, the mountain of his boyhood, but then the awful thought occurred to him that he might return to The Street some day as a roll of newsprint.

Although tormented by massive haemorrhages and insomnia, the Pictish Pagliacci managed to write his wry pieces from what became his death-bed including one, inevitably, about a man he knew who suffered intolerably from both rheumatoid arthritis and St Vitus's Dance. He concluded with his own epitaph:

When the time comes and I am not
Some friend no doubt will say, 'His head was hot.'
While some fair charmer when the tale is told
Will sigh and murmur, 'And his feet were cold.'

And then I hope they'll walk off arm in arm
And say together, 'But his heart was warm.'

There can't have been many master-columnists more unlike in appearance and style than the polymathic Ian who left Wick High School at the age of fourteen and William Neil Connor, known the length of the Street as Bill or Cass. Ian's face resembled a lump of Ailsa Craig with a revolutionary shock of hair which, burnt or unburnt, seemed constantly in motion as if the north wind played about it. Bill had next to no hair at all, at least not within the twenty years I knew him. He resembled an owl not least when he peered over the top of his horn-rimmed glasses. Whereas the urbane Mackay wielded a rapier or shook his jester's rattle under your nose, the predatory Connor-bird struck deep, sometimes just once or else, when offended by mealy-mouthed libertarians, he whirled one of those huge spiked balls on a chain round and round his head like a battle-drunk Viking. Combat and satire were his specialities. Moderation was scarcely within his understanding.

Connor became the King's champion during the Abdication crisis, accusing Baldwin and the Church of England of downright hypocrisy; Connor flailed both Hitler and Chamberlain long before it became a fashionable exercise. During the war, he lambasted Whitehall in company with his tabloid's brilliant cartoonist, Phil Zec, saying that 'wits and brains will win this War. The Army is starved of both.' Herbert Morrison, the Home Secretary and a former pacifist, threatened to close the *Mirror* down on the ground that what Bill wrote was demoralizing the Armed Forces where it was the most popular paper. At this the acid-tongued columnist resigned his job and joined up. He returned to his rostrum five years later and began his column: 'As I was saying when I was interrupted, it is a powerful hard thing to please all the people all the time . . .'

He still breathed fire. He described the H-bomb tests on Christmas Island – which he witnessed – as being 'like an oil painting from hell'. When he saw rabbits bleeding and blinded by the 'unspeakable, unspellable plague of myxomatosis', he devised ways of infecting the scientists responsible for its spread with a hefty shot of the virus. Some of his victims struck back. Liberace, on whose sexuality Cassandra cast doubts, sued the *Mirror* for libel and won a vast sum.

Yet the columnist who called Billy Graham 'the smartest, the smoothest, the slickest and the most graceful opponent of iniquity I have ever met' could write like the psalmist about the plight of child refugees, the needs of the poor and solitary pensioners and things he loved such as growing old-fashioned flowers, the character of cats, the confinement of goldfish, white mice and hamsters, and cookery especially when, condemned to gruel and Lucozade, he wrote from his sick-bed.

Even from that supine position he lobbed a firework into the lap of the Marriage Guidance Council entitled 'Scrap Cakes' in which he suggested that young matrons should get advice in the matter of cooked foods suitable for projectiles to correct infuriating husbands. As he saw it, they should hurl handy-shaped meals that came easily to the fingers and had a reliable trajectory in flight. Wives who found a deep sense of contentment in watching their husbands wash gravy from their faces should realize that the basic principal was that women always did the bowling and the men the catching, the hard way. Tinned pie dishes and bowls of spaghetti in a thick tomato sauce were recommended for beginners.

Old Incorruptible, like the Great Mackay, died fighting and for much the same reasons. The last message from the battle-front at High Wycombe Memorial Hospital read: 'Normal service in this column is temporarily interrupted while I learn to do what any babe can do with ease and what comes naturally to most men of good conscience – sleep easily o' nights.' He died on 6 April 1967.

Up the Street of Ink Which Has All But Dried, the drunks were sleeping it off on benches below the slim shadow of the wedding-cake spire of St Bride's. Seen from afar the octagonal stages of this 'madrigal in stone', telescoped and, with diminishing perspective, look like an enormous hollyhock. With its limed oak beams, its gilt and gleaming white paint, the interior reeks too much of the garnish of the press barons who paid to have it done up after the Second World War but its cunning proportion demonstrates that nobody could lessen the power of Wren's hand.

Looking round, as if seeing it all for the first time, I recalled how, years ago, I sent dispatches to New York about the discovery of tons of bones in the newly opened crypt, the product of the graveyards of churches that had originally stood on the site. Why they were important for forensic criminology or the vital statistics of our forebears I have forgotten but I quoted a Cambridge anatomist who said it was probably the biggest ossuary in Britain. The original 'Bride' was Brigida who, in the fifth century AD, married the High Druid of Connaught. Outside, the plane leaves danced in the sunlight. A drunk stirred, sat up and reached for a bottle under the bench. Had I really been there before?

From the Street, St Bride's is totally eclipsed by that vast hulk of New Delhi designed by Lutyens for Reuter's News Agency. Its putty-like Portland stone looks drab by comparison with the jet-bright sparkle of the *Daily Express* building, Lord Beaverbrook's palazzo, on the opposite side. Predictions that the black glass in chromium frames would collapse like a greenhouse at the first whiff of powder were wholly refuted by events. Not a panel was cracked during those nights of hell. Three doors up on the same side lies the home of the *Daily Telegraph* which the proprietors say is about to be moved away. With its fluted pilasters and Graeco-Egyptian twiddly bits turned modernistic, it fits my notion of Cairo town hall, a building I have yet to see.

Wine Office Court runs alongside the shadowy side entrance to the Cheshire Cheese. The parrot that bit Belloc died God knows how many years ago, they told me, and I hadn't the heart to find out what lay behind our old office door. I ventured into the labyrinth, along Little New Street, into Gough Square where the house inhabited by Sam Johnson is now flanked by LBC Radio and David Gibson Advertising Ltd, a fact which would have pleased the great communicator. Tourists mooched about. There are always tourists in Gough Square.

In 1965, the year in which the circulation of the *Mirror*

(5,000,000) far exceeded that of its closest rival the *Express* (3,400,000), a good friend of mine with a somewhat rhetorical turn of speech spoke to an American tourist who was photographing Johnson's house from several angles. He said, 'I take it, sir that you are a Johnsonian?' The man looked both surprised and pleased. 'I *sure* am, sir,' he replied. 'I always say *all* the way with L.B.J.'

Back in The Street by way of four distinctly unfamiliar pubs in Fetter Lane, I stopped to listen to a guide speaking from the open deck of a stationary tourist bus, his voice enormously amplified. '*Each night in this street over a thousand tons of paper used to be trucked in from the London docks. The total length of the webs would stretch four times round the equatorial girth of the world.*' Could be stretched by whom? The intriguing fact occurred to me that I had walked further than that in my time. '*One Sunday paper alone, the* News of the World, *used to print 13,000,000 copies which in terms of wood pulp represents ten square miles of Scandinavian forest. The pulp is now grown in Scotland.*' Hokum on all counts. I began to dislike the man more and more. Forestry Commission pulp is fit only for palings and coarse strawboard. '*There used to be twenty-four pubs in or just off Fleet Street and there are many journalists who claim that in one night they have drunk in them all.*' This is oft-repeated mythology.

Tiring of the fellow I crossed the road and looked into El Vino, packed out with young lawyers and, of course, I couldn't recognize a soul. But, like the Apostles in the Garden I needed solace and ordered a large plain malt. A stout lady with the look of J. Walter Thompson about her sat in Hope-Wallace's chair with its brass plate between her shoulder blades. It's stupid to go back.

Stacy Aumonier, that much under-rated writer of short stories, wrote one, perhaps his best, called *Where was Wych Street?* It swung on heated arguments in a law-suit between barristers and witnesses who could not remember – only a few years after its demolition – where that little street, famous for its bookshops, taverns and shaving saloons used to be. It had been demolished by the creation of Kingsway. I recalled the story in my search for that long dark passage which led to the Rainbow Tavern where Belloc in cape and floppy hat used to stride in and look round imperiously for Chesterton and his companions. An old street-cleaner didn't know. 'Only been here twenty years.' No good asking a young policeman. He didn't look that old. But a bookshop, L. Simmonds at number 16 Fleet Street, looked wonderfully familiar. Short of some premises in Delft, it could well be the tallest, narrowest bookshop in the Western world. Certainly the best in The Street. With some trepidation I went in.

The same shelves of books in curious disorder. The same sense of confinement. Ten feet wide at its widest on all five floors including the basement; seven feet at its narrowest. But somebody always knew where everything was, from Astronomy to Zen Buddhism and Zymotic diseases, and that man was Louis Simmonds, born Stiglitz from a ghetto in Poland. I had bought second-hand books from him since our days in Wine Office Court. 'Is Lou still with us?' I asked a young assistant quietly. 'Like hell I am,' said a white-haired gnome emerging from behind a partition, 'and where the hell have you been as if I didn't know.' He held up his arms and we embraced.

Business time and space at number 16 preclude all but the flavour of what we gossiped about in his back office. Whether he's changed much in his eighty-first year I can't say but at times he could be, as Arthur Sarl put it, 'an awkward little sod'. Perhaps with uppity customers but this atheistic Jew, so quick to detect anti-semitism, has always been an extraordinary good friend of mine. So where was the long dark passage to the Rainbow?

As he led me down to the basement, Lou grinned. 'You should know,' he said, 'you stumbled down it often enough.' He pointed to a curious overhang between the wall and the low ceiling. With the pride of a freeholder he explained that the old passage to the Rainbow and Nandos, the oldest coffee-house in London, ran through a portion of what is now his shop.

Elated at finding the Gnome and the end of the rainbow, I made towards Temple Bar and the eastern end of the Strand where 'in file, each breasting their way against the traffic, stately, pretty as great swans, swim those splendid sisters,

St Clement Danes and St Mary-le-Strand.'[1] Temple Bar is crowned by an exotic dragon or gryphon in bronze which, with teeth bared appears to be snarling at Westminster, although it can be seen that, with tail upturned, the impudent creature is presenting its backside to Fleet Street. Immediately above the dragon, jutting out from the fretted parapet of the Law Courts, hangs the great clock. The story is that when a janitor went to wind it up one Saturday night just before the war he fell into the works and of him no more was seen until the next morning somebody noticed stains like tomato soup on the pavement.

Within a couple of hundred yards the Strand divides around the 'monstrous island of the Aldwych'. The lumps in order of lumpiness are India House with its fidgety Asiatic detail, steel-framed Australia House described by the Master as 'commonplace', and Bush House 'big-business classicism', the headquarters and one of the many transmission points of the forty channels of the BBC World Service. Before I dwell lightly on my poor relationship with that service, something can be said about the infinitely more powerful transmissions which spray the world with cosmic rays. Fragments of them were being captured nearby.

Work as a science writer for a newspaper into which some scientists were immoderately pleased to get their names simplified the task of finding worthwhile stories. Much work was being done on the possibilities of space flight and the genetic hazards of exposing the astronauts of the future to whatever lay beyond the earth's protective envelope of air. Using the usual anonymity of Reliable Sources Close to Government Projects I learnt that physicists from Imperial College were setting up a small laboratory in one of the deepest holes in London, the disused underground station at Aldwych.

There beneath I've forgotten how many hundreds of feet of protective clay the scientists were exposing tell-tale gas chambers and inch-thick plates of photographic emulsions to rays from outer space of almost unbelievable velocity. Only

[1] David Piper.

the most penetrative particles could arrow through that protective mass. The cosmic chaff, the less potent stuff, was
filtered out, deflected or arrested on the way down. It stirs the
imagination deeply to realize that these rays, the after-birth of
stars that were born billions of years ago, are the most
plausible causes of human aberrations, pre-natal and possibly
throughout our span of life. Here indeed is the substance of
practical astrology. Let the credulous rely on the movements
of stone-dead planets. And whilst the Aldwych team probed
far underground, the aerials of the BBC World Service were
transmitting all that the Controllers thought that the world
should know.

The staff had moved there years after their war-time
occupation of Peter Robinson's, the huge drapery store over-
looking Oxford Circus where I joined them without really
knowing what it was all about. With more experience of the
Manchester Guardian's relaxed, conversational style the chances
are that I might have grasped more quickly the essential
differences between the written word and what comes over
the air unsupported by strong headlines and mild hyperbole.

Hindsight makes it abundantly clear that I had joined an élite
corps which chafed, occasionally, under the keen scrutiny of
the resident censors but which, if left alone, I suspect, was
perfectly capable of putting over the essentials of the world's
news during a world war without any trimmings.

The trick or, to be more fair, the skill, the essence of their
difficult craft lay in their ability to study sheets of telex from
the agencies and their own correspondents and then walk over
to a typist and dictate what sometimes within minutes would
be snapped up by news subs, taken to the studios and broadcast to millions of listeners. By contrast, the newspaperman
writes and rewrites his opening paragraphs, makes additions
when he's finished his draft and perhaps re-jigs the whole piece
before it goes to the subs and splash-writers.

This chiel amang them made notes, doodled with his leads
and inserted nicely phrased inessentials to the point where the
marvel is they put up with him as long as they did. During the
war, the Overseas Service, as it was then called, played a large
and most often unrecognized part in informing and encourag-

ing the temporarily conquered, and spreading dismay among the King's enemies. There were the propaganda services, too. The innocent became an odd-job man and moved among eccentrics such as Hamish McPhee who, in between recourse to much liquor told obscene stories to the Arabs in fluent Arabic as a means of putting across hard military 'facts' that brought no comfort whatever to North African Muslims. He had an enormous audience. The task of this novice was to ensure he appeared at a studio on time with the news he inserted between the plain damned dirty jokes which he ad-libbed.

On one occasion I remember finding him asleep in the canteen with his chin deep in a dish of grilled halibut from which he emerged with a Father Christmas-like beard of white sauce. Yet in front of the microphone that evening his rasping voice with its phlegmy gutturals never wavered.

A whisper of Intelligence and espionage flavoured some of the dispatches which came in on tape from correspondents at action stations and, in turn, various interested parties overseas could interpret in their own way what was compounded at 200 Oxford Street. We were not without our problems. Furious complaints from South Africa made it clear that the man who translated our bulletins into Afrikaans had a distinct bias towards Marxism. They fired him and I had the somewhat opaque task of simplifying the English bulletins for the new Afrikaans translator.

About eight o'clock one night the receptionist phoned up to say that, in the temporary absence of the departmental chief, General Smuts would like to speak to whoever was in charge of our South African service. This apparently was me. I lifted up one of the international phones. No response. The General was downstairs.

It took some time to straighten out the matter but before long we were in a Soho restaurant where the little man in sombre khaki relieved only by ribbons and crossed swords on his shoulder-tabs talked not of war and propaganda but of the unique flora of Table Mountain and of those famous men, his friends Louis Leakey, Raymond Dart and Robert Broom who had discovered the bones of ape-men in the limestone caves of the veld. Those three men were, later, to become invaluable contacts.

Life on the corner of Oxford Circus was austere. When flying bombs buzzed about us we slept on tiered bunks in the basement, ready to take up alternative news rooms and studios in what was always referred to as 'an emergency'. On the staff were George (Lord Weidenfeld), Bob (Dougall), Edgar (Lustgarten), William (Empson), Peter (Quenell), Vera Beatty (wife of Sir Gerald Barry) and a newsreader called Mike (Major General Sir Michael Gambier-Parry).

We worked round the clock in eight-hour shifts under conditions not far removed from those in HM Prisons. Bernard Moore, the Head of External News Services, thought it 'not unreasonable to imagine that gloomy inspiration for George Orwell's *1984* came to him in his washed-brick cell on the second floor.' But it wasn't for me. When rockets began to fall on London and my apartment was reduced to rubble in my absence, I yearned for the freedom of The Street and handed in my security pass.

Thanks largely to the tutelage of Arthur, the Mackay, Bill Connor, the *Guardian* and the *New York Times* I emerged with sloth-like alacrity as a science writer. Given the opportunity to talk only about things that interested me, I returned to radio from time to time by way of the less austere Home Services and went off on my first commission to the Canadian Arctic to record the songs of the caribou hunters and wolves and the abundant life of the Barrens.

Upstream with Essex

Essex Street and Devereux Court – as you may see them today – are all that remain to remind us of that great Gothic mansion, home of the impetuous Robert Devereux, Earl of Essex, the last and most comet-like of Gloriana's favourites. With its panelled galleries and tapestried interior it overlooked the river from the Strand. Every vestige has vanished. Not surprising this, perhaps. The world is strewn with shingle from the dwellings of the past. At the other, the extreme end of the social scale, not a stone remains of the appalling slums on which the extravagant-looking Law Courts were built in the Strand just over a hundred years ago. To see something of the slopes of the river as the hysterical Essex saw them for the last time, I followed a knot of lawyers, walking in step, across the road and down through that narrow passage which today is Devereux Court.

At one o'clock when the sun sits high and bright, it's almost impossible to get a seat inside the cosy, crowded and curiously concealed Devereux Arms, and this was such a morning. We stood outside, drinking, gossiping and one of us, the narrator, listening. 'Well, that's the end of *that*,' said a barrister in winged collar and band. 'Satisfaction all round, as far as I can see.' He looked round for approval.

'For all except your poor bloody clerk,' said another. 'Don't forget he's still rotting in gaol.'

I looked up at the pub sign, the heraldic device of the Devereux which, according to Debrett, is pronounced *Deverooks*. Considering that Robert's father had in him blood from all the great houses of medieval England, the Earls of Huntingdon, the Marquisate of Dorset, the Lords Ferrers, Bohuns, Bouchiers, Rivers, Plantagenets, the device is remarkably simple: the crest a ducal coronet surmounted by the head of a white hunting-dog (*Talbot argent* in heraldic language). The shield (*Arms*) below is conspicuous only for three pancakes (*Torteaux*) with on either side (*Supporters*), another collared dog and (*Sinister*) a leashed reindeer. The enigmatic motto is *Virtutis Invidia Comes*: Envy is the attendant of Virtue.

In that small courtyard bounded by the Judge's Gate and a stall for the purchase of excellent sandwiches, fruit and coffee, the lawyers chattered, consulted notes and dispatched clerks for heavy books from some nearby chambers. What, I wondered, would have happened to this hive of close-set streets and squares and gardens with the gracious seemliness of a cathedral close had it not been for the long survival of the four Inns of Court: Middle Temple, Inner Temple, Lincoln's Inn and Gray's Inn? Like the law itself, their origins are lost under the dust of antiquity. Despite the prodigious research of the learned Inderwick and Williamson, the early history of all those societies is conjectural. They had unexpected champions. When a would-be developer tried to build more houses around Lincoln's Inn Fields, the Privy Council railed against attempts 'to fill upp that small Remynder of Ayre'. Some think the lawyers encamped there to take toll of rich merchants going west; others see them like a sort of Swiss Guard, defending Westminster against the encroachment of the City. Essex essayed the very reverse of that endeavour. He tried, treasonably, and failed, miserably, to incite the City against the Crown.

Not the least strange thing about his relationship with Elizabeth is the disparity in their ages. When they were scarcely ever apart for long, she was fifty-three and he not yet twenty. Then came that later period when, each in different fashion, they bickered, sulked, yet made it up. She showered him with honours, land and very personal gifts including a famous ring with the promise that, if ever he sent it back, it would always bring forgiveness. He, in turn, poured out letters of adoration. He was after all of the age of Shakespeare. Clearly she loved the learned, high-spirited lad with his martial air, open and boyish manner, mane of auburn hair and a strange capacity to say and do the wrong thing.

She had, of course, loved others. After the downfall and death of Leicester there had been the handsome Heneage, De Vere of tilt-yard fame, young Blount who sorely wounded Essex in a duel. Gloriana, uncommonly sexual though not, perhaps, physically penetrable, had loved them all. It was said of her nicely 'that nature had implanted in her an amorousness so irrepressible as to be obvious and sometimes scandalous. She was filled with delicious agitation by the glorious figures of men.' She had other frailties.

It was on the expedition Essex led to Cadiz that the Queen displayed to the full her capacity for dissimulation, ambiguity, procrastination, downright parsimony, a seemingly total inability to make up her mind and a touch of masochism. And behind her were the Cecils and the ever-watchful Raleigh. Events burst like a rocket at apogee when Essex, created Lord Deputy of Ireland, failed to subjugate the kerns and, worse, insulted the Queen. Apprised once of what somebody referred to as 'Her Majesty's condition' he exploded, 'Her conditions are as crooked as her carcase!' His words reached the ears of Elizabeth. She never forgot them. Essex acted with characteristic stupidity. With cautious support from James of Scotland he reckoned on bringing the Irish over to depose the Queen. Within six weeks high drama turned to abject bathos. The Court, subtly guided by Francis Bacon, got wind of the affair. The mutinous, desperate Essex failed to get the support of the City. Great gates, including Ludgate, were slammed shut in his face.

Judge's Gate in Devereux Court leads into the cul-de-sac of Essex Street where, by looking west from the steep steps down to the Temple, it is just possible to imagine the great house in which Essex spent his last cold night, Sunday, 8 February 1601 in relative freedom. He was surrounded by a press of the Queen's troops and artillery under the command of the Lord Admiral. Three weeks later he went to the block.

I say 'with imagination' since almost all we know of the last three of those Strand palaces, Essex, Arundel and Somerset, comes from Ogilby's map of 1677. It shows the Temple Gardens and the great houses cluttered about with small buildings and streets. The troubles of the Civil War, the Plague, the Fire and a constant pall of smoke from sea-coal had by then induced the nobility and the not-so-badly-off to sell out for estates in cleaner air. The speculators were moving in and prime among them arose the self-styled Dr Barbon, son of Cromwell's fanatical mob-raiser, Praise-God Barebone, whose puritanism was matched by a keen eye for profits in the leather trade. The son, Nicholas, went in for bogus medicine, property development and fire-insurance. He bought Essex House which the Fire had threatened from a mere 200 yards away, and demolished it. Not until the creation of the Victoria Embankment, where today you may walk or ride on a thoroughway raised from the tidal mud of the older and much wider river, was dignity restored. I strode that way, upstream, with the tide.

Paris pins down the Seine in a light grip but one that, like a judo hold, cannot be got out of easily. There is as much, perhaps more to offer on the Left Bank as there is on the right. London is wholly different. Millions of self-satisfied metropolitans next to never see their own river. It's the bridged boundary of something vaguely referred to by many as 'south of the Thames', as remote from common experience as Potters Bar. And, apart from all too few ventures across the bridge, I must confess to being among those short-sighted millions from north o' Euston to whom the Embankment is no more than a breezy Rubicon.

Due, perhaps, to a tunnel effect it blows as briskly at the river's edge as ever on Hampstead Heath. Two dinghies ran before a stiff north-easterly, bucking the wash of a Tilburybound tug towing garbage. A whirl of featherlight gulls called *kee-ah, kee-ah* as they broke aerial ranks and dived for whatever can be imagined among the wind-thrown paper in the barges' wake.

Here it was, not so long ago – just past the dilapidated-looking *Wellington*, the only floating premises of a City livery company, the Master Mariners – I saw a river manœuvre as intricate to me as a long-thought-out chess move, a manœuvre I thought I might never see again. Since I don't know the Watermen's name for this particular skill, I shall call it a multiple cast-off of dumb barges, those huge iron hulks, towed behind tugs, which seem to have neither life nor way-leave of their own.

The tug, a jaunty blue and white affair with next to no free-board, was chugging downstream against the tide, hauling three barges which appeared to be empty. Before my eyes, as if the spectacle had been performed for my benefit alone, she went from half to full speed ahead. The *dunka-dunka-dunka* quickened. Her diesels spat out oily smoke-rings. The skipper tooted, first once and the last barge was cast free. She tooted again. Two sharps toots this time and the second barge followed her, swinging over in a generous curve, towards the far bank.

A man appeared on each barge, not hastily. They might have been bored passengers on an empty tourist launch. To my surprise they didn't haul on their tillers. Those almost statuesque figures wielded long sweeps from somewhere aft, and with the co-operation of fast-flowing Father Thames they made those barges do wonderful things, avoiding each other as if they had all the time in the world, until, by the time the last barge had been cast off further downstream, the first two to be liberated had nosed into their moorings with scarcely any visible way on them. This seemed to me, a most land-lubberly sort of reporter, to be of the very essence of watermanship and as though I had witnessed a small miracle carried out by men to whom a moving structure underfoot is more natural than dry land.

★

I have known a professional Waterman for many years. He is, in fact, a retired Lieutenant Commander RNR with an Order in his bedroom drawer. But to those of us who meet irregularly in a noisy ale-house in West End Lane he is George the Boat to mark him out from George the Cop and Just George, a former magistrate. We are all of us concerned with the dispensation of Christian knowledge and excisable fluids.

What with his experience of the Merchant Navy and the Royal Navy, his Master's and Lighterman's certificates that authorize him to command ships in blue water and shallow, George comes closer to my notion of an all-round seaman than any other man I know. But until he swallowed the anchor a few years ago, he skippered a little coaster, the *London Stone*, that went up and down the Thames thousands of times probably unnoticed except by the discerning few who could appreciate the explosive nature of her cargo.

Giant oil tankers seize the imagination. The *London Stone* carried a mere 500 tons, the maximum tonnage permitted by the Port of London Authority. But it wasn't crude oil. Her tanks were full of petroleum or, on her return trip unloaded, with petroleum vapour more dangerous than dynamite. A trim little ship, chartered by the Regent Oil Company, her pedigree is on a plaque in the wheelhouse which affirms she was built in Charles Hill's yard, 'Ship Shape and Bristol Fashion'.

From the landing-stage below Westminster Bridge I have waved to George at the wheel as he hung about, waiting for those vital few feet of rising water, but he vehemently denies waving back, saying he had a damn sight more important things to think about. It's only in recent years that I have learnt something about the tensions, the responsibilities involved.

At high springs in the Basin the Thames has a rise and fall of just over twenty feet. On the return trip, that is to and from the Wandsworth depot where he offloaded what the company called 'the product' picked up at Canvey Island, George had fourteen bridges on that serpentine river to contend with. Their navigable arches vary in height. The up-and-down trip under the best of conditions could take about eleven hours. But he never knew when he might encounter delays in loading, fog or intractable shipping such as those 'bloody little scoots', small Dutch coasters, which are apparently responsible to nobody except the whims of their skippers.

When they could see fumes coming off the deck, fire hazards were a constant threat and on Guy Fawkes Night with rockets falling around and youngsters on the bridges with fireworks in their hands, George says he and his Mate Fred pretty well died a thousand deaths. But with the exception of a minor blunder on the part of one of Her Majesty's frigates, the *London Stone* always managed to land 'the product' on time.

A pity the representatives of the people of Westminster can't do more about giving the Embankment at least the air of a port on an historic river. Here we might have, say, the Quai des Ducs or, perhaps, the Quai des Mouettes – for here the Black-headed gull, the Herring and the Lesser black-back are the noisiest of the inhabitants – and a few more moored ships would add to the appeal of the scattered few. Scott's *Discovery* has been banished to Dundee; the *President* looks disgraceful; the *Tattershall Castle*, formerly a Humber ferry, a paddle-steamer on which my wife, Katie, at a very tender age, got stuck on a mudbank for an hour, serves refreshments as does a venerable old Thames barge, one of the scores which George used to see tacking against strong westerlies on the Long Reach.

She looks shipshape with her baggily brailed main. These ancient craft didn't go in for booms which are strictly for yachtsmen. I write with only small experience of trying to do the right thing when, slightly seasick, I was a grossly inexperienced deckhand aboard a rich man's weekend Dutch *botte* on a trip to Boulogne and back. But in the days when my mother-in-law lived at Whitstable I have seen a noble squadron of brown sails set out for a barge race from that port.

There was nothing of a yacht race about their endeavour. At the second gun, the crew rushed forward, broke staysails and shook out their mains whereupon the *Mercy Jane*, the *Tom and Mary*, *Genesta* and *Sara* and half a dozen more paid off nicely against the wind. The pity is that these fine craft are now mostly mastless house-boats much in need of love which, for an old wooden ship, means scraping, caulking and paint.

★

Among the laurel bushes of the Embankment Gardens I recalled the mildly improper story of the KPP, the Keeper of the Private Parts. During my early days on the *Guardian* an indignant letter appeared in *The Times* from a reader who claimed that two 'almost nude' statues of classical figures below the Adelphi had been re-erected the wrong way round, that is after being stored for safe custody during the war they were now standing among the bushes as if ashamed of one another, cheek to cheek as it might be described. They represented, I seem to recall, Castor and Pollux, the Dioscuri, the brothers of Helen who were ranked by Zeus as equal to the gods.

Ian Mackay scented a story and told us in El Vino about a week later that the London County Council, as it then was, referred him to the Ministry of Works who, in turn, put him through to the Ancient Monuments Commission, who said that such a matter lay within the discretion of the KPP who was, I presume, a Privy Councillor, the man who held watch and ward of some hundreds of pieces of stone genitalia, all stored away in numbered and documented tin boxes somewhere in Lambeth. They were the private parts of famous statues which had been replaced by fig leaves on the insistence of the Good Queen, then an imperious old lady who divided her time between Osborne, Windsor and John Brown.

That night I duly notebooked the fact that Mackay claimed to have handled 'some truly Herculean instruments for haughmagandie'.

'*What's* that?' asked Bill Connor.

Ian repeated it. 'Hurdies fyke,' he said. 'Buttocks in action.'

Bill sniffed. 'They'll never print that,' he said.

'By God they will,' said Ian.

'Pollux,' said Connor.

The sad fact is that I can't remember whether they did or they didn't.

The enormous riverside façade of Somerset House leaves me in awe but not inspired. Eight hundred feet in length, it can be seen best from the top of Waterloo Bridge, not the Embankment where the round-headed arches used to come right down to the river. Today they mask all but the top of the infinitely more graceful façade proper with its elegant colonnades, pillars and pediment which lie behind and above them. Though it is, of course, the back of the great building with a formal frontage in the Strand (1776 by Sir William Chambers) my impression of the riverside outworks is of a Victorian aqueduct.

The building stands on the site of Protector Somerset's palace where, later Queen Elizabeth lodged as a princess. Chambers, a brilliant architect and the Surveyor-General of his day, demolished the palace and set to work with an official commission to build imposing municipal offices around a vast courtyard. Chambers seized the opportunity. It would enable him to outdo his closest rivals, those ambitious Scots, the impatient Brothers Adam – Robert, James and William – for whom he had no time whatever, who had begun to build their *magnum opus*, the Adelphi, eight years earlier.

The two riverside giants, so close to each other, were erected. Two buildings more unlike one another can scarcely be imagined. Somerset House was academic, even educational. No classical Order was ever a hair's breadth out of line. As a sagacious contemporary critic put it, 'the work of the Adelphi leaped about. It looked so light, so airy.' The arches were fan-lit, the pediments nicely swagged and the pilasters decorated with the Brothers' hallmark, that trailing honeysuckle in stucco. Into architecture they introduced the idea of movement. But there were fierce critics – Chambers, of course, and Walpole who, in a much-quoted line, described their elegant frontage as 'warehouses laced down the seams like a soldier's trull in an old regimental coat'. But it is Sir William's building which survives.

Financially, everything went wrong with the Adelphi. The Ordnance Department failed to rent the vaults for storage. The scheme for embanking a whole group of first-class residences on an arched sub-structure was opposed by the City and the jealous Livery Company of Watermen and Lightermen. The houses were admired but few were sold despite Garrick's purchase and friendly patronage. Had it not been for a State lottery which at the time drew vast sums of money into the Treasury, bankruptcy would have faced the adventuring

Brotherhood. They were obliged to sell their art treasures and the speculation hung round their necks, heavily, for years.

What was eventually built on the site of the only piece of sustained town-planning completed to the Brothers' designs in their own lifetime can be seen from the Embankment a little to the west of Waterloo Bridge, the new Adelphi building: 'savagely ungraceful with the reiterated uprights of the twentieth-century's commercial idiom,' comments Pevsner, obviously disturbed. Its despoliation dates from 1936. There in the original Adelphi lived Hardy, G. B. Shaw, Galsworthy and J. M. Barrie. There the peripatetic Savage Club had its first handsome home. There on the levelled floor of that huge building were the old offices of the *New York Times* where, in my comings and goings, I looked at what fragments were left of the Golden Age of Architecture, notably what are now the homes of the Royal Society of Arts and the office of *The Lancet*. The whole complex was built, originally, for people with a certainty of their own importance.

On the basis of stakes found in the river, some think there were Celts in London before Claudius arrived with his legions and elephants. Others will have it that the Romans were the first to bridge the Thames at Southwark and it took Londoners about 1600 years, an astonishingly long time, to build a second bridge at Westminster, erected in 1750. Many bridges followed relatively quickly and the finest in my view is Waterloo, a worthy successor to the one the Scottish engineer James Rennie built in 1817.

The Victoria Embankment, that handsome boulevard between that bridge and Westminster, is notable for its tree-flanked gardens, its so-called Cleopatra's Needle of still faintly pinkish granite, hewn from a quarry of Syenite in Upper Egypt, the Geologist told me, and some extremely hard seats guarded by cast-iron camels *couchant*. Since in company with Muhammad I know quite a lot about camels, I think these were modelled on thoroughbred Omanis, too good in my view, to be burdened with packs. The trees are splendid too.

There are yellow-green Ginkgos or Maidenhairs which are among the oldest trees in the world. A fossil of one of their characteristic leaves, like little long-stemmed fans, was found in Palaeozoic rock known to have been laid down 150,000,000 years ago. If it hadn't been for the care bestowed on them in Chinese temple gardens, the species once so abundant (the fossil came from Yorkshire) might have died out in Sechuan within living memory.

Other exotics include the now common Catalpa from North America, the rare Pignut, the beautiful Dove or Ghost tree *(Davidia)* with petals like dainty white handkerchiefs which, together with the Giant Panda, was discovered in the mountains of western China by the French missionary, Father David. Near the bandstand you may see the noble-sounding Tree of Heaven with its stinking flowers. It's better known as the Tree that Grows in Brooklyn where it has spread like a weed. Its roots are opportunistic and prehensile. This is not uncommon among plants. A friend of mine returned to his maisonette after six month's absence to find that a willow had come up through the bathroom plughole. E. H. Wilson tells an engaging story about a particularly happy-looking ivy on the walls of Magdalen College, Oxford which turned out to have got into the cellar and drunk half a barrel of port.

Appropriately enough the London Plane is at its best in the Embankment Gardens, both the hybrid, by far the commonest form, and its ancestors, the Oriental Plane, a native of Turkey, and the Western Plane which the Americans call the Buttonwood or Sycamore. In winter silhouette its weeping twigs form countless little Gothic arches hung about with dangling bobbles, three or four to the string. It has been immortalized in Handel's 'Largo', Shade of my Soul.

Among those trees are the dark effigies of Great Men and their Works: statues of Gilbert and Sullivan, 'Dry Wilf', that is Sir Wilfred Lawson MP who tried to put a jinx on what he called the Demon Drink. He wouldn't have got on at all well with Robert Burns whose full-length bronze, says David Piper, is one of 'compelling awfulness'.

Our Bard is in the Poets' Corner of Westminster Abbey and, despite his doublet and hose, looks rather pious for the creator of some of the finest bawdy and finest elegiacs in the English language. Perhaps the man behind the mask. Sam Johnson nearby (by Nollekens) is of the gravity we expect and a very fine bust it is too. Almost human in that company of stony-faced ghosts. With his head slightly bowed, Wordsworth seems to be turning over a thought or two. Could it be about a lonely cloud? Thackeray, Scott, Ruskin, Camden, Dryden, to name but a few, they are (almost) all there and if you don't look at the incised captions too closely, there is thoughtful opportunity here for a sort of Rorschach blot test. What are your first impressions? Who are they, these whited sepulchres? What did they *do*?

David Garrick, very properly taking a final bow from behind parted curtains, strikes just the right note. It is, one feels, precisely what he would have wanted. I walked a few paces forward, towards John, Duke of Argyll (how on earth did *he* get in?) for a different perspective and found I was standing on Charles Dickens, on a foot-polished flagstone I mean. Sam Johnson's beloved Davie, the man who all but worshipped the Bard, still looks the Great Player. The pity is he couldn't have been facing Shakespeare. The whole crew look towards the central aisle and that great rose window which at sundown gives them a touch of colour.

Around the corner, in what the red-robed Marshals refer to as the Eastern Annexe, is a fine armless bust of John Milton, high up but not so high that, a year or two ago, I couldn't spot a huge spider scampering across the nose of the author of *Paradise Lost*. This was *Tegenaria parietina*, the biggest spider in Britain – vital statistics 1.9 centimetres (body); 5 centimetres (legs). This spider, known as The Cardinal, is believed to be the species, common at Hampton Court, which scared the wits out of Wolsey as it scampered around his corridors. I incautiously related this discovery to the editor of *The Times* diary (PHS) the day before the right royal wedding between Andrew and Sarah and sure enough the next morning PHS 'hoped the imminent princess was not daunted by very large spiders since he had been informed . . .'

I have dwelt, some may think disrespectfully, on the cream

of our literati. But is there no whisper of geniality, sunniness, high spirits, animation, sociability (I am warming up to this), of sheer damned cheerfulness in the Corner devoted to what we honour them for? Is there no poet, no phrase-master with soul so dead that he can't brighten them up a little? There is and his name honoured in my calendar is Adrian Mitchell.

> You stony bunch of pock-skinned whiteys,
> Why kip in here? Who sentenced you?
> They are buying postcards of you,
> The girls in safety knickers.
> Tombfaces, glumbums,
> Wine should be jumping out of all your holes,
> You should have eyes that roll, arms that knock things over,
> Legs that falter and working cocks.
> Listen!
> On William Blake's birth we're going to free you,
> Blast you off your platforms with a blowtorch full of brandy,
> And then we'll all stomp over to the Houses of Parliament
> And drive them in to the Thames with our bananas.[1]

To reflect on Godly matters we shall now have five minutes of silent prayer in St Faith's Chapel.

The Master makes no bones about it. He says we are entirely in the dark regarding the early history of the Abbey. Its first association with royalty is the recorded burial there in 1040 of Harold Harefoot, son of Cnut the Dane. Edward the Confessor began to rebuild the church and monastic buildings about ten years later. The actual fabric that we now see dates only from the middle of the thirteenth century.

The official guides – which are among the best in the

---

[1] *London Lines, The Places and Faces of London in Poetry and Song* selected by Kenneth Baker, Methuen, 1982.

country – make much of the fact that, in plan and proportion, the Abbey is the most French of all English churches. But this is far from obvious if you stare at its bleak skyline or the twin towers of the West Front, built to the designs of Wren and Hawksmoor. They look as if they have been grafted on and are not really a part of the whole intricate complex.

We Londoners can, so to speak, quarry the abbey visually, taking it in leisurely, chapel by chapel, walking from the museum to the Dark Cloister, returning only, always to that groin-vaulted one dedicated to Henry VII, 'an admirable foil for the consummate virtuosity, the aerial acrobatics in stone that go on overhead'. The last fling of Gothic, probably the most beautiful in England.

The orange and yellowed with age, uncomfortable-looking Coronation Chair, a bit of furniture that wouldn't look out of place for the sauce-cook in a baronial kitchen, signifies, we are often told, the unification of England and Scotland. The Stone of Scone – which you can't see – lies underneath, bolted down with cunning devices, a reminder of that day when it was mischievously and skilfully carried off under the red faces of the Marshals.

The chair itself is curiously pattered with *graffiti*. You can just make out the names of Tom and Robert. Visitors, perhaps Scottish Nationalists? 'No,' said a seated Lady Marshal, smiling. 'They were mostly scratched into the wood by the boys of Westminster School. In the eighteenth century they were easy-going lads. Very irreverent. Perhaps like today.'

With a complexion the colour of ancient parchment, Elizabeth I lies in effigy on a four-poster tomb in the aisle of the Henry VII chapel. With such a prominent nose it could well be that of Edith Sitwell. A little boy peered through the iron grille. 'Look,' he said to his sister, 'there's the Queen.' I wonder which one he had in mind.

The Abbey has suffered less from rebuilders than restorers. Since the early years of the seventeenth century they have swooped on the work of Henry of Reyns, John of Gloucester and the great Henry of Yevele, builder of the nave in addition to the tremendous hammer-beamed Westminster Hall across the road. Most if not all details of the North Aisle are by

George Gilbert Scott, Master Surveyor of the Abbey and designer of St Pancras Station, the Albert Memorial and much else. Because of its texture and colour, Scott loved marble and in his search for the best he got caught out on a number of occasions.

There is a very Irish story of how a far-seeing gentleman from County Down, also called Scott, offered to supply him with some good grey granite from the Mountains of Mourne – far-seeing because he got the contract signed before he secured the quarry. Unfortunately he knew little about weight-lifting and the limitations of public transport. When the first of the blocks were hewn, the rail-trucks were quite inadequate to bear them to Newcastle, the little port in Dundrum Bay and a special one had to be constructed. There were no cranes powerful enough and immediately available to lift them on to the freighter and the harbour had to be dredged to enable the ship to clear the bar.

I left the Abbey by way of the crossing and the North Transept where, outside in the Broad Sanctuary, more knots of visitors were being shepherded by guides, ready to pour in. The sheer weight of numbers in and around the Abbey recalls a typical remark made by the Duke of Wellington. After fire destroyed the Houses of Parliament in 1834 he was asked by Sir Charles Barry if he thought the Embankment should be extended so that the new building could be seen from all sides. 'By God, no!' said the Duke. 'Would you enable it to be surrounded by a damned mob?'

From Queen Anne's Gate you may enter St James's Park as if you owned it and at six o'clock on a fine spring morning when only cats are about and even the streets are suppressing yawns, there is no finer example of landscaping to be seen anywhere in London. The favourite viewing platform, the bridge across the lake, lies immediately opposite that entrance, but there is more enterprise in a circumambulation of the whole ninety acres. It's quite a small park.

Before turning right alongside some truly enormous Wych-elms, glance back towards Westminster where the twin towers of the Abbey rise serenely above a pale green shimmer of trees. Wren and Hawksmoor are vindicated by your intake of breath. Nearby, to the north-east, the cupolas of the Admiralty are my idea of the Kremlin (which I've yet to see) and below them the Horse Guards Parade was built for barking s'arn majors, boot-stamping, butt-slapping and pageantry.

Cling to the clamorous fowl by the water's edge but don't forget the Mall and Nash's Carlton House Terrace seen through the trees where, with luck, you may see a posse of the Household Cavalry, upright fellows, jog-jogging to or from Buckingham Palace, like tulips on horseback.

Two huge fig trees at the north end of the bridge are much resorted to by chatterings of sparrows and tits which, knowing there are few times when they are not fed by visitors, have taken to hovering over out-stretched palms, much to the delight of youngsters who can seldom have seen tamer birds. It was just below that bridge one polar-cold morning in December a long time ago that I witnessed an almost unbelievable event.

Except for a black hole about thirty yards in diameter, the lake had frozen over thickly. In that hole some hundreds of wildfowl bickered and fought noisily under a whirl of gulls. Not just common fowl but teal, smew, gadwall, widgeon, shoveller and many others.

I was leader of a group from the London Natural History Society, and bird-spotting couldn't have been easier. Suddenly a falcon plunged out of the sky almost vertically. There could be no mistaking it: blackish head, the distinctive anchor-like outline of the wings, its terrific speed. It was that urban rarity of rarities, a Peregrine falcon. The fowl rose in a cloud. Perhaps confused, it struck at and missed a terrified moorhen on the edge of the ice. It flattened out, banked sharply and stooped again and again unsuccessfully. It flew off towards the Abbey. All this took only seconds. Restraining my own excitement, I gave the impression that I knew anything might happen in St James's Park.

But nothing could match what happened there when John Nash came within an ace of setting fire to a fantastic bridge

across what was then a canal. The Treaty of Paris had been signed. The Prince Regent had ordered celebrations on the grand scale. Nash, never short of ideas, arranged a feast in honour of the Duke of Wellington in a newly built polygonal hall of twenty-four sides at Carlton House to which, among many others, came Louis XVIII and the Tsar. 'Displays of joy still more striking and appropriate to the occasion' were planned for the commonalty the following month. Fireworks on the Vesuvian scale.

On the Serpentine the American fleet in miniature was defeated, driven ashore and burnt. An illuminated balloon rose from Green Park. Artillery announced a terrific bombardment of fireworks provided by Woolwich Arsenal. On the canal in St James's Park Nash had designed a Chinese bridge that might have come from Brighton Pavilion. Towers at each end with a seven-tiered pagoda at the centre. From the pagoda, magnified by half a dozen reflectors, poured 'fiery showers and rockets springing from the lofty top in majestic flights, almost presuming to out-rival the first inhabitants of the universe'.

Here were all the elements of impending disaster. At midnight, as a bystander saw it, 'the pagoda exhibited an appearance that excited many doubts'. They were quickly resolved. The upper structures burst into flames. A man leaped from the tower into the water but cracked his skull on a floating stage. Another rushed out in flames and died soon afterwards. Most of the pagoda toppled over into the canal, a sizzling mass of burnt carpentry and exploding squibs. A memorable occasion for all concerned. A pity we don't know what Wellington said about it.

The Duke, not a man to be trifled with, had a poor opinion of the great scenery designer. As Prime Minister he resented Nash's influence over George, who by then was King; he opposed what was virtually a royal command that Nash should be made a baronet on the grounds that 'as far as the public knew' his conduct was 'still under enquiry'. That conduct concerned the public money Nash had been spending on the conversion of the carcase of the old Buckingham House into the new Buckingham Palace. Together Nash and the

The modern bridge

King had tricked Parliament into providing funds for what George IV had originally conceived as a mere *pied à terre* to replace Carlton House which, despite the money lavished on it, looked dilapidated and had been declared unsafe. Between them, without much being put to paper, the King and his private architect had worked out a mutually advantageous scheme with Mrs Nash as part of the deal.

When the work began at a feverish rate in June 1825, Nash admitted privately that he had no stomach for the job. At seventy-three he felt too old. He foresaw the difficulties. He wanted to retire to his castle on the Isle of Wight. Yet, as a loyal servant, he buckled to and a five per cent commission on a massive enterprise wasn't to be sneezed at.

Within three years things started to go seriously wrong. The original designs by Pugin with no central feature enclosed within forward-projecting wings were, in the opinion of Sir John Summerson, 'a ludicrous jumble'. They would have to be pulled down and, in some trepidation, Nash went to the Government for more public money. He was told, typically, he could pull down what the Devil he liked but as Prime Minister, Wellington would be damned if he got another penny.

The fortunes of Nash, his royal patronage, his protection and his reputation foundered disastrously in 1830 when George IV died at Windsor. His enemies, the Whigs, came to power. The Treasury demanded to know – not how – but *why* Nash had over-spent his estimates by at least £46,000. He was summarily dismissed from the Board of Works, ordered to attend an enquiry and suffered what seems to have been a serious stroke whilst attending the funeral of an old friend in St Paul's Cathedral one bitterly cold day in February. Exit Nash amidst much execration. Sad, this.

Before Queen Victoria held her court in Buckingham Palace, lampooned by one coffee-house wit as 'the Brunswick Hotel', three other architects, Edward Blore, James Pennethorne (in 1852) and Aston Webb had their hand in what we see today, the grand, unsmiling façade surrounded by gilt-topped railings through which hordes of visitors indulge in orgies of loyalty or gape unsmiling at grand and unsmiling guardsmen.

Gossip columnists seize on what they can learn from bribed servants about what goes on within, but I have it from reliable colleagues who, together with a few other guests, have had lunch with the Queen and Prince Philip, that the interior of the palace is truly palatial. From the interior courtyard the red-carpeted stairs lead up to ante-rooms and an array of glass doors that look out on the huge garden to the west. They felt, they said, somewhat over-awed by the vast oval dining-table, the gold plate and the Regency-dressed servants who never spoke, but the food was exquisite and the conversation, skilfully led by HM and HRH, made them feel 'almost relaxed'. They remembered that the Queen asked David Attenborough if he knew why her flamingoes stood on one leg.

Perhaps the most delightful, certainly the most appropriate fact to emerge from our biological survey of the Queen's garden years ago was that ornithologists discovered, among the nineteen breeding species of birds including the Pied wagtail and Spotted flycatcher, twelve pairs or four-and-twenty blackbirds. The chief correspondent of the *New York Times* seemed impressed by what I wrote but asked for meticulous confirmation since it sounded improbable.

The high-walled garden of nearly fifty acres has been under the rigid control of the church, the aristocracy or the Crown since the Domesday Survey and royalty at least are anxious to keep their habitat as private as possible. Most of it consists of mowed lawn, the parade-ground of royal garden party-goers in hired togs. There is also a sinuous lake of three and a half acres fed, like Regent's Park lake, by the filtered Tyburn, one of the ten metropolitan tributaries of the Thames.

The survey showed that in 1965 the Queen's Beasts – in the strictly mammalian sense of the word – had declined to two, the House mouse and the Brown (or Hanoverian) rat. Why no Grey squirrels which are common enough in the adjacent parks? Possibly because HRH is a dab hand with a gun or rifle of any calibre and the Grey squirrel, an alien, is a damned pest much given to pillaging birds' nests. Amphibians, too, are very scarce because the waterfowl, including the pelicans and flamingoes, gobble them up.

More lowly beasts with six or eight legs seemed to be doing pretty well under the benign despotism of Mr Nutbeam, the Queen's head gardener. The late Dr Bill Bristowe, who was Britain's, if not the world's leading spiderologist, the man who, a few remember, identified Miss Muffet (or Mouffet) of nursery-tale fame as Patience, daughter of Dr Thomas Muffet, a celebrated sixteenth-century arachnologist, nobbled, classified and released fifty-seven species. Beetles were disappointing (87 species) but many plant bugs and moths were attracted to the mercury vapour night-traps. As might be expected there were few butterflies on the royal rose-beds and herbaceous borders. Amongst the moths was a caraway-seed sized specimen, *Eareas biplaga*, a native of East Africa. It probably got in during the garden party for Commonwealth prime ministers staged a few days before it was caught, which just goes to show that ceremonials on a royal lawn may have ecological significance.

Of the ten metropolitan tributaries of the Thames, the Lea to the east is by far the biggest and, historically, the most important. In Romano-British times it provided useful communication between Londinium and Verulamium (St Albans) where the patricians lolled in steam-heated luxury. After the Legions pulled back to Rome, the Lea became the frontier between Saxon Wessex and Danelaw or, to put it another way, between Christendom and paganism.

The Walbrook, as we saw in the venture below Cannon Street bridge, degenerated from a salmon-breeding ground, a Roman defence point with a fine Mithraic temple on its eastern bank into a stinking stream. But of all the tributaries of the Thames the four that rise on Hampstead Heath – or just to the south of that open, airy, high catchment ground – are my familiars. I know every spring, every well, every ditch, conduit and runnel that sends them gurgling into a dozen lakes or, too frequently, into underground sewers before they can claim their birthright. These tributaries in order of my affection are first and foremost the Fleet, then the Brent, followed by their two still-born sisters, the Westbourne which can be heard but not seen a hundred yards from this apartment and lastly the Tyburn that flows somewhere under the grounds of Buckingham Palace. Rivers can be diverted but it is a hard thing to lose them altogether.

Two large manholes can be seen just inside the gates of the Royal Mews. A van pulled up and I followed it in. Two courteous policemen promptly closed in on me. What was my business? Tracing the lower course of the Tyburn sounded wildly improbable but I brandished an official-looking map and pointed towards the grilles. Had I an official pass? I had not and it wouldn't have helped if I had. Apparently the manholes led down to electrical junction boxes.

For the next half-hour I trod the length of Birdcage Walk, Victoria Street and Horseferry Road, looking for lines of sewers, slight dips in the ground, anything that might support the contention that, over a thousand years ago, the Tyburn slid into the Thames around the desolate Isle of Thorney on which Westminster Abbey was first built in Saxon times.

An intriguing notion is that long before the Thames was deep dredged and its width greatly reduced, the river could be forded at a number of points. An important one lay just above Westminster Bridge between the Houses of Parliament and the Albert Embankment. Lord Noel Buxton, an occasional correspondent for the *Guardian* on esoteric matters, sought to prove this by gallantly wading in during one exceptionally low tide and got more than half-way across before he was obliged to retreat and dry out in his noble house and then take the bus back to Fleet Street. What is certain is that whilst ships could neb their way into a few of the tributaries, the majority, if not all, of them were flanked by sandbanks, reed-beds and a labyrinth of channels with here and there raised gangways of osiers and pebbles which became the resort of wildfowlers and felons.

The red-robed Marshal in the Abbey assured me that his distant predecessors were supplied with corn from a mill which stood on the banks of the Tyburn where present-day Millbank rims the river. This suggested one or two things.

First that the old Tyburn stream must have been pretty nimble to have driven a heavy mill-wheel. Nowadays there's not much in the way of a contour drop from Buckingham Palace to the Thames. Second, one would have thought that the mill would have been built as close to the Abbey kitchens as propriety allowed. Where better than behind the Victoria Gardens, and though they are a nineteenth-century creation, wouldn't the stream's outfall still be visible? I peered over the wall of the Embankment, nervously – much to the delight of passengers on a pleasure-boat who shouted, 'Don't jump!' – but not a trace of it could be made out.

With the exception of the Vickers Building with its con-cave-sided tower, which is as good as the Shell buildings on the other side of the river are bad, there's not much to be said for Millbank in my view. All the pedestrian can do is to saunter or scamper along and, with a date with the Apothecary in one of the most remarkable gardens in London to be kept in mind, I scampered until I reached the Tate Gallery, stopping only to put my foot down, hard, on a wind-blown five-pound note and pocket it. I have no explanation for this. An aspect, possibly, of our affluent society to be compared with the old dog I once saw which sniffed at a large portion of grilled chicken at the foot of a dustbin in Soho, pissed on it and trotted off.

Expert opinions differ widely about the external architecture of the Greek temple-like Tate but never about what it houses. Nikolaus Pevsner, wise and waspish as ever, says the designer, Sydney R. J. Smith, ('an unfortunate choice') used the accepted late-Victorian grand manner 'with neither discretion nor originality'. David Piper, urbane to his fingertips, hedges his aesthetic bets by going a bundle on the Portland pomp of its pillars surmounted by Britannia among unicorns 'queening it over the busy river'. Personally I rather like the place and wonder what else architect Smith could have erected to relieve the hotch-potch of that portion of the bank. Inside there is a quiet riot of all that's best in British painting from the fifteenth century onwards, and much American too. A great place for meeting cultured birds with sandwiches and aspirations. If only everyone could start doing something artists only dream about, mused the poet Herbert Lomas.

The Tate was built out of the generous pocket of the sugar magnate, Sir Henry Tate. The Millbank site originally housed a vast early-Victorian slammer known and dreaded as the Tench, an enormous penitentiary. It contained more than a thousand cells and three miles of radiating corridors which can still be traced in some pleasant surrounding streets. *E miseria surgit ars*.

Millbank lies in a mind-bewildering whirlpool of traffic where, through field-glasses, I scanned yet another tributary of the Thames, the Effra which pours in through a mean culvert on the opposite bank. It rises in Norwood to the south of Herne Hill where John Ruskin lived for many years. As a young lad of thirteen he wandered up and down her cowslip-laden banks and sketched her, recalling, when he became old and famous, 'this sketch was the first in which I was ever supposed to show any talent'. It is to be wondered what the vitriolic critic would have said about the Effra's condition today. She worms underground through neo-fashionable Kennington, encircling the Oval cricket ground whose banks were made out of earth from her deep grave. Within half a mile her filtered remains are lost in the Thames.

For these facts I am deeply indebted to Nicholas Barton whose *Lost Rivers of London*, a work of quiet scholarship, first set me to thinking about the source and saturation point of almost every ditch around my lodgings on Hampstead Heath over forty years ago. It was from him I learned that the location of the well-known ghosts of London have been mapped and for the most part they haunt the courses of well-known subterranean streamlets. In short, rising damp.

> They return, spectrally, after heavy rain,
> Confounding suburban gardens. They infiltrate
> Chronic bronchitis statistics. A silken
> Skin haunts dwellings by shrouded
> Water courses and is taken
> For the footing of the dead.[1]

[1] U. A. Fanthorpe, in *London Lines, The Places and Faces of London in Poetry and Song*. Selected by Kenneth Baker, Methuen, 1982.

Events took a dramatic turn eight years ago when, during a phenomenal storm, seven inches of rain fell on Hampstead over a period of three hours. Several elderly people were trapped in cellars and drowned. Gospel Oak at the foot of Parliament Hill on the Heath resembled a canal. West End Green became a pond three to four feet in depth. A woman standing in a telephone booth with the water above her knees was heard to say to someone, presumably her husband: 'The car won't start, dear. No, I don't know where I am but it's somewhere south of Potters Bar.'

In a wet dash to our apartment I saw waterspouts arise from gratings on a steep hill and one of them threw the manhole cover into the air where, momentarily, it spun round and round like a ping-pong ball in a shooting gallery. Resort to the map in Nicholas Barton's book showed that I lived close to the source of the Westbourne which flows down to the Serpentine in Hyde Park by way of Paddington and Bayswater and, after a brief affair in Sloane Square, where it is piped above the platforms in the tube station, it enters the Thames below the home and gardens of those cheerful fellows in scarlet and black, the Chelsea Pensioners. And there, at their gates, I met my old friend, the Apothecary.

Frank Allen, a man of many parts, upheld an enviable reputation as Group Pharmacist at one of the largest regional hospitals in the vicinity of London. He has a capacity for enhancement, for being able to transmute things through his sure grasp of essentials. In another book I referred to him as the Alchemist but Apothecary is nearer the mark since we were heading for the nearby Chelsea Physic Garden where the growth and study of plants led to systematic botany and, eventually, pharmacology.

Apothecary means, literally, a store-keeper, an excellent, an evocative word but it brings to mind that sorry, that life-weary fellow in the last act of *Romeo and Juliet* to whom our hero resorts for a dram of 'soon-speeding' poison that he might lie down and die beside his beloved. But except in one small particular, his eyebrows, Shakespeare's apothecary no more resembles my friend than I do. Romeo's poison-dispenser is described as:

> In tattered weeds, with overwhelming brows,
> Culling of simples. Meagre were his looks;
> Sharp misery had worn him to the bones:
> And in his needy shop a tortoise hung,
> An alligator stuffed, and other skins
> Of ill-shaped fishes . . .

White-haired Frank is an ebullient Humpty Dumpty, too stout to touch his toes easily without a shove from behind. When his pendulous under-lip curls into a quip, as it so often does, his rugger shoulders shake, his eyes half close and one huge hair of his bushy brows doth 'rouse and stir as though life were in't'. Frank swung through the wrought-iron gates of the Garden with me behind in the role of the Apothecary's apprentice.

He looked around. He had been there many times before but not for some years. With nose uplifted like a labrador he sniffed the air. 'Hawthorn somewhere around but at quite a distance I should imagine. Smells fragrant from here. Do you get the undertones of aniseed? Ah yes! There's a bush. Now you'll notice that as we approach the sweetness gradually disappears to be replaced by a fishy smell. It's due to the carbon compounds of ammonia, trimethylamine and propylamine which are among the first products of putrefaction.'

Frank pointed out that there's good reason for the variable smell. Pollination is brought about by dung-flies and midges which go for foul odours. When the flowers begin to open they smell pleasant. Pleasant to us I mean. God knows what a fly smells. This is lost when the flowers are ready for pollination. Immediately after that act the unpleasant smell disappears entirely. The anthers of the flower are purple with brown pollen which to flies, I suppose, looks like decaying flesh.

He paused in front of an evergreen and crushed one of the small dotted leaves between his fingers and said: 'Perforated St John's Wort, the commonest of the Hypericums. Smells slightly goatish. Caproic acid. Look at the minute glands. In the old days the plant had scores of uses, from keeping evil spirits at bay and treating wounds from poisoned arrows to

curing bedsores, coughs and bed-wetting. The red sap was believed to represent the blood of the saint, that disciple "whom Jesus loved".'

We went from plant to plant examining, smelling flowers and crushed twigs and leaves but before I unravel my notes on that memorable afternoon something must be said about the garden, founded in 1673. It was necessary to have some place where plants, old and new, could be studied, compared and referred to.

The Chelsea Physic Garden never found its financial feet until 1714 when Sir Hans Sloane, Isaac Newton's successor as President of the Royal Society, purchased the freehold of the garden from Lord Cheyne and presented it to the Worshipful Company of Apothecaries of London on a peppercorn lease. Exotic plants such as cotton arrived. It was sent out to found the staple crop of the new colony of Georgia. Others such as the periwinkle *(Vinca)* from Madagascar were suspected to have medicinal properties which has been confirmed by modern research. Gardeners' dictionaries were compiled. For 150 years Chelsea remained one of our main centres of botanical teaching and research in Britain. I forget how many species grow there today. This botanical oasis of a mere four acres lies within two and a half miles of Piccadilly Circus. It is probably the most intensely cultivated ground in the country.

With that forty ducats worth of 'soon-speeding' poison in mind I asked the Apothecary to introduce me to a few of our botanical malefactors. He glanced around. He made for beds of plants in the potato family *(Solanaceae)*. He lifted up his hands. He brought them down with forefingers pointing at one stout plant with jagged leaves and white trumpet-shaped flowers and another evil-looking thing with large purple flowers I wouldn't have touched with the traditional barge-pole. 'By no means the worst, but behold the Rosencrantz and Guildenstern of our saturnine cast,' he said (his father was an actor and later a theatrical manager). We were looking at specimens of the rather rare Thorn-apple and the more wide-spread Henbane once believed, probably wrongly, to be the supplier of the 'juice of cursed Hebanon' that killed Hamlet's father.

177

The Thorn-apple or Devil's Apple *(Datura)*, an introduced alien, contains the hallucinogenic drug stramonium from the plant known in America as Jimson Weed. Thirty small boys in a dormitory who incautiously ate some seeds were temporarily demented. A few hours after bedtime the dormitory was a pandemonium. Some of the boys were barking like dogs, some crawled moaning under their beds and others tried to pluck imaginary objects out of the air. Emetics all round brought about some recovery by next morning, except for a deep red flush, high temperatures and an intense thirst.

In the seventeenth century the powdered seeds of Thorn-apple were used as knock-out drops by ale-house thieves. Wenches slipped half a dram of it into their lovers' ale or wine. Apparently some could make men mad for as many hours as they wished: 'an early example of biological standardization,' observed the Apothecary drily.

Culpeper records that the root of Henbane, another deliriant, is 'so like a parsnip root – but that it be not so white – has deceived others'. But not Culpeper. Like Thorn-apple, it is today a rare poisoner. A book published just before *Hamlet* notes that an oil is made from Henbane seed 'which if it but be dropped into the ears is enough to trouble the brain'.

There are three nightshades in the potato family, the Black, the Woody and the Deadly. The first two are common and the latter, a tall shrubby plant, fortunately, is rare. But who would eat a glossy black berry, the size of a small cherry within odd-looking calyx lobes? Perhaps inquisitive children attracted by the smell and taste. Women used to use the deadly one, *Atropa belladonna*, to brighten their eyes and imagined it might brighten their other capacities. The plant, dedicated to Milton's 'blind Fury [who] with abhorred shears slits their spun life', is also known unpleasantly as Dwale – and just say that word slowly. An astonishing and dreadful outbreak of poisoning with two deaths occurred in London in the last century when the berries were offered for sale under the novelty name of 'Nettleberries' by an ignorant fruit-seller subsequently convicted of manslaughter. The poisonous element is atropine and nobody seems to know how much of it can be anticipated in the other two common but not deadly nightshades.

High on the Black Record stands Aconite, a fine ivy-green perennial whose spikes of helmeted bluish-violet flowers adorn our gardens and south-west England in the wild under the name of Monkshood, a member of the buttercup family. To quote the Apothecary: 'Although its cardiac effects might be used to counterfeit a coronary catastrophe, the immediate symptoms of numb and "drawn" cheeks and lips don't make aconite an ideal homicidal poison. Some have tried to get away with it, but were nobbled.'

Hemlock, an umbelliferous plant which might (just) be confused with parsley, Pignut, Wild carrot, or caraway is a right improper killer known in the north of England as Dead Man's Oatmeal and Break Your Mother's Heart. One can see why. If, as many believe, the deadly ingredient (coniine) put paid to Socrates, it isn't surprising that friends had to throw a cloak over the philosopher to conceal frightful convulsions, 'salivation, bloating, dilation of the pupils, rolling of the eyes, laboured respiration, diminished frequency of breathing, irregular heart action, loss of sensation, uncertain gait, falling and complete paralysis with the mind clear to the suffocated end'.

At this I felt we had gone sufficiently deep into the Lethean prospectus and sought to bend my mentor's thoughts in the direction of the delightful, such as wallflowers, those haunters of castle walls, sweet *Chevisaunce*, Edmund Spenser's comforter, or violets, perhaps. Certainly roses. Surely none could say ill of the *Rosaceae*. A dire error. I should have known better. The Apothecary snorted like a horse.

'If you mean the genus *Rosa*, yes,' he said. 'It contains some of the most exquisitely scented ingredients of all flowers, the principal constituents of attar of roses. But they are a bit complicated. The true old rose scent is present in the Gallic and the Damask rose. The Field rose smells of musk and the Dog rose of mignonette and so on. But, by God, if you examine the rose *family* you are into some appalling stinkers. Cotoneaster, June berry, wild pear and sorbus can smell of rotten fish and cat piss, all in the aminoid group. Remember that hawthorn.

'Let's think now. Wallflowers. H'm, cabbage family. Used to be planted near the windows of manor houses so that the scent could enter musty rooms. Enormous complexity here. The elements of violets, roses, orange-blossom, even hawthorn have been extracted from its attar. Violets – and I mean of course the wild species, *V. odorata* – are a very old simple. They were used to cure headaches, relieve melancholia and insomnia. Aschar, a sixteenth-century herbalist, wrote: "For he that may not sleep, seep this herb in water and at eventide let him soak well his feet in the water to the ankles and, when he goeth to bed, bind of this herb to the temples and he shall sleep well by the grace of God."'

How the conversation in the garden's tea-house shifted from the vulgarity of the folk-names for Meadow saffron to the possibility that Dracula was more than a fictional figure, I cannot for the moment recall. But this is of the essence of the Apothecary's conversational gift and nicely oblique method of reasoning. Saffron *(Colchicum)*, that haunter of moist meadows, is a curiously naked member of the lily family, that is until the leaves emerge in the spring and all her popular names draw attention to this: Naked Nannies, Naked Virgins; in French *dames sans chemises* and *cul du tout* (naked bum). With Teutonic directness the Germans call them Pudenda or Naked Whores *(Nackende Huren)*. Could there be an allusion to the relationship between nudity and delinquency in this, since Meadow saffron is truly dangerous in all her parts?

The successful use of the Autumn crocus, *Colchicum autumnale*, in the treatment of gout goes back to ancient times. However, various medieval practitioners misused it, even killing their patients by over-dosage. The great Thomas Sydenham in 1683 omitted this unique cure from his famous Treatise on the gout for this very reason. 'That one act,' said the Apothecary, pausing for dramatic effect, 'was of far-reaching historic importance. Both William Pitt and Benjamin Franklin suffered badly from gout. It happened that they were each in the throes of an acute attack at the time when they might have effected a satisfactory *entente*. But they were in no mood for diplomatic discussions. Had it not been for Sydenham we might have kept our American colonies.'

Dracula turned up unexpectedly when I mentioned that I had been physically driven out of a beechwood in the Chilterns while searching for the rarest of British orchids, the Soldier *(O. militaris)*. My eyes watered profusely and my nose tingled from the reek of a carpet of crushed ramsons, one of our wild garlics. The Apothecary chuckled. 'Serve you right,' he said. 'You shouldn't have been there. Garlic is apotropaic; by that I mean it has the power to avert an evil influence. That's why it scared the hell out of Count Dracula.'

Did he really believe in the existence of that blood-deprived blighter? The Apothecary scratched his nose, slowly. 'Put it this way,' he said. 'The desire to drink human blood and to avoid sunlight and a marked aversion to garlic are the symptoms of an incurable disease which is often congenital. It is conceivable that so-called vampires and werewolves were suffering from a class of diseases known as the porphyrias which are caused by a metabolic defect, a depletion in haem, the red blood pigment, which seems to have put paid to George III. The diseases today are alleviated by the injection of red blood pigment but in earlier centuries the sufferer could treat himself only by drinking other people's blood. Folklore suggests that the victim of a vampire bite becomes a vampire. The sudden loss of a lot of blood would trigger the disease in a person already congenitally disposed to it. This might well occur in isolated communities such as Transylvania where there was much inbreeding.

'My view is that stories of vampires having long canine teeth and an inherent fear of daylight are not inconsistent with the symptoms of the disease. The effects of exposure even to mild sunlight can be dramatic, resulting sometimes in skin lesions so severe that the nose and fingers could be destroyed. The teeth, of course, don't become any longer but they are far more prominent when the lips and gums are extremely taut.

'Sufferers also tend to become extremely hairy. Now what do you suppose a simple peasant, walking home in the dark, would make of an animal-like creature with a hideously scarred face and what looked like protrusive teeth? By God, I'd make a run for it! I think there is reasonable evidence for what might be called the prototype for Count Dracula.'

'But the garlic,' I said, 'how came that to be regarded as, what did you call it, apotropaic?'

'We are on rather dodgy ground here,' he said. 'The principal constituent of that plant is a sulphur derivative, diakyl disulphide. It has been widely used for centuries to disguise food without a marked flavour as any restaurateur knows. There is a reason to believe it would increase the misery of haem depletion. I'd bet sufferers would have tiptoed round your wood in the Chilterns.'

Somewhat in the manner of Isaac Walton's Piscator and Venator we parted, temporarily, my friend the Apothecary and I, above that confluence of streams the Westbourne and the Thames – but whereas they looked down on the limpid, gently purling Dove we stood above a sorry sewer.

Down to the Borough

How James Whistler saw Battersea Bridge just over a hundred years ago can be seen in Room Eighteen of the Tate Gallery, an exquisite high-arched pontoon in sapphire and sepia that owes much to Hakusai, Utamaro and other Japanese masters so popular among British and French Impressionists from 1860 onwards. John Ruskin didn't think so and in *Fors Clavigera* he accused the artist of flinging a pot of paint in the public's face. Whistler sued for libel, won a farthing in damages and went bankrupt over the costs.

The 'modern' bridge (1890) is a squat thing in cast iron which doesn't appear to owe anything to anybody. The notice ordering troops on foot to break step is mildly amusing since it is difficult to believe that even a squadron of tanks could depress the arches by a millimetre. Yet the bridge is of sociological importance. It's the checkpoint, the valve through which 'the posh lot' (as they refer to them in the Prodigal's Return) is advancing from fashionable Sloane Square and points west to 'the screaming wastes of south London' (Sherlock Holmes). That little triangle of London bounded by the river, Albert Bridge Road and the west end of Battersea Park Road is (or was) solid, terraced, working-class Victorian. The attraction now for the Sloane Rangers is, of course, the chance of getting something well-built around

Surrey Lane with a garden as a bonus for at least half the price, maybe much less, than what's up for ferocious grabs among the white-washed brick and window-boxes in the converted stables and mews of Chelsea.

Over a pint of ale in the Prodigal I learnt a little about the neighbourhood from a quartet of what I took to be regulars. The caste was as follows: Joe, a retired Waterman, now a part-time school caretaker; a surly young Australian who swigged fortified cider; a hugely cheerful young Asian, a Gujarat from Nairobi; and an elderly lady, clearly genteel, who sat in a corner over a small G and T, crocheting what appeared to be an Afghan hound.

Why this inquisitor lightly disguised as a book-researcher doesn't get promptly brushed off never ceases to surprise me. White hair and a white beard help and all went well with the possible exception of the surly Australian who, as I understood it, strummed a guitar for a living. With my slight knowledge of the depth of the Thames at high springs and multiple barge cast-offs acquired from George the Boat and the mudlarker under Cannon Street bridge, Joe the Waterman and I got on like old chums. Used to work in Plaistow and inherited his dad's house just across the road, he said. It had cost the old man only a few hundred quid in 1935. Knew everyone locally and wouldn't move anywhere. Worth a packet the place was nowadays and two lodgers 'helped considerable'. The newcomers? He sniffed. A bit toffee-nosed. Didn't matter so long as they didn't get in your hair, of which I noticed he'd none to spare. Mind you they gave the place class. Look at the house prices nowadays. Kids, now, they was different. Needed a clip on their ear-'oles them little sods did. Specially them as came in cars. Nearly lost his job over one of 'em.

Jambo! said I to the young Asian and back came *Jambo sana!* and a grin that showed all his front teeth. *Habari gani?* How did things go with him? I asked, incautiously, since he answered in fluent Swahili, away beyond what I remembered from days in Kenya years ago, yet still very useful for talking to ex-East African traders kicked out by Kenyatta. They mostly run small supermarkets or work in those of their innumerable relatives. Starting with a little news agency, their businesses then sprout in all directions like water weed. My new friend worked for his uncle in Lavender Hill with four other nephews. Nine in the morning until nine at night. Seven days a week. No racial problems whatever except for *wamazungu senji* which is a down-to-earth comment on less successful white traders who hate their guts. The newcomers? He shrugged. *Maskini sana* . . . their pockets were deeper than those of the old folk, he reckoned.

The clearly genteel lady, a widow from the military belt in Surrey, thought the new young people were *such* dears. Not like the . . . she looked round, nervously. I was being pursued by the Australian who felt he was missing out on something. 'Whatja want?' he asked thickly. 'Ever been to Austrylia?'

I said I hadn't but implied, mendaciously, that there were few places on earth I would more like to visit, adding truthfully that a close friend of mine had taken part in an expedition staged by the University of Adelaide to study a newly discovered tribe of aborigines who lived in the outermost outback. They honed the cutting edge of boomerangs with their teeth. The fellow-countryman seemed singularly unimpressed.

'We call the bleeders Boonks,' he said.

'Boonks?'

'Yeh! That's the noise they mike when they hit yer rydiator.'

Battersea Park is truly an artefact, all 300 acres of it. During the ten years it took to prepare the ground, starting in 1846, millions of cubic yards of earth came upriver from the Victoria Dock, then under construction, to be dumped on the marshy land. With its lake and funfairs, refreshment rooms and tennis courts, the park maintains the traditions of the famous gardens of Vauxhall, Ranelagh and Cremorne. There is some good statuary there, too, by Hepworth and

Henry Moore
Whom we all adore
For his massive Maggies
And craggy Aggies.

An oldster told me that more than anything else he regretted the disappearance of the waterfall that fed the lake. Did his courting on that bank he said. He could show me the spot.

I took to the path immediately above the river the better to look back on the spider-like lattice-work of the most entrancing bridge on the Thames, the Albert which looks as if it has been knitted by a giantess. Swifts screamed over the water. A stiff breeze toyed with the kites of three kids and I felt on top of the world. But not, alas, for long.

Among an alcove of trees alongside that path there stands a strange oriental temple dedicated, I believe, to the cause of peace but, before I had time to reflect on its curious proportions, an apple-headed cur scarce larger than a Yorkshire terrier streaked out from behind the building and made for me with the resolution of a torpedo and much high-pitched yapping. Had it been bigger I might have had cause for concern but this animal seemed inconsiderable until it jumped like a squirrel and snapped at my knee. I took an ineffectual swipe at the creature whereupon it fell away and attacked from the rear, battening on to the back of my ankle with needle-sharp teeth. Total injury near-zero but I swore loudly and felt a damned fool.

Far from being apologetic, its mistress, a middle-aged woman in an expensive boiler-suit, implied I had no right to be so aggressive and that, with a little encouragement, her pooch and I might have been friends for life. Everyone loved the animal, she said. This is the very essence of the doggie-woggie stuff dished out by the exercisers of untrained tykes. I said . . . but what does it matter what I said? I stamped on, but not at peace with the world.

My relationship with dogs is something I find difficult to describe. It's not fear; it's not ambivalence bordering on disrespect. I like dogs. If we didn't live in a London apartment and travel abroad quite a lot we should own one. Yet the fact remains that over the years I have been bitten by more dogs than most people in their lifetime are stung by wasps. It happened several times, once extremely painfully, on my British and trans-European walks. Dogs on the Heath have drawn blood. Not fierce dogs, mark you, nor even particularly large breeds. I recall an animal about the size of my Battersea assailant which my wife and I encountered outside a village in the Chilterns.

It was trotting obediently behind a pleasant enough woman whom we greeted and stopped to ask the way. As a landmark she pointed out a church which she had attended for many years. We had an agreeable chat about the neighbourhood and were on the point of saying good-bye when the creature trotted round behind my back and, to her consternation, not to say my complete surprise, bit me sharply on my calf, drawing blood. Now why? Dogs are alarmed by abnormalities. Normally, when on my own, I carry a pack as do postmen, and they, together with walkers with a pronounced limp or unusual gait, are frequently bitten. I have called this the Rigoletto syndrome, that hunchback who lamented he was *solo e deforme*. But on that occasion, as on others, I don't recall that I was carrying anything. And the three of us had been chatting amicably. No dog could have detected a trace of hostility.

But soft, as they used to say, I had been observed when that damned animal attacked me in Battersea. And by as charming a dark-eyed wench as ever you saw. Sue Bradbury and I, she gently reminded me, had met at some awful publisher's party. We were, I dimly recall, the nicest people there. She is in the business herself under the sign of a distinguished house. Until that encounter I didn't know she lived nearby. Happily married I hasten to say, since, as sprawling London becomes as a village when two even lightly associated friends meet in its outer suburbs, we warmly embraced. What ensued must, after a slight throat-clearing exercise, be simply reduced.

Under the byline of 'Beachcomber', the late, great J. B. Morton created for the readers of the *Daily Express* a dozen or more characters and institutions which will be remembered when his employers have been long underground and forgotten. Among them we had that crazy German newspaper, *The Arbeiterbitten Once, Twice Shy*, or something like that. Sue, unseen witness of the pooch's attack on me, told me she had been very badly bitten in Gloucestershire the previous year. By what sort of dog?

'Everyone asks me that,' she said. 'I really don't know, it all happened so suddenly. Some sort of hound, I think. A darkish animal. My husband and I were walking towards a stile and a young couple approached, coming in the opposite direction. As we climbed over I must have frightened the animal – anyway it latched on to my face.

'Christopher drove me to Cheltenham General. Not the best of times. A Sunday afternoon. A young casualty officer appeared in jeans. An Australian. He looked about twelve. He took the point and smiled sweetly when my husband suggested it might be best if we got back to London straightaway. "Well," he said, "I may not be the best stitcher in Britain but I am certainly not the worst." He got to work at once and it took him just over an hour. Seventeen stitches. Fortunately the dog's teeth missed the corners of my mouth and eyes. As you see, they are all in the lines of my face.'

I looked hard and couldn't see a thing. Ungallantly I pulled up my left trouser-leg to the knee and round the calf and ankle displayed the *reliquiae* of encounters with dogs from Wester Ross to a hill above Rome. 'How did the owner react?' I asked her.

'I must say they were absolutely horrified,' she said, 'and when we left the hospital they were waiting outside. One of them said, "We realize it must be of little comfort to you but the dog has already been put down."'

Before Sue and I parted she told me more about their friends and neighbours. Riparian Battersea, or South Chelsea as some have taken to calling it, seems to be divided between natives, mostly working-class and immigrants, both Asian and from across the river. Some of the older inhabitants remain aloof from things like the Neighbourhood Watch scheme. Probably they deplore the fact that the loss of community spirit makes it necessary. However they are still the first to notice anyone acting suspiciously, and the first to come round and tell you.

'Y'know, some friends you haven't seen for months who, when you're out, maybe at a party, peer through your windows. And some very old customs survive here. My husband – who's lived here a long time – has seen a newborn child's palm crossed with silver.'

I walked on. A mile ahead can be seen the squat profile of Battersea Power Station which used to belch smoke from its fluted chimneys, like two Mississippi river-boats steaming neck to neck. It happened to be water-sprayed cotton-woolly smoke not hideous stuff, languid on fine days and Wagnerian against a flaming sunset. Its working life now over, this dinosaur of the electricity generating age reminded David Piper of the cinema organs of the 'thirties. Even Pevsner gives it more than a nod of approval . . . 'one of the finest examples in England of frankly contemporary industrial architecture which set the pattern for the power stations of the next two decades'.

The Master mentions decorative motifs on the walls which are hidden by a sprawl of warehouses. With an eye to seeing them by clinging to the river frontage, thereby avoiding a dreary mile-long detour around the back of the station, I ventured down a truckers' drive-in reckoning, perhaps unreasonably, that once I set foot on the slimy pebbles I had a *strandlooper*'s rights of way-leave, *princeps ambulare* and other fanciful notions. The unvarnishable fact is that I felt nervous among notices that told me plainly that I had no right to be there.

'Oy!' shouted a ferrety looking fellow with a massive German Shepherd dog at his heels. 'Where you going, like?' A polite fiction about wanting some spraying done or hiring a container truck wouldn't have got me anywhere except back where I'd come from since I had walked into a cul-de-sac where only a low wall and a gate barred me from the river. I asked him how I could get down to it. He told me I could jump off the bloody bridge if I'd a mind to but first I had to get back to the main gate and sharpish, too. So back I went, with the dog scarcely three feet from my backside.

Although I had planned to hug the south embankment as far as possible on this walk and visit the Battersea Dogs' Home on another occasion, it occurred to me that I might look into that temporary home for all London's strays at a time when close exposure to two entirely different breeds had given me something to think about. On the way to those extensive kennels in the Battersea Park Road I turned over my stock of experience.

A candid friend once asked me, bluntly, whether at heart I was nervous if not scared of dogs. I said not in the least as long as I knew what they were up to, especially the truly wild species such as wolves in the Canadian tundra and packs of Lycaons or Cape hunting-dogs in East Africa where, inquisitively, they encircled our night camps, attracted by the pungent reek of the camels. Unless they were rabid, wolves in the Americas have never been known to attack man. Russia is rich in what seems to be wolf mythology. Trained dogs I have always respected and admired but the operative word is 'trained'.

Dog-food manufacturers work on the assumption that there are between six and seven million dogs in Britain. Uncountable numbers of those companion dogs (I deeply dislike the word pets) have very little training and I am at odds with their owners and perhaps I sometimes show it. Therein might lie my susceptibility to attack. Dogs can sense the indefinable. Two men I have questioned at length on this subject both said you can learn a great deal about people from the way their dogs behave. The men are David Churchman, a chief inspector who kept an eye on the trainers and handlers of all the dogs used by the Metropolitan police, and Arthur Phillipson, formerly director of training for the Guide Dogs for the Blind Association. What those two classes of dogs can be taught to do and what they sometimes do on their own often surprises those in charge of them.

Police dogs on the trail acquire the capacity to assess different situations. They soon learn to distinguish between a frightened lost child, a harmless mentally disturbed wanderer and a desperate criminal on the run who, if cornered, might try to fight it out. With a bite pressure of 250 pounds per square inch, the marvel is that German Shepherd dogs can be taught to hold down a strong man without harming him. As the policeman put it, his men are taught to 'read their dogs', encouraging and guiding their reactions.

When an animal has undergone basic training for the police force, the chances are that it will show particular abilities in one direction, perhaps locating dead bodies, explosives, narcotics or strange objects such as a safe dumped in a field overnight. Or a deserted building in which someone is hiding. Rewards and punishments are confined to praise and scolding, briefly uttered by tone of voice alone. After what may have been a hectic day cornering an armed robber and pinning him down the dog trots home with his handler and probably plays with his youngsters on the hearth rug after supper.

German Shepherds (Alsatians) have extremely good memories. The inspector recalled a day when one of his own dogs cocked its leg up against what must have been the faulty base of a street lamp on the Thames embankment. It received a sharp shock where it hurt most and couldn't be persuaded to walk that way again. A good dog can hear a pin drop on a hard surface at a distance of twenty-five paces.

The trainer of trainers for dogs for the blind always preferred labradors because, unlike Shepherds ('Excellent dogs, mind you') they are socially acceptable almost everywhere. They have short coats and, being gun dogs, are not worried by noises. Basic training, starting when they are ten months old, takes about six months, when they are taught to stop and sit down and move backwards or forwards or turn to the left or the right on command. For the job they have to do they are taught to walk correctly, that is slightly to the fore and on the left of their handlers, keeping to the centre of the pavement. The vital period is when they are matched and instructed with their first blind owners. Tall, fast walkers need big nimble dogs and elderly owners slow animals. They have a working life of eight or nine years.

Some dogs with patient, sensitive owners show remarkable virtuosity. He recalled one animal which, in a large food store, could, at a word of command, locate cheese, bacon and, elsewhere, packeted soap and fire-lighters. In the days when all Woolworth's stores used the same kind of pungent floor polish, it could find Woolworth's in a strange town.

Dog petters and dog spoilers should note that both these master supervisors were at one in believing that dogs are by nature primarily motivated by self-interest. Given half a chance they take every advantage they can get. Not a few dogs owned by the blind become accomplished thieves, especially in butchers' shops. The animal accepts obedience as a form of self-preservation and reward.

At feeding-time the Dogs' Home, Battersea can be heard at a range of a hundred yards in a neighbourhood that really comes to life only when the trucks start to roll in at night to where Covent Garden fruit and flower market is now located in Nine Elms Lane. As I wasn't expected at the Dogs' Home that day I took a pint in the pub opposite, the Pavilion, and phoned the manager to be told, politely, that he was busy with two clients but could see me in half an hour.

An uncommonly friendly pub, the Pavilion. Everyone seemed to know everyone else and total strangers like myself got a heavy wink, a greeting and place at the crowded bar. In the big bar, a juke-box all but set fire to the wallpaper yet in what had been the snug they played pool and gossiped above the whimper and gurgle of babies in prams.

The Guv'nor Ray Reynolds bustled around like a ship's purser on the first day out. He greeted me and, hearing I'd got an appointment across the road, promptly sat down. 'Lost one, have you?' he asked solicitously. I hadn't the heart to say what I'd really come about but enquired, cautiously, about the dog seekers.

In the rapid lilt and clipped syllables of County Sligo, he said that about a dozen a day came in. He was, as he put it, 'what ye might call the comforter and shoulder to cry on,' and some of 'em did cry on him, they did. Sometimes men, too. If they were on their way in for the first time, it was 'a drop of Dutch courage' they needed before they joined the queue. 'But mind you, if they come several times, maybe four or five and from right across London, too, and there's no trace of their dog you can see the sadness in their eyes.'

What were their chances of getting their dogs back? He

shrugged his shoulders. Hard to say but he reckoned most of 'em did. And then, by God, you should see them. Many's the time he'd had to stop a man buying the whole pub a drink. 'Cost 'em a fortune it would.' We shook hands and I joined the queue on the opposite side of the road.

A small crowded office. Babble of voices. Barking dogs. Everybody busy. A girl with a ready smile asked my name and business. At her feet sprawled a huge marmalade-coloured chow with its nose perilously close to the feet of comers and goers. 'Hallo, dog,' said I. The chow wagged its rear end, slowly. 'That's Shane,' said the girl behind the desk. '*My* dog.' Shane looked up, obviously pleased.

In came the Manager-Veterinary Surgeon, W. M. (Bill) Wadham Taylor. 'Yes, what do you want?' he asked, somewhat testily. He'd forgotten my call. Could he give me twenty minutes of his time? Somewhere quiet, I suggested. He shrugged his shoulders and took me upstairs to a little room and a cup of tea where I emerged an hour later with a more than favourable opinion of a dedicated man.

Aged I should guess between sixty and seventy, Wadham Taylor knows what he's about and answers questions with the speed of a television quiz winner. Something just under a third of their funds comes in from the Metropolitan police who delegate their legal duties towards stray dogs (and cats) brought in to police stations to the Battersea Home; that is, they must be retained for a week for which board is charged. How many dogs passed through their hands last year? About 15,000. How many were claimed? Between fifteen and twenty per cent. What about the rest? Here his voice rose, slightly. 'Those dogs were purposively abandoned, kicked out. Their owners had no intention of trying to get them back. What makes this job so worthwhile is that most people who come here looking for their lost dogs usually find them.'

Under what conditions were they prepared to sell dogs? 'We carefully cross-examine prospective purchasers about what they want the dog *for*. Where do they live? What is their occupation? What facilities have they for exercising a dog? We never sell guard dogs which are much in demand around here.

We are in business for what you rightly call "companion animals". A good dog might cost them £50.'

Rather a rough neighbourhood, wasn't it? 'Nonsense,' he said. 'A lovely place to live in.' He and his wife have 'a nice flat above the shop. Five minutes from a park which has got just about everything. Mind you, you don't want to walk about the streets at night.' Before they became vets 'donkey years ago', he restored classic Rolls Royces in Scotland.

In general terms he was averse to distinguishing the characters of different breeds, reckoning that, like human beings, they varied a great deal. 'But they know on which side their bread is buttered.' I steered him round to German Shepherds and labradors. He smiled. Labs, he thought, 'liked to please everybody, especially those who feed them. You could teach a lab to jump over a cliff. Not so a Shepherd. They are individualists. They stop and think what to do next.'

As we parted a man turned to him, profusely grateful for harbouring his scruffy-looking mongrel, lost for nearly a week. The dog tried to jump up on his shoulders to lick him. 'But how would it have reacted if the man had regularly thrashed the animal?' I asked.

'In just the same way,' said the Master-Pinder. 'Dogs don't bear grudges.'

Lovely as that district might be to a dedicated man with a job to do there, the area to the south of the four bridges, the Park and the power station, is today an almost unmitigated eyesore. Elms Lane, Cringle Street and a dozen cul-de-sacs harbour the fossils of the Railway Age, rusting sheds, vacant lots and red-brick business centres. But in our mind's eye let us go back in time and not so far back at that. Say just over a hundred years. From the recorded evidence of the birds that nested in Battersea Fields, especially the predatory harriers and that haunter of thick reedbeds, the Bearded tit, the riparian marshes must have resembled the fringes of the Norfolk Broads. And behind them lay rich grassland.

William Cobbett – who could not bear the thought that the

best food in the country was destined for central London – was
enraged by the fat oxen he saw there.

> . . . this primest of human food was, aye, every mouthful of
> it, destined to be devoured in the Wen, and that, too, for the
> far greater part by the Jews, loan-jobbers, tax-eaters and
> their base and prostituted followers . . . literary as well as
> other wretches who, if suffered to live at all, ought to
> partake of nothing but offal and ought to come but one cut
> before the dogs and cats.

When the Marsh Wall was built and cultivation became more
and more intense, Battersea emerged as a market-gardening
area. The population rocketed from 5,500 in 1830 to about
200,000 within a hundred years. Today the population density
is about thirty people per acre. Industry has been replaced by
offices and warehouses in the Nine Elms area.

Nobody who has swept down to Heathrow in an aircraft or
walked east along the embankment with his eye on the sun can
fail to notice that, after much meandering, the river seems
hesitant about which way to turn between the huge market
and the Pimlico Gardens on the opposite bank until, a little
beyond the Vauxhall Bridge, it strikes due north into the
flanks of Westminster. Since there is precious little to be
seen on the southern shore for close on a mile, I resorted to
imagination triggered off by trivialities.

The low outgoing tide offered for my inspection red-brown
algae, shell marl, shattered pottery, baulks of timber, the
grinning carcases of long-dead cats and bits of that ubiquitous
fluffy polystyrene which has been found as far afield as the
shores of the South Polar Seas. Trapped in it all, like stranded
jellyfish, were knotted condoms, increasingly common since
the new pandemic. A girl I know who now works as a Refuse
Disposal Consultant was asked for her qualifications for the
job. She replied that she had spent five years of her life as an
archaeologist, studying nothing but what other people had
thrown away. Evaluating rubbish is what archaeology is all
about.

I walked on – marched is perhaps the better word since, lost in an ever-widening whirlpool of thoughts I tend to quicken pace. Ambulatory overdrive. In our walks around the Heath at first light, Katie, in the way of a sympathetic wife, is well aware that if from our normal well-matched pace I suddenly stride ahead I am in a scarcely describable thought-world of my own, only subconsciously aware of her presence and that, given distance, usually about fifty yards, I shall revert to reality and stop and turn round and look apologetic. 'Profitable?' she sometimes enquires and, if I nod, she motions to my left-hand breast-pocket where a small tape recorder is a more efficient substitute for pinning down the fugitive thought than what used to be called a twopenny notebook, red-backed and ruled feint.

On and on I marched, past the outfall of the Effra, beyond Vauxhall Bridge with its strange carved figures between the breakwaters. Seen through glasses the façade of the Tate gave some distinction to the west bank; upheld, too, by the Vickers Tower but smudged by the Millbank home of the Department of Energy. Tugs tooted as they hauled garbage to some bourne far downstream and, above their freight, the spindrift of harsh-calling gulls. For how many millennia has this ancient stream, once the tributary of a far bigger river that arose in Central Europe and emptied out on Dogger Bank, carried craft? The answer by sub-atomic reckoning is about 300,000 years.

Far down the estuary, beyond Gravesend on the Kentish shore, lies Swanscombe, a fine-sounding name but today an eyesore of sand and gravel pits. Among the spoil the quarrymen began to find hefty flint axes in thousands until, on one memorable day in 1935, Alvan Marston, a local dentist, discovered the first bits of a human skull, Swanscombe Man, one of the oldest in Europe. The makers of these so-called Acheulian axes lived among straight-tusked elephants, woodland rhinos, huge cats and fallow deer on the banks of a river at least two miles wide. From the distribution of those axes they must have crossed the water regularly in dug-out logs of oak.

The ice came down again and again. When it finally melted,

the Mesolithic people poled over from Scandinavia. They were followed by the Celts, the Romans, the longships of the Vikings, the Saxons under Alfred who 'honourably restored and made habitable' the Thames valley, the Normans – successively with more sophisticated sailing craft. The Bayeux Tapestry tells us what they looked like. The Plantagenets gave manœuvring-room for the Lancastrians and Yorkists until Gloriana with her hennaed hair and ropes of jewellery constantly queened it up and down the river. Envisage then *Regina*, the royal barge breasting the shoals between the shingle beds at the river's sharp turn.

Thomas Puckering's men had built her at Rotherhithe, forty-five feet in length and carvel-planked from good Wealden oak. Twelve pairs of rowers aft of the gilded coach house gave her sturdy drive and four pairs of rowers right for'ard could turn her at a word of command. The huge standard blazoned with the Tudor arms, six golden lions *gardant* and quartered with *fleur-de-lis*, clattered in the downstream breeze.

Inside the palatial coach house Gloriana lolled on a bank of scarlet cushions raised at her head, and beside her Essex half knelt, his fiery hair about his shoulders, his anxious eyes searching the powdered face, the quizzical smile of Henry's wholly unpredictable daughter. Was he or was he not in favour? Everything depended on her mood.

In that month of May, ten years before he went to the block, events seemed reasonably propitious for ambitious Essex. The Armada had been sunk or scattered. Leicester was dead. Unfortunately his counter-attack on Spain with Drake had proved near disastrous despite his own gallantry. It turned out to be easier to repel an invasion than to make one. The expedition had cost a fortune and they had missed Philip's treasure-ships. Gloriana had blown her royal top and ordered him home on pain of the Tower.

What would be his fate? With no loot to stem the ever-mounting debts of the poorest Earl in England, the impetuous Essex immediately begged audience at Court, relying on his eloquence, his long-professed love for his royal mistress. At least reckoning he believed she needed the support, the good will of his noble kinsmen. But she foresaw the move. And there was the matter of an expensive expedition to be paid for. Queen to Knight check.

No word for six anguished days before Sir Edward Dimmoke, her Champion at Large, arrived with a curt summons. Her royal barge would stand off the steps of Essex House at an hour before noon, the following day. Let him prepare himself accordingly.

Came noon. Bells tolled from a score of towers but no barge appeared. With a conspicuously unarmed squire at his side, Essex paced the length of his watergate, up and down, up and down until, not long after two o'clock, he heard the soft chant of the rowers as the ship inched in, slowly. More delays. Covertly, from behind veiled curtains, she watched him until, at a slight movement of her hand, her barge-master brought him aboard in a mean cockboat used by the crew.

About what passed between them at first meeting we have no record but from his subsequent correspondence with his guardian, great Burghley, it seems that royal disfavour included a demand for £3,000 which she had lent him or, in default, its equivalent in land. This she got, eventually, at considerable profit to herself. What is certain is that from that period until at least the Francis Bacon affair, Essex returned to the Queen's regard. She even sold to him for a considerable term of years the right to farm the customs on imported white wine. What brought this about? A relatively simple case of seduction on those huge velvet cushions? Simple, perhaps, on the part of Essex. There were those who said it had happened before.

Agile, able, handsome, uncommonly eloquent even by the standards of that age, he could pen elegant lyrics as easily as he spoke, and he was a born flatterer. From the kneeling position, a slight movement forward, perhaps to kiss those heavily bejewelled fingers and more might easily follow. For diversionary tactics, there were the cushions to be arranged, an exquisite pendant to be admired, and below it, a purple corded placket to be simply undone. What at least he hoped for can be easily imagined. 'He could conceal nothing,' wrote Henry

Cuffe, 'he carried his love and his hatred on his forehead.'

Not so the Queen. Her overt sexuality in common with her other courses of action and inaction were not so much subject to her whims, her rapid changes of mood; they were stupidly perverse and harmful to herself. Advisers of the sagacity of Burghley and Bacon often tried to persuade her that, in acting the way she did, she injured none but herself. Freud could have made much of her tempestuous childhood shot through as it was by hideous fears, alternations of neglect and over-indulgence and, not improbably, sexual abuse. For her mother Anne Boleyn, and for many others, her birth in 1533 had been like the birth of fate.

It was preceded by what Edith Sitwell called 'the Sophoclean drama of King Henry's escape from real or imagined incest', that of his marriage with his brother's widow, mother of Mary Tudor, 'cursed by the gods with the decree that no male child of that marriage should live'. When Elizabeth was a very young girl, scarcely three, her father 'that lonely being, a giant in scale, a creature of powerful intellect and insane pride, of cruelty, vengeance and appalling rages' cut off her mother's head. Was she then the heir to England or a mere outcast bastard? Until the old king's death she could never be certain.

Even in her fifteenth year in the house of her stepmother, Katherine Parr who had married Lord High Admiral Seymour, she had to put up with his lordship's premeditated gallantry in her bedroom for, when her stepmother died not long afterwards, his lordship with more than an eye to the throne, proposed to her. For which grievous offence his own brother, Somerset the Protector, ordered him to be flung in the Tower and eventually beheaded. Those were harsh times.

The years rolled on when, as Queen but still unmarried and childless, the Protestant cause in England depended entirely on her continued existence since the next heir was the Catholic Mary Stuart. Was Elizabeth at heart homosexual? Virtually impossible. She loved men. At the least provocation even the Ladies of her Bedchamber, her woman friends and the wives and daughters of her ambassadors got short shrift in voluble English, French, Italian and Latin too which she could write and speak rapidly. From Leicester to Essex, with nobody

knew how many in between times, Gloriana assumed her role
as puppet mistress, prepared at any moment to change the cast
if it suited her obscure purpose.

Somebody put it about, possibly Ben Jonson, that 'she had a
membrana upon her which made her incapable of man though
for her delight she tryed many'. Had Essex not burned his
intimate diaries together with a mass of incriminating papers
that bitter cold night in February 1601 we might know the
truth of the matter.

The bulk of Lambeth lies behind the exceptionally dreary
Albert Embankment and, apart from an affectionate glance at
the Archbishop's palace in buttressed warm-red brick, the
very epitome of Gothic, I have scarcely a thing to say about
that section of this perambulation. A pity this, since Black
Prince Road down to Kennington hints at royal connections
still vested, as I understand it, in successive Princes of Wales
and Dukes of Cornwall. I wonder if they are proud of that
property? The Palace now, that's a different matter. Seen from
the outside the whole complex with its lantern tower and
Tudor chimneys is a joy to look at. I have yet to meet
His Grace. Wasn't it the Smith of Smiths who said, 'I have,
alas, only one illusion left, and that is the Archbishop of
Canterbury'?

Across the water lies the Palace of Westminster. Although I
never belonged to that curious Westminster lobby group of
reporters and broadcasting celebrities for whom the media has
turned out to be the message and the message the media, I
spent a year or two pestering northern MPs in the sump-
tuously palatial neo-Gothic Central Hall of Parliament, the
dividing line between the House of Lords and the House of
Commons. At that time the Commons sat in the House of
Lords quarters while their own House, bombed and burned
out during the war, was being re-built. In the Central Hall any
reporter could ask to see particular Members of Parliament
and Badge Messengers – House servants got up in full evening
dress no matter what the time of day and wearing heavy
polished necklaces to dangle their portcullis badges from –

would deliver a Green Card to the MP. Then as now, MPs had no objection to being at the beck and call of anybody who could provide the publicity that in turn would provide the votes when an election came along.

More than forty years have passed since then and most of what I am relating comes from a near-lifetime friendship with David Wood of *The Times* who took me into that trading-house of parliamentary news and gossip, Annie's Bar. Much has changed. Women now sit in the House of Lords, as well as life peers whose titles are not hereditary. It has been accepted that not every peer, either hereditary or lifer, can play the senator at his own expense, so they may all claim a daily attendance allowance to encourage frequent calls at one of the best and most exclusive clubs in town. In a busy week a peer can make nearly as much as a London bus driver. Socialist left-wingers who have spent a lifetime campaigning for the abolition of the House of Lords no sooner get there than they proclaim its merits over the House of Commons. They have taken the Tory bait: 'Reform that you may preserve'.

The Commons as a House has also changed, not necessarily for the better. In the old days a Member had only a locker to store his papers, and when he was not dictating a constituency reply to a part-time secretary in full view of every passer-by he would be talking politics in tea-rooms, bars or dining-rooms. The Chamber dominated his life. Your modern MP sees himself as a company executive who needs a fairly spacious office (with cocktail cabinet), a full-time secretary, and if possible a research assistant. (Many of the research assistants are American students of politics working for doctorates; and the increased research activity has placed a heavy load on the Commons library and research staff.) In a normal day's debate only ten or eleven backbenchers can be called by the Speaker, and House Committees have had to be devised to give back-benchers some role where they can behave like company executives, usually taking up the time of Ministers and senior civil servants. Meanwhile, as the Chamber becomes less important, or at any rate less well attended than in the old days, so the club life of politicians declines; and as backbenchers seek an executive role they increasingly hanker for their parliamentary

salary to be fixed at the level of a high rank in the civil service.

One good thing: David Wood tells me that Annie's Bar, Fred Peart's great achievement as Leader of the House, flourishes. There are more than a dozen specialized bars in the Palace of Westminster, but Annie's Bar and the House of Lords staff bar alone allow MPs and journalists to trade news and gossip on equal terms. Elsewhere journalists are guests of politicians, or the politicians are guests of journalists, as in the Press Gallery bar where you could once find the largest range of malt whiskies in London. Your daily newspaper would be thin gruel at breakfast time if Annie's Bar did not exist, for that is where the seeds of big political stories are planted and nurtured. And if you ask why 'Annie's' the answer is as literal as you suspected: Annie ran the bar when it stood in the Members' inner lobby. As the division bell rang MPs set down their drinks and walked out of one door; journalists walked out of another door into the Ways and Means corridor. After the count of Ayes and Noes they all returned to Annie's to pick up the theme and the drink. But the original Annie's Bar was destroyed with the Commons Chamber during the war, and its site is now occupied by the Opposition Chief Whip's staff.

Kings Reach, that portion of the Thames between the slopes of *La Straunde* and those public buildings directly opposite, the Royal Festival Hall, the Hayward Gallery, the National Theatre and so on, can be hugely praised as there's always something to be seen there in fair weather and foul and it's a great place for striding out. My intention had been to look at the outfall of the Fleet into the Thames under Blackfriars Bridge and to scan the northern shore from the high roof of that very modern pub that almost overhangs the river, the Doggetts Coat and Badge, to see whether anything resembling the general topology of Ogilby's map of 1677, a copy of which I carried, could still be made out. The first proved difficult, the second impossible.

The outfall, a huge pipe, can be seen (just) from an angle. A muddy swirl in the river might well have been all that was left of the torrential rain that had fallen on Hampstead Heath the previous night but, equally, it might have been sewage. Or both. The pub manager had gone off for the day and his deputy was out of sorts and markedly unhelpful. Not so a well-founded barmaid who had overheard the argument. What was I looking for? Her previous job had been in the Information Bureau alongside St Paul's where, she told me, they handled nearly a thousand enquiries each day.

I showed her my section of Ogilby, originally eight feet in length, the first plane survey of London after the Great Fire. She looked, fascinated at where Essex, Arundel, Somerset and Buckingham had lived but knew nothing about them. What had visitors asked her? Just about everything, she said and recalled the Japanese gentleman who, she thought, was trying to sell them a fridge. It transpired he wanted Selfridge's. She mentioned, too, an American intent on reaching Canterbury cathedral where he wanted to see the exact spot where Becket was shot. With something of a family affair to attend to near the old Clink prison, I hastened on.

With the exception of the great loop it makes to ensnare Millwall and Cubitt Town on the Isle of Dogs, London's river heads more or less due east from the bridge of the Black Friars (Dominicans) to Gallions Reach and Barking Creek where the Roding drops into the Thames. Thereabouts on that sombre morning at the end of January 1965, the launch *Havenger* bore the coffin of Winston Churchill from the Tower to the Festival Pier. The old-fashioned guns along the river boomed a nineteen-gun salute. The great steam cranes on the wharves dipped down like prehistoric creatures. Big Ben stood still for half a day. The crowds were silent and so was I, emotionally gripped by it all.

There is at Southwark with its fragile ruin of a great ecclesiastical house the feel of an ancient Liberty or Burgh – it's still called the Borough – which has existed there since the fourteenth century. London had grown at a tumultuous rate. The Tower symbolized royal power; Westminster stood for government and law-making; but the Tower and Westminster were connected by a river and for over six centuries, that is from 1197 to 1857, that river from the mouth of the Medway to Staines some forty miles upstream remained under the jealously guarded jurisdiction of the City of London.

For the simple geographic reason that all traffic from the south and the south-east poured across London Bridge, Southwark has been an important suburb of London since Roman times. The Borough became famous for its inns, good food, the brewing of ale and famous, too, for the town houses of the church dignitaries, the bishops and abbots of southern England. With the exception of Winchester House, by far the grandest of them but now a mere shell with the socket of a rose window (see overleaf), all have disappeared. To that house belonged a Liberty known as the Clink which, because it lay beyond the range of City authority and the incomers called for entertainment, gave rise to an extensive rookery of gaming-houses, whore-shops and bear-pits, the precursors of London's playhouses.

The stew, according to Eric de Mare, 'was originally a sweating or steam bath which came to Britain from the Imperial City during the Roman occupation. This hygienic type of pleasure resort continued in Russia, Finland and Turkey and the near East and was brought back to England again in the twelfth century.'[1] Today they are called unisex saunas.

The Knights Templars were notable wenchers and where more easily could they be ferried from across the river than to Bankside in the Borough, 'the repaire', in Stowe's phrase, 'of incontinent men to the like women'? He adds that few English women were found in the houses; the inmates were mostly lusty strumpets from Flanders.

On Bankside, a little to the east of Southwark Bridge, lies Park Street and a boarded-off enclosure, the site of the most famous theatre in the world, Shakespeare's Globe. Built in 1599, burnt down fourteen years later, rebuilt, demolished in 1644, it is once more, we hope, to emerge, phoenix-wise, from the ashes. Here were played most of the late tragedies including *Hamlet*.

---

[1] Eric de Mare, *London's Riverside*, Reinhardt, 1958.

In one of the many bars of a nearby pub, the famous Anchor with its double walls much used for smuggling, sat my good friend the Apothecary accompanied by his wife, Crokie, and my wife, Katie. There could be few more informative couriers to the Liberties of Southwark. He knows every street and back alley in the Borough. He rose to greet me and with a wave of his hand informally introduced me to a knot of fascinated American businessmen out for the day after a conference and resumed his eloquent discourse.

'I need not remind you, gentlemen,' he said, 'that just as trade follows the flag, so around here were subsidiary trades which flourished on the fat wallets of travellers and merchants. They came to the City to buy and they came to sell: furs, jewellery and musk from Russia; silk, spices, fire-arms and books from Venice; swords and armour from Milan; wine and citrus fruits from France and Spain. The manifest of a ship from the Baltic records, I have heard, half a dozen live wolves although I can't for the life of me imagine who'd want them. When the day's trading was done and only the Watch and the bellmen were supposed to be abroad, they sought venial diversions.

> The stews in England bore a beastly sway
> Till the eighth Henry banished them away.
> And since those common whores were quite put down,
> A damned crew of private whores soon came to town.

'Mind you, Henry never really put the whores down. Who could? The Bankside stews had been an accepted part of London's cultural pattern for centuries. In effect the stew-keepers were given a royal licence in a Liberty where even the Lord Mayors had to be cautious where they trod. There were about a dozen precepts about what could and what could not be done in the knocking-shops.

'No stew-holder or his wife should let or stay any single woman to come and go freely at all times where she listed. No single woman to take money to lie with any man, but she lie with him all night till the morrow. Not to keep any woman that hath the burning infirmity nor keep any woman in his house on the holy days but the bailiff to see them voided out of the Lordship. Their Lordships, of course, were the bishops who levied rents and collected fines from those who broke the regulations. The whores themselves were known as Winchester's Geese.'

Much enlightened, no doubt, the Americans thanked him and trooped upstairs to the restaurant. The Apothecary sighed and looked round. 'Marvellous place this,' he said. 'At least it was. It's just changed hands. God knows what's going to happen to it. Some multiple group has just carried off the chains and leg irons from the old Clink prison just round the corner. And, worse, a first edition of Sam Johnson's *Dictionary* has disappeared.'

I knew that Shakespeare, Burbage, Massinger and Ben Jonson had tippled in the original pub. Their theatre stood within hailing distance. But until the Apothecary in the booming voice of the Grand Cham quoted the actual lines from memory, I had not known that it was in the Anchor that Johnson had prefaced his reading of Henry Thrale's will – of which he was one of the trustees – with the words: 'We are not here to sell a parcel of boilers and vats but the potentiality of growing rich beyond the dreams of avarice.'

The nappy strong ale of Southwerke
Doth keep many a gossip from kirke.

What's nappy? 'Smooth, I believe,' said Frank, 'as in babies' naps with their smooth or raised surface. Probably from the Old German *noppen*. The Thrales owned the pub and several others which eventually became the famous Barclay Perkins brewery.'

In addition to its double walls and a resident ghost, there is a 'secret passage' in the present Anchor, much used in the old days for the clandestine admission of liquor and tobacco. A huge beamy tavern yet intimate. Little snugs have their own cliques of regulars. The one immediately beyond the creaky side-entrance is regularly enlivened by the advent of The Skipper, a former ship's captain (RN) with an uncommon thirst. He turns up at two o'clock and before the pub closes at

three he has downed six pints, supped from his own pewter pot that holds a quart.

From upstairs, in the glossier bars and eating-places, comes the sophisticated chatter of young City gents, lawyers, ad-men and Sloane Rangers who, as in Battersea, are snapping up local property around the Clink. 'Heavy Buzz', they say and 'Weirdos' meaning anyone a few years older than themselves. All things large and small are reduced to 'mega' and 'micro'.

Dr Oliver Goldsmith who, in Johnson's words, 'wrote like an angel but talked like Poor Poll', struggled hard to run a practice on Bankside. His lack of success was marked; his contemporaries noted that he dressed in a shabby suit of green and gold 'whilst a want of neatness and of money for the washerwoman' was betrayed in his shirt and necktie often worn for a fortnight.

Conditions in the prisons varied enormously and depended on whether or not the prisoners, especially those confined for libel or debt, could eventually pay for their upkeep. Tobias Smollett, that entertaining if ill-tempered novelist and critic nicknamed 'Old Smelfungus' by Sterne, served a term in the King's Bench where, despite limited confinement, he was treated like a guest. He described that 'comfortable asylum for the unfortunate' in the novel he wrote there, *Sir Launcelot Greaves*, the story of an eighteenth-century Don Quixote. King's Bench he wrote:

> . . . appears like a neat little regular town, consisting of one street surrounded by a very high wall, including an open piece of ground which may be termed a garden where the prisoners take the air, and amuse themselves with a variety of diversions. Except the entrance, where the turnkeys keep watch and ward, there is nothing in the place which looks like a gaol or bears the least colour of restraint. The street is crowded with passengers. Tradesmen of all kinds here exercise their different professions. Hawkers of all sorts are admitted and vend their wares as in any open street of London.

In the days of the Tudors, punishment for the destitute 'and those of the poorer sort' was barbaric. Without a standing army or a police force the Crown had to rely upon men of influence and power for protecting property, pursuing criminals, suppressing rebellion and defending the country against invaders. Private persons were encouraged, indeed obliged to carry arms and be ready to use them. The instruments of violence were ready to hand.

Theft of goods over the value of twelve pence could rank as grand larceny which carried the death penalty. Hanging involved slow strangulation rather than the swift dislocation of the vertebrae and the felon's goods were usually forfeit to the Crown. Towards the end of the sixteenth century a penurious government decided to use convicted men as oarsmen in the royal galleys where conditions were appalling. Physical mutilation in public places was commonplace and imprisonment considered a relatively lenient punishment, a reprieve from death. But such were the conditions in most Tudor prisons that the reprieve was often short-lived.

For complaints about deliberate starvation, the emaciated felons were flogged and flogged until they dropped and were left to die or, under pretext of giving them a palliative, they were drugged and struck on the head. Murder by poison or attempted murder by that means carried a special penalty of boiling to death.

In his *Chronicles of the Greyfriars of London*, Thomas Timbs quotes a few cases that no doubt provided an hour or two of entertainment for the commonalty of the City and the Borough in the sixteenth century.

> This yeere was a cooke boyld in a caldron in Smythfielde for he would a-poysond the Bishop of Rochester, with dyvers of his servants: and he was lockd in a chain and pulld up and down with a gibbet, at dyvers tymes, til he was dede . . . x day of March was a maid boyld in Smythfield for poysoning of divers persons.

Other public diversions included hanging, drawing and quartering, hurling anything to hand at unfortunates in the pillory or the stocks for petty offences; battles between apprentices, the hue-and-cry after thieves and murderers as well as bull-baiting and bear-baiting. Even in the days of the Puritans, the first arguments against the accepted pastime of flogging and worrying blinded bears to death were not that it caused almost unimaginable pain to the animals but that it was liable to attract unsavoury characters 'leading to thieving, gambling and the like'.

With the Apothecary in the lead like a questing hound, looking around, sniffing, we slipped down Stoney Street, quartered the Market, glanced at Thrale Street and went thence into the heart of the Borough where, half a century ago, he and his wife had spent the first night of their honeymoon at another hostelry, the George, probably the White Hart of *Pickwick Papers*. A fine four-poster as he recalled it with a little pair of steps to get in and, nicely symbolical, a Tudor rocking-cradle at the foot of the bed 'into which we pitched our confetti'.

In the morning he found he hadn't enough money to pay the bill and was obliged to phone his best man to come round at once and bail them out. 'Bring some ready,' he recalled having said. 'Much of my married life has been like that.'

The Borough abounds in some excellent taverns, the product first of travellers and visiting merchants; the publicans' trade stimulated, no doubt, by the sale of hops that first began to arrive in quantity from Flanders in the late sixteenth century:

Hops, Reformation, bays and beer
Came to England all in one year.

'This is approximately, but not exactly true,' said that ever meticulous botanist, Geoffrey Grigson. The word 'hop' and the practice of flavouring and preserving beer with its dried flowers has been known since the Middle Ages. Hops became worthy of wholesale at the advent of the big breweries with their stored ale. When London telephone numbers were prefaced by three letters and not three figures as they are today,

the area code for Southwark was HOP. A few fine old warehouses with their floridly painted signs and curlicues still exist
in the Borough.

It began to grow dark. The bastions of Tower Bridge were
hung about with a garland of lights. Because I wanted to show
the Apothecary a nature reserve on a vacant lot below the
southern approach to the bridge, the four of us hastened down
Tooley Street back to the sullen river. In 1976 as part of the
Silver Jubilee celebrations, Max Nicholson, a former director
of the Nature Conservancy, put forward the idea of an ecology
park on a small area of natural vegetation then being used as a
lorry park alongside the bridge.

The reserve was named after that great eighteenth-century
botanist William Curtis, who during many surveys had found
relatively rare marsh plants growing not far away and regretted they were disappearing 'as a result of development'. The
idea flourished, literally.

Over 150 different kinds of plants and trees sprang up
around a reed-lined pool where, gradually introduced,
dragonflies and butterflies including the Janus-eyed Peacock
and the Small tortoiseshell danced in the sunlight. Foxes
visited this urban water-hole. Thousands of school children
regularly studied natural history there. I remember the delight
of a street child from Wapping gingerly touching the first
hedgehog she had seen. Katie and I had visited the pool about a
month before we took the Apothecary and his wife there.

Imagine our dismay at finding more than two acres of
luxuriance bulldozed flat for the new Thameside Plan. We
looked across the river upstream, where nothing caught the
eye except vulgar conformity, the work of group architects
repeating what for thirty years had been done time and time
again, on the sites where one man, Christopher Wren, and a
corps of craftsmen built over sixty exquisite churches, each
one of them completely different.

City for all seasons

No single word, no single phrase gives a reasonable impression of what it feels like to *live* in London. Trollope, uncommonly terse for once, described the monstrous splodge as 'unintelligible'. Henry James, conscious of what he called 'the fatal futility of *fact*', deplored the 'horrible numerosity' of metropolitan society. V. S. Pritchett, taking up Mr Podsnap's suggestion that there are within the capital, 'Many Evidences that Strike you . . .', commented quietly, as he always does, 'that the place is *all* evidence, like the sight of a heavy sea from a rowing boat in the middle of the Atlantic where you are surrounded by everything and see nothing'.

When sophisticated visitors, especially Americans who have seen a great deal between Hampton Court and Harry's Bar in the City during a ten-days' tour ask me, as many of them have done, what it feels like to live here, I lean heavily on ambiguity and say that it depends on where you are and at what time of the year.

Right now spring hath truly sprung. By spring I don't mean those unfulfilled promises in early March when in between flurries of foul weather we take brief delight in lawns alight with crocuses and snowdrops, described by Yeats as 'candle-like foam on the shores of the spring tide'. The all too brief season upon us now is what's implied by that evocative

word *primavera*, the first truth as if it had never been revealed before.

On the Heath one enormous survivor, a very old elm known to me for years, prepares a book-plate entry. The birches are as if painted by a *pointilliste* with a mouse-hair brush, mere dots of the limpidest green, whilst chiff-chaffs, those little immigrants that pronounce their name over and over again are chiffing and chaffing like mad. Tits are jiggling too and should anyone imagine I have in mind those most beautiful of female adornments, I am referring specifically to the Great tit which for hours on end chants *jigger-jigger-jig* or, as Anne Hathaway's bedmate has it, *Hey-dinga-dinga-ding*. In short my masters, this is the weather the cuckoo likes. Maids have come forth sprig-muslin dressed; citizens dream of the south and the west, and so do I.

Ebullient finches and that counter-tenor of the tree-tops, the Mistle thrush, can sing their heads off in the spring and then shut up, sulkily resuming their winter silence if a mere calendar proves them not so much wrong as adaptively right in being able to survive on alternative diets. Not so the warblers. Their arrival carries the conviction of a prophet who has burned both his bridges and his boats and, since they're plighted to settle down, they sing and they sing.

Outside St James's Park station the other morning I came across two young brides of God peering in a puzzled sort of way at one of those big stylized diagrams of the Underground system. From their accents and wholly with-it habits I took them to be Americans, perhaps from St Ursula of Wichita Falls or perhaps Our Lady of Sioux City. With becoming gallantry I bowed, slightly and said: 'Can I help you, Sister?' whereupon the younger of the two responded with a delicious smile. 'You sure can, Brother. How in the heck do we get to St Paul's?' Trala! Trala! With my good deed done I pranced off like a young buck.

Young and old are infected. On my way to one of the most distinguished clubs in the West End, a shared place within a bowshot of Berkeley Square, a toddler touched his dad for the equivalent of a bob to shove into the chest of a macabre model of a crippled child. That simple act of charity done, he smacked the thing on the side of its head so hard that he all but knocked it over.

One of the *most* distinguished clubs? Unquestionably yes. Membership of the Savage is restricted to those who have achieved distinction by doing something rather than somebody. Because the authors and artists, the musicians, lawyers and scientists who are to be seen homing down to our rooms like bees to a hive at hours roughly defined by the licensing laws, are required to hang their haloes up in the hall, I shall say no more about the place, at least not here, but in light-hearted manner we might look around for a minute or two at some of the characteristics of other adjacent but very different shelters for chauvinists protected by the most efficient hall-porters in the world.

We might first consider the locale. The best clubs for gentlemen are in St James's Street, for many of the great palaces which line Pall Mall are regarded with condescension by the more exclusive. One such palace for motorists, I learn from Major Douglas Sutherland whose line goes back to the thirteenth century, is generally known as the Chauffeurs' Arms. When the Conservative Club merged with the Bath it was referred to as the Lava-tory. The United Services Club on the east side of Waterloo Place was the Duke of Wellington's favourite club, and the members benefited by his intrepidity, for he bearded the Committee and had the price of the midday chop reduced to a shilling. Peace hath her victories. Yet another with a surplice of bishops is commonly called the Clergyman's Rest.

As a guest in the dining-room behind that Athenian façade I once heard a very eminent cleric ask his companion with a purple vest whether he took coffee after lunch. 'No,' he was told, 'I find it keeps me awake in the afternoon.' The chance of admission to a good club comes about only through having one's name put forward by some member with sufficient confidence in his own standing to believe one is more than likely to be accepted by a caucus elected for that purpose. Unless invited it is a grave social error for an aspirant even to suggest that he would like to join the fraternity. Some gentlemen are reluctant to put forward candidates, not the least reason being that in certain clubs they themselves would feel obliged to resign – or worse – if their nominee were turned down.

I am again indebted to the gallant Major for his story about an elderly and distinguished member who, on learning that his cousin had been blackballed, decided to do away with himself. However, before he squeezed the trigger he carefully entered himself under the category of 'various' in one of his most precious possessions, his Game Book.

All clubs worth the name are divided over the issue of whether or not to allow their members to bring their wives or women friends to dine on specified nights of the week but, as somebody rightly remarked, most clubs with the exception of the Savage have the atmosphere of a duke's house with the duke lying dead upstairs. After the first rush of curiosity many ladies are unwilling to join the gentlemen in their own fastness of fumes and foxed leather chairs.

All the best clubs are within a saunter of the three central parks where at this season the infant leaves of the great planes are dancing against a sky as blue as a fisherman's pants. All seems set fair, but for how long? Because, topographically speaking, London is an estuarine swamp between two extensive ridges, it is inconsistently wet and the sky means a great deal to us. It often changes from hour to hour and never more variably than during Lent.

Southern uplifts of warm air from south of Blackheath and north of Highgate mean the serenity of the sky between those breakwaters is torn apart. Billowing clouds of anvil-shaped cumulo-nimbus tower over the Thames. They are unzipped by lightning. Thor thunders. Veils of rain scatter the nursemaids and their charges. Shoppers shelter, peevishly, but it's all over and done with within minutes. Soft spring rain hurts nobody. The skies are shredded, leaving us with immense banks of cottonwool daubed with blue like an apocalypse by Tiepolo.

For bird-conscious weather-watchers, the dawn and just-before-dusk flights of starlings are our barometers. During periods of low pressure they are roof-skimmers, making their early way up from night roosts on ledges in the West End.

During periods of sustained high pressure they fly high, sometimes so high that the impression is of a sprinkling of pepper on an empty plate. This pattern is repeated throughout the country.

For countless thousands of Londoners the country is represented by Hampstead Heath, Blackheath, Wimbledon Common and points south-west of Kew Bridge. Gentlemen think otherwise. The country, or at least selected parts of it, is where they actually reside. It is where you may find their draughty *seats*. The Major remembers a conversation with an elderly friend of his about a mutual acquaintance who they both agreed was a bounder. Although there are few worse things that one gentleman can say about another, his friend went further. 'He is not only a bounder,' he declared, 'he is also a liar,' a declaration which, overheard in White's, Boodles or Pratts might provide reasonable grounds for action for slander. It came out that the fellow in question had told him he had a house in the country whereas it was discovered he lived in Surrey.

To me, a vulgarian, the country is that largely uninhabited portion of the earth beyond our own toe-hold on the North Yorkshire Moors, a mere bothy; and our early-morning preoccupation with the Heath, those 800 soul-saving acres between Parliament Hill and the Hampstead Garden Suburb. Our top-floor apartment stands on a rise above windy winding West End Lane in the not so fashionable district of West Hampstead. In addition to an abundance of space, it has vast views to the south-west whilst in those quarters of her own where Katie puts herself in quarantine against my writing fevers, she can see far below a road and a rising roofscape through the crown of an immense lime tree in which birds nest and sing and to which a small host of identifiable moths resort.

We are warm, we are high up and almost sound-proof. An amenity unrecognized by many is the proximity, a mere 300 yards away of a large cemetery thickly planted with berried bushes and mature conifers, a ready-made nature reserve of some thirty acres. Like that Victorian Valhalla for the eminent on Highgate Hill, our local cemetery abounds in statuary and I recall my surprise on discovering that the upturned palms of a

downcast angel were liberally spattered with blood. But not a miracle. The kestrels, nesting in the tower of the adjacent Chapel of Rest, were using it as a chopping-block for slain sparrows and fieldmice.

It would be tedious to catalogue the avian residents and visitors, the screaming of swifts, the high-pitched shrilling of goldcrests from the tops of sombre cypresses, the *hoo-hooing* of Tawny owls at dusk, but the sight there of half a dozen or more curiously crested waxwings on a telephone wire during a bitterly cold March attracted more rarity-chasers than I care to remember. They literally chased the birds away.

There is, within sight of the railed footpath that bisects the cemetery, a massive tomb about six or seven feet square and almost wholly obscured by a pall of rambler roses. Two wrens, presumably male, since the sexes are much alike, were disputing their right to nest there with an indignant *tic-tic-ticking* noise. Under that tenacious rose I made out the inscription with some difficulty: *Sacred to the Memory of His Imperial Highness, the Grand Duke Michael Michaelovitch and his wife Sophie* who was Countess of Merenberg and grand-daughter of the poet Pushkin.

I find that for eight years they leased Kenwood, the great house on the Heath, 'entering fully into the glamorous social life of the times' until they offered the place as quarters for men and guns that fired at Zeppelins. So we have the bones of Karl Marx in Highgate, and as far away from there as they could be laid to rest, those of the last of the Tsars and his wife.

Although the 'Red terrorist doctor' died before the exiled Duke arrived, Marx also walked the Heath after his long daily stints in the library of the British Museum. By contrast with the elegant goings-on at Kenwood, his abject, his almost unbelievable poverty was such that the marvel was that he managed to survive at all. Before he moved to Kentish Town from his disease-ridden lodgings in Soho, two of his children died because he had no money for either food or medicine. At a time when patriots like Kossuth and Garibaldi were being fêted and publicly cheered in the streets, Marx was constantly hiding from debt collectors. The International added to his duties and gave him hope, but did not add to the pittance he earned writing articles for the *New York Tribune*, and that, too, stopped when his language became too strong for the editor. A Prussian spy who somehow managed to worm his way into the rooms of the Marx family reported that 'everything was broken, tattered and torn and thick with dust over everything . . . manuscripts, books and newspapers lie beside the children's toys, bits and pieces from his wife's sewing basket, cups with broken rims, knives, forks and spoons'.

Marx wanted to dedicate *Das Kapital* to Darwin, but Darwin cautiously refused, saying he was unhappily ignorant of economic science. As for the book itself, Isaiah Berlin says: 'It acquired a symbolic significance beyond anything written since the Age of Faith. It has been blindly worshipped, and blindly hated by millions who have not read a word of it, or who have read without understanding its tortuous prose. In its name revolutions were made; counter-revolutions which followed concentrated upon its suppression as the most potent and insidious of the enemy's weapons . . . it has called into existence an army of interpreters and casuists whose unceasing labours have buried it beneath a mountain of controversy which has outgrown in influence the sacred text itself.'

However apocryphal, there is a story of how, years ago, an American scholar came to London, intent on all the original material written by Marx. He haunted the British Museum Library, asking the oldest people present if they could remember anyone who might have seen the great man at work there. And then at last he tracked down an oldster who said he well recalled seeing him. 'He never spoke to anyone and always looked prematurely old. He sat there, writing, surrounded by books. And then one day, you know, a curious thing happened. He failed to turn up, and nobody ever heard of him again.'

The two south-bound motorways, the M1 and the A1, converge like a pair of callipers on Scratchwood, a little to the north of Hendon where, in those days when engaged in the Heath survey we took time off in the late spring to glory in the clamour of four or five pairs of nesting nightingales. Within a year of the coming of an army of bulldozers and the like to complete one of those super-highways, the pairs had fallen to two and they failed to return the following year. They were, as far as I know, the last of their kind to nest within the conurbation.

Yet Scratchwood remains as part of a geological monument as important in its way as Lulworth Cove, the Devil's Dyke, Haytor and the Fossil Forest, a monument to the prehistoric past. It's part of a ridge where, half a million years ago, a great wall of ice advancing south-west across East Anglia, screeched, crunched and came to a halt. It had run out of momentum. As the earth, our Ever-Mother, began to warm up again the ice started to melt. Enormous cataracts of Windsor-brown water bearing sand and gravels poured down on what today is Hampstead Heath.

For evidence of this my friend, Eric, the geologist took me up to East Finchley and showed me the grey-blue capping of clay so unlike the ochreous yellow and brown clays of Hampstead and Highgate. Eric can decipher the texture and appearance of clays and stone in the way that a master-tailor, sitting cross-legged, needs only to look at and finger material to tell us whether it's wool, the real thing, or a mixture of recycled stuff which perhaps contains synthetics. Eric would like to see a monument erected on the edge of that glacier, a reminder of that time when the North and South poles were running as planetary refrigerators. But what of the post-Ice Age period, that almost indescribable spring of the world of the high latitudes?

For many years my interest in that period, the Mesolithic – which began about 12,000 years ago – has been two-fold. It dates from the purchase of our cottage on the North Yorkshire Moors where I began to do what I did in Hampstead at the end of the war: I started a survey of the immediate neighbourhood and combed Ryedale for support. With one golden exception, the late Catherine Robb, probably the best-known botanist in the north of England, I elicited no response from my neighbours, mostly sheep farmers with a strictly utilitarian attitude towards plants, birds and other animals. However in the adjacent village of Hutton-le-Hole I struck up what eventually became a valued relationship with Raymond Hayes, an elderly, modest and endearing man who has been twice honoured (MBE and FSA) for his obsession with local archaeology. He is a person always worth listening to. In the mid-'thirties, he and his associates located the world-renowned Mesolithic site of Starr Carr near Scarborough.

The hunters of the Mesolithic, meaning the middle Stone Age, migrated to north-east Britain after the Great Melt. They came from southern Scandinavia, poling their way across the swamps of the North Sea. Their characteristic tools were microliths which are flints with carefully serrated edges about the size of a blade of a penknife. At Starr Carr in the fertile Vale of Pickering, an ancient lake, John Moore, a friend of Raymond Hayes, noticed discolouration in a field of barley. He dug down, located peat, an abundance of animal bones and a veritable arsenal of microliths.

John kept his archaeological grand slam close to his chest until, repeatedly nudged by his associates, he disclosed the location and the site became one of great importance. But all this is not immediately evident from the copious writings of the late Professor John Graham Douglas Clark, former Master of Peterhouse, an authority among much else on the Mesolithic. By tape-recorder talks with Raymond Hayes I sought to straighten the record in the *New Scientist*. And now back to Hampstead Heath.

At about that time (1976) the *Hampstead and Highgate Express*, probably the best regional paper in Britain, came out with a front-page story of the discovery of a Mesolithic camp site alongside a pond on the Heath, one of the sources of the Brent, a tributary of the Thames. Alec Jeakins, a perceptive local archaeologist, had seen some of the little tell-tale flints sticking out of the eroded sand and clay. Members of the local archaeological society promptly got to work and within two years they had literally brush-and-combed the railed-off site and unearthed many thousands of small artefacts, the component parts of tools and weapons for hunting and spearing animals and fish. And at the announcement of that initial discovery – quickly picked up by the national press – I felt somewhat humiliated.

In our survey described in the first chapter of this book we concentrated on the fauna and flora of the Heath, my concern being with our six-legged inhabitants. Savants in those towers of fragmented learning in the Victorian museum-land of South Kensington – not always the easiest people to deal with since their scientific ambitions are all too often frustrated by petty day-to-day work and by a succession of bureaucratic directors – assured me that there were next to no fossils to be found in the hundreds of feet of London clay below the skin of the Heath; there was no evidence anywhere, they said, of prehistoric human habitation. Some of them implied or had the downright impertinence to say that if there had been anything to which a scientific name could be attached their colleagues would have found it long ago.

Enter Philip Hartley, a student of zoology, textile merchant (retd.), gifted natural historian and lovable eccentric. He and I shared the same desk at an infant school in Headingley more than sixty years ago and have been close friends ever since, not least because he has the fossil hunter's equivalent of green fingers. With a geological map and uncommon sense he knows what's likely to be found at critical levels. As a youth of eighteen, that is about the time we shared the same girl, Philip located a prehistoric fish bed in a public park scarcely three miles from the noses of the geological department of Leeds University. Forays among the mudstones of Whitby produced relics of Jurassic crocodiles and Ichthyosaurs, those enormous marine lizards; he found the palatal plates of giant rays and armour-plated sturgeons in Hampshire, and much else in the Isle of Wight.

When peace broke out in 1945 the man, who today puts you in mind physiologically of a toby jug, sent me a characteristically irate letter, demanding to know why I now chose to inhabit the barrens south of Potters Bar rather than where he and our old companions, he implied, were running the country. Several weeks elapsed before the epistolary smoke cleared.

Philip then came down here, briefly. On our first foray into a wood near Erith on the Kentish shore of the Thames, a location which is now designated as a Site of Special Scientific

Interest, he struck the jackpot within an hour by the (relatively) simple expedient of following an exposure which he knew to be one of the boundaries of the Basement Beds of the London clay and kicking deeply into mole-hills. From one such mound he kicked out two shark's teeth, exquisitely incised and looking as polished as when they first sank to the floor of the Eocene Sea seventy million years ago. 'There's some good stuff here,' he said, and dug down like a ferret.

We brought away more fossils from that exposure than nowadays I care to think about, fragments of animals from an era when a much smaller Britain lay between the prehistoric continents of North Atlantis and Great Scandia. They included the lower jaw of Eohippus, the proto-horse, a creature scarcely larger than a fox terrier.

The following morning, before he drove back to Leeds, we walked round the Heath together. On a woodland path within a few yards of that site where, thirty years later Alec Jeakins and his colleagues located the Mesolithic encampment, Philip bent down and picked up a sliver of flint with a serrated edge. 'By God! That looks like a microlith,' he said. When I told him the museum people had assured me that most of the flints thereabouts had been imported from a central dump as hard-core for footpaths, he shrugged his shoulders and chucked it away. 'They could be bloody well wrong,' he said. 'They often are.'

From time to time it happens that the Jewish Passover and Christian Good Friday, that most solemn of days within our calendar, either follow one another or exactly coincide. When this took place a year or two ago I hastened down to the nearest pillar-box with an important letter, anxious to get it away that evening. An elderly man wearing either a skull cap or a small black beret approached the box with his own letter. We were almost the same distance apart. Perhaps with that sundowner as a stimulus I stopped, bowed slightly and said, 'On this commemoration of your deliverance from enslavement, Sir, please step forward first.'

He smiled, pushed his letter in the box and turning to me

said, 'As a matter of fact I'm not a Jew but I can see that you are and I'd like to say I always get on very well with them.'

On Good Friday the altar of All Saints is stripped. No Holy Eucharist can be celebrated. The Church fasts because the Bridegroom has been carried away for the Supreme Sacrifice. It will not be considered sacrilege, I hope, to relate how I have seen this enacted among a troupe of one of the gentlest animals in the wilderness. It happened some five miles to the south of an oasis without a name in North Kenya.

We were hungry. Our tracker reported the spoor and droppings of Klipspringer, a small animal with large beautiful eyes. When startled they bounce away like rubber balls in a series of erratic zigzag leaps. There were many of them. *'Mingi, mingi.'* But where were they? He shrugged his shoulders. The spoor were several days old. They crossed and re-crossed each other. I sent out three men to look for them.

One came running back within an hour to say there were at least ten animals among thorn bushes around a foul water-hole. But no cover for at least 200 yards, a range beyond my competence. We all but crawled up to find them huddled together which is unusual. And then to my surprise one little animal bounced out into the open, calling *zic-zic*. It spun round and round as if engaged in a dance. At that my headman stiffened and muttered *'Simba'*. There was a lion about some-where nearby. And the little animal wanted to entice it out into the open.

From some concealed hollow a lioness streaked out, but the *dik-dik* didn't bounce away. One chopping motion from that great paw and it lay there dead, almost decapitated. The sacrifice had been made. The rest of the troupe fled.

What is the message of April? Pack up. Your situation is untenable, your loss irretrievable, *y no hay remedio*. Lamas do not die but on reincarnation are said to change their bedding. 'Why didst thou promise such a beauteous day . . . ?' Within an hour of sunrise, the prospect of another long stint at this desk became intolerable and so, like that mysterious fellow in Sonnet XXXIV, I ventured forth without my cloak and strode up that most royal length of the river towards Hampton Court where every mile is dyed in history. Montaigne, I think it is, bids us always have our boots to hand and be ready to leave since the land of our better selves is surely reached by walking.

London has no asset more precious than the Thames. Whilst it may no longer be the city's commercial life-line, it remains its backbone, its identifier, its most distinguished landmark as well as its greatest open space. Dwell on those words. As a regular Left Bank promenader, by which I mean I walk the lower Thames at least half a dozen times a year, there's no temptation whatever to leave the tow path between Hammersmith and Kingston Bridge where, once across the water, you are among the deer of Hampton Court Park and the palace Wren rebuilt with the Louvre in mind can just be seen through the rook-loud, the mistletoe-topped elms.

Once on that stretch of river I move rapidly from ambulatory neutral which is a period for adjustment, for ensuring that, by means of zip fasteners, I am not at the start too chilly, that boots, or more usually on short walks my shoes, are comfortably tied, to cruising speed. Thereafter, if I am feeling at peace with the world and my immediate surroundings in particular, I find that sub-consciously I have slipped into ambulatory overdrive which is an almost super-charged form of motion difficult to describe, a gliding form of motion in which the body from the waist downwards seems scarcely to exist.

As usual I started from Hammersmith suspension bridge, by Bazalgette the engineer, with its cast-iron towers and whacking great eyebar chains of forged steel that look better from a distance. There are locals who will tell you – or at least say their fathers told them – that, during the troubles in 1917 a group of Fenian extremists attached bags of fused cordite to a concealed section of one of those chains at night and watched from a deserted warehouse, expecting the bridge to fly apart as if the taut guy-ropes of a marquee had been suddenly cut. But they were Irish with no gift for pyrotechnics. The fuses fizzled and blew out like penny-bangers.

The riverbank thereabouts is famed for its massive Black poplars more than a hundred feet in height with their trunks so

228

deeply fissured that a disc cut from the bole looks like a cog-wheel. At their feet is a small forest of the rare Giant hogweed – taller than a man, it looks monstrous especially when its umbels, bare in winter and almost as wide as a bicycle wheel, are ice frosted.

In midstream, Chiswick Eyot, an ancient island, strains at her moorings of matted mud. There one bitterly cold afternoon in November three of us were marooned until the tide rose and we were able to paddle my friend's amphibious motor-car back into deep water. Since conviviality at the club had much to do with that ignominious venture I shall not name him and will say only that the other passenger was that fine actor, the late Teddy Chapman, who in city togs was indignant at having to wade through mud.

We had taken off in fine style in that weird-looking mechanical hybrid from the place where they lodge the Boat Race eights above Putney Bridge. There were surprised looks and a shriek from an elderly lady as we plunged into the water, and then it was *chug-chug-chug* to Hammersmith and beyond, at peril only from huge baulks of floating timber almost wholly submerged. Sheer bravado prompted us to nose into the Eyot where we stuck for an hour sustained only by about seven inches of scotch. My most vivid recollection is that the bare branches of the willows on that island were festooned with old condoms 'like Christmas day in the work-house', observed Ted drily.

I repeat: London has no asset quite so precious as the Thames, not least because of the wide variety of its wildlife, especially birds and plants. Behind the towpath on the left bank lie the extensive Barn Elms reservoirs, the haunt of innumerable wildfowl during the day and a safe dormitory for gulls at night. Wisps of teal rocketed backwards and forwards across the river as I walked, although what they were doing there during the late spring I cannot say since both resident and visiting birds breed in heather and gorse on dry ground, often at a considerable distance from any water except a brooklet.

An elderly well-dressed military-looking fellow walked up, watching the teal with evidence satisfaction. 'Couldn't hit 'em

231

now,' he said. 'Got a touch of the screws in me right shoulder. No matter,' he said, chuckling, 'I've had me share. I've had me share,' and I had the impression he wasn't merely referring to the wildfowl.

Striding out now, fast, on the peak of overdrive, the trees, the plants, the birds, the craft on the river, especially the fragile skiffs like water-boatmen, the sweating oarsmen on the sinuous eights being bawled at by coaches on bicycles, all became intermingled, overlaid by thought-streams, except where one vibrant spectacle or burst of bird song pushed aside the memory-store and brought me up short with a twinge of conscience – but never for long.

Those late-blossoming Goat willows, for example, with bee-laden catkins in colour somewhere between powdered sulphur and newly-hatched goslings. Not rough-and-tumble bumble bees. These were slavish hive-born honey-makers and together they hummed like an old-fashioned tin top.

Frank the Apothecary who, as might be expected, is a thoughtful apiarist tells the story of how a friend presented him with a pot of honey which for a time he could make nothing of. Some honey has a fairly distinctive colour – it tends to be slightly greenish from, say, ivy flowers. All that he could say about this sample was that it was curiously sweet. But from what? It turned out to be Pepsi-Cola. He tracked the hives down to a site close to the Tower where we lamented the loss of the William Curtis Nature Reserve. The bees had been browsing on the dregs of scores of almost-empty bottles on a rubbish dump.

With the songs of chiff-chaffs as cheer leaders I hastened on. This zest for brisking springs as much from the sheer physical pleasure of moving fast as any quarrel with Stevenson's distinction between travelling hopefully and arriving, but it does mean that I am infinitely more of a bird-listener than a bird-watcher, which involves hanging about peering through field-glasses.

If birds sang or merely called, which is a different thing, with monotonous regularity – and thank God they don't – the sound could be reduced to sonograms which are graphs that represent sound in different dimensions such as frequency or pitch, time or duration, amplitude or loudness. But they are devilishly difficult to interpret unless you are a brain specialist or cardio-vascular surgeon acquainted with the outpourings of electronic hardware. Think what a machine would make of a starling's standard repertoire which includes clicks, cork-pops, murmurings and gurgles with varieties of the wolf whistle, *phwee-phwee-oo*.

Descriptions of birds' songs and calls in books are rendered in three different ways. First there is phonetic gibberish in which the redwing, according to the best field guide on the market (Peterson's), appears to produce 'a thin *see-ip* or harsh *chittuc* or more typically *trui-trui-trui-troo-tree*'. To an Englishman the chiff-chaff says *chiff, chiff, chaff, chiff* but, curiously enough, to a German it's *zilp, zilp, zalp, zilp* and to the Danes it's something else.

Second, there may be an actual description of the song such as 'a rather high musical warble interspersed with buzzing phrases of varying lengths and ending in an upward inflection'. This gets you nowhere. It's like trying to look up a word in a dictionary when you can't spell it. Lastly some go in for a sort of Mad Hatter's tea-party in which the Coal tit says 'teacher teacher'; the yellowhammer fancies 'a little bit of bread and no *chee-eese*'. For some reason the Wood pigeon wants to 'take two cows, taffy' and the Tawny owl very properly asks 'who? who?' The fact remains that innumerable finches, buntings, pippits and wagtails say '*Twit!*'

At Barnes Bridge, a useful place to cross over to Chiswick House, the most elegant Palladian villa in London, the river completes yet another loop almost exactly delineated by the Greek letter Omega. It is impossible to describe this capricious meandering except in terms of the geology of the Ice Age and I don't intend to try, an evasive way of saying I really can't get the hang of it beyond the fact that the proto-Thames changed its course at least four times before it settled down in a swamp which has been progressively drained and banked since Roman times.

Most of the river frontage of Barnes is not worth looking at but for a hundred yards on both sides of the bridge there is some elegant eighteenth-century property within smelling distance of a large and ugly brewery and the biggest sewage works on the left bank. But don't ignore it. To avoid getting wet by whatever it is that is squirted down on to their enormous feeding ring, Pied wagtails go for joy-rides on the long arms of the revolving sprinklers. And within a mile you are at Kew Bridge with the finest botanic gardens in the world to wander about in, and beyond them if you cling to the river as far as Hampton Court there are three hours of brisk walking in almost open country which can be seen panoramically from the top of Richmond Hill.

Because Kew is a governmental institution which until thirty years ago used to be under the wing of the Ministry of Agriculture, it follows that the official guidebook relates rather primly how the gardens evolved from the small private estate of Princess Augusta, mother of George III until it was acquired by the nation in 1841 and became a scientific institution and public show-place of nearly 300 acres. The facts are more lurid. The Princess loved plants. It is not perhaps surprising that before he went completely off his chump, her son George chose his bride from lists of German princesses as if he were a gardening enthusiast going through flower catalogues on winter evenings. He actually discovered three sub-species as yet unthought of in the Gothic Almanac. Quick! Get someone to look at them. Are they blight-resistant, hardy, sweetly scented?

Marketed by the very small firm of Mecklenberg-Strelitz in the Duchy of that ilk, Princess Charlotte was the last flower on the list but she harboured two psycho-physiological drawbacks: unqueenly manners and a flat face. Poor Charlotte! If, as a famous encyclopaedia puts it, she eventually passed away at Kew after 'a peaceful and happy life', she worked damned hard for her pension. Her unfaithful husband forced his attentions on her, giving her over a dozen children in fifteen years. He died blind and wildly insane. Her favourite son Prinny, Nash's royal patron, was not only a notorious drunkard and rake but behaved abominably towards her. She got unfairly involved in a political tangle, not of her own making and in which she had no desire to meddle; she was not even allowed to go back to her beloved Duchy.

Thrown back on her own resources Charlotte employed the famous architect Sir William Chambers to design the beautifully proportioned Orangery, the Pagoda and three classical temples which, clad in ivy and clematis, still stand there today amidst the luxuriant gardens, lakes and greenhouses. Under the direction of a succession of outstanding botanists such as Sir Joseph Banks and the Hookers, Kew became the world's botanical Mecca with every plant known to man listed and described in that serial publication, now computerized, *Index Kewensis*.

A former director, Sir George Taylor, whose name frequently appears in my early notebooks, gave me a list of heathers to plant in our moorland garden and said that if he hadn't already got more than enough to do, he'd have joined our expedition in 1957 to the Ruwenzori, the Mountains of the Moon. Together with the late Patrick Synge he'd been there several years earlier, collecting plants beyond the imagination of a writer of science fiction.

I met the new Director for the first time on this walk. Professor Arthur Bell is by my standards a young chap with a ready smile and an uncommon ability to put across the complexities, the relationships and the importance of the teeming world of plants in a straightforward uncomplicated way – which is just what the Trustees want since the Gardens are there for scientific purposes, for general education and for the sheer pleasure of visitors who pour in all the year round. One of us thinks that Arthur Bell and I got on fine.

He is a much-travelled Geordie with a passion for walking and irrepressible curiosity, who got into the botanical business not so much through the back door as through the necessity to find out what plants were made up of, fundamentally, that is inside their tissues from their seeds to their roots. He is a biochemist who took up an important job at Trinity College, Dublin at a time when the medics there were using Jack beans, sub-tropical American plants as a source of urease, an enzyme or go-between chemical that breaks down urea into ammonia. Purely academic research?

235

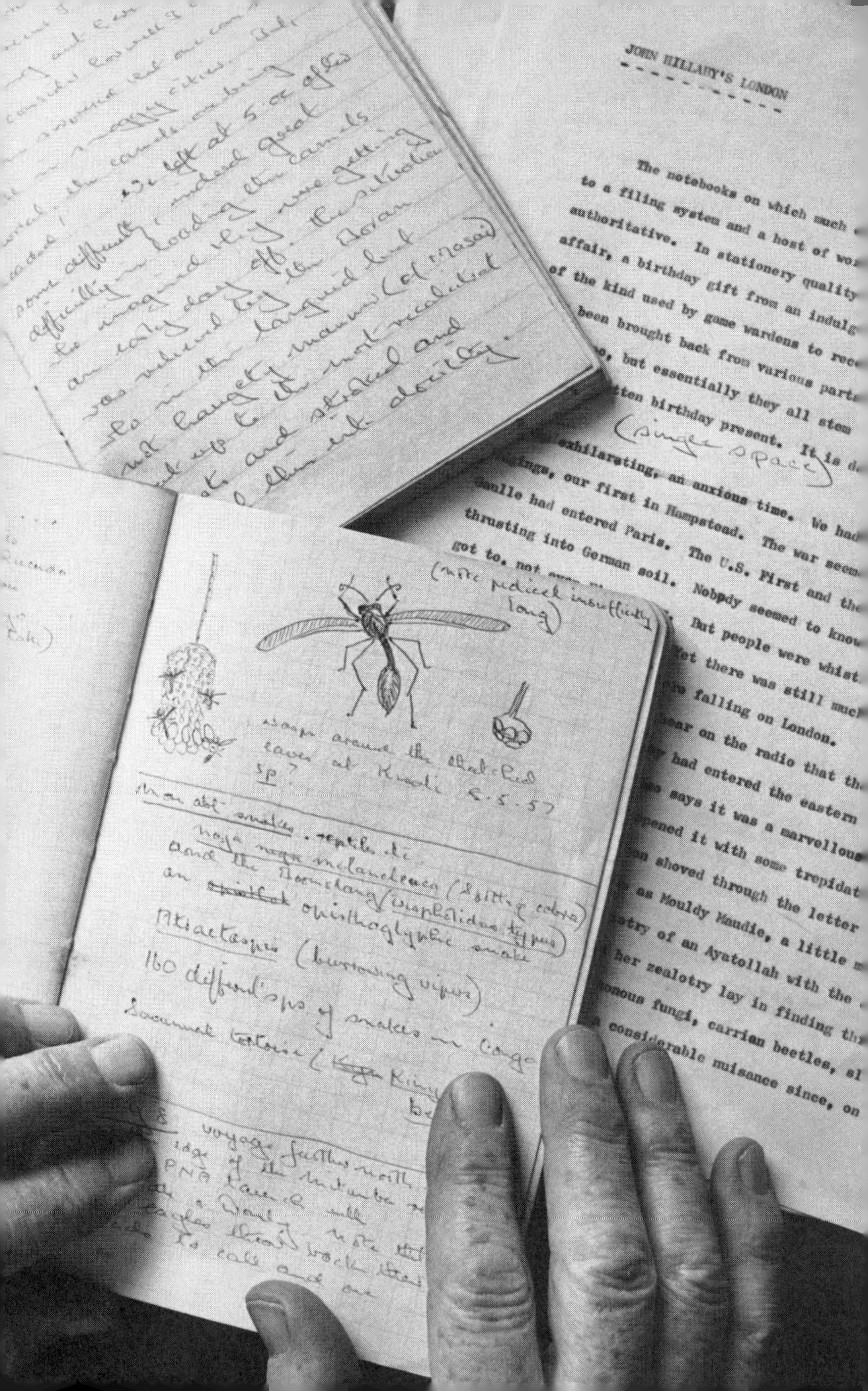

The notebooks on which much ...
to a filing system and a host of wor...
authoritative. In stationery quality ...
affair, a birthday gift from an indul...
of the kind used by game wardens to rec...
been brought back from various parts ...
..., but essentially they all stem ...
...tten birthday present. It is de... *(single space)*
... exhilarating, an anxious time. We had ...
...ings, our first in Hampstead. The war seem...
Gaulle had entered Paris. The U.S. First and the ...
thrusting into German soil. Nobody seemed to know ...
got to, not ... ...
... But people were whist...
...et there was still much ...
...re falling on London. ...
...ear on the radio that the ...
...y had entered the eastern ...
...ho says it was a marvellous ...
...pened it with some trepidat...
...en shoved through the letter ...
... as Mouldy Maudie, a little ...
...try of an Ayatollah with the ...
...her zealotry lay in finding th...
...onous fungi, carrion beetles, sl...
...considerable nuisance since, on ...

(handwritten notes, partly legible)

...worm around the thick-red leaves at Kivoli 2.5.57
(note pedicel insufficiently long)

Man ate snakes. reptiles etc
naja nigra melanoleuca (spitting cobra)
And the Boomslang (Dispholidus typus)
an opisthoglyphic snake
Atractaspis (burrowing vipers)
160 different sps of snakes in Congo
Savannah tortoise (King...
...voyage further north
...idge of the Mitumba...
PNG hauled off...
...a dove note that...
...Eagles threats work their...
...to call and ...

Not a bit of it! Urease enables diagnosticians to estimate the amount of urea in urine and in that way to learn a great deal about the efficiency of the kidneys, on which swing a whole range of diseases. Arthur Bell went through the European relatives of Jack beans in search of alternatives. He found what he wanted and this survey led him into chemo-taxonomy which is now, years later, a wholly different way of determining botanical affinities, the relationships between many hundreds of plants. It also led him to study the chemical defences used by plants to resist attack by predators, mostly insects. Much of today's work is due to the young man from Gosforth.

There are as many sides to Kew as there are to the royal family. There are the Gardens best known to visitors for their riots of rhododendra, azaleas, blossom-laden trees and noble groves of conifers. There are the tropical houses, sprayed and temperature-controlled by computers, in which you can roam in the vegetation of palm-shaded beaches, Arizonian deserts and simulations of equatorial jungles for the current price of half a pint of indifferent beer. There is the Herbarium, vulgarly known as the Haystack, where about six million plants from right across the world are pressed, documented and filed for reference and enquiry. The plants come in at the rate of about a thousand specimens a week. There are the laboratories. There is a total staff of more than 400 of which about a quarter are botanical scientists.

There is Kew in the country at Wakehurst Place set high and proud on the Sussex Weald where the horticulturists put their ideas into practice on good soil and physiologists refrigerate a great range of seeds, keeping them alive against what might happen in the future. I have visited scores of scientific institutions in my time but the Kew complex is by far the most beautiful of them all.

Back on the towpath, flanked by a veritable Golgotha of beetle-ridden elms, I turned my field-glasses on to Syon House on the opposite bank. Although better by far inside than out, Syon is superb. Once a monastery and still the home of the Percys, Dukes of Northumberland, a mansion wholly transformed from 1760 onwards by Robert Adam, 'Bob the Roman', it helped to swell the Brothers' coffers for more than twenty years. Building and rebuilding had become fashionable among the Quality who were forever changing their minds. By that time, 1780, although they had come within an ace of going bust over the Adelphi, the Brothers had established a small army of perhaps over 1,000 artificers.

As I have wandered, through Syon's Grand Hall in black and white marble, stucco and statues, I have often pondered on Sir John Summerson's suggestion that this might be the place where the Adam style was actually initiated. It blended together a great variety of motifs from many sources, Roman, Greek, Etruscan and Palladian among them. What they did which none has done better was to unify the whole, right down to the carpets and what are now famous paintings, ordered in those days by the half-dozen. A reflection, possibly, on contemporary taste is that the majority of car-borne visitors have come to look mostly at the exhibition nearby of living butterflies. 'Better than the telly,' one of them said.

On we tread through that riparian avenue of trees, the cascading willows and their curious family relatives (*Salicaceae*), the poplars especially the Grey species (*P. canescens*) with its boughs encircled by necklaces of black lenticels. The seeds of both willows and poplars germinate only on wet mud, a fact which may account for Virgil's belief that the trees arose by spontaneous generation. Kew told me that twenty million elms may have died in the last twenty years. The yew, the oak, and the elm have probably had as much effect on the military and social history and the landscape of England and Wales as all other kinds of trees put together. The death of the elm symbolizes the spirit of an age which learnt too late to value things which it could no longer have.

There is a curious obelisk in the Old Deer Park, now used by Mid-Surrey Golf Club, and I couldn't make out what it was until one of the many indolent fishermen told me it lay due north of the Kew Observatory. But of what use was an observatory, with satellites constantly encircling the earth? He said bugger all but what with these computers and things everything was becoming too mechanical these days.

I looked down at his bag of carbon fibre rods with antenna-like fluorescent bite-detectors all packed away on a trolley of the kind trundled around by golfers, and couldn't think of anything to say. They have already got around to polarized spectacles and echo-sounders to locate shoals of fish for those who squat all day in moored punts.

Seen from the barge-bordered boat-houses close to the bridge, royal Richmond is one of the finest sights on the river especially when, during a light breeze, a long line of almost evergreen willows trailing in the water on the far bank wafts gently backwards and forwards in unison, like a *corps de ballet.* Avoid the main street which is cramped, noisy and ultra-suburban but make for The Green by way of high-walled Old Palace Lane.

Since the Palace built by Henry VII is today an almost incomprehensible mosaic of 400 years of building, pulling down and more rebuilding, and is known superficially in its original state only from Wyngaerde's drawings of 1502, it is enough to sample one or two of the courtyards, peer up at the great gateway, the tiers of mullioned windows and remember that it was here in March 1603 that Elizabeth died on a great pile of cushions, 'fading slowly like a spent fire, Gloriana till she lay grey'.

She had been a long time a-going. In her seventieth year she fought death as she had fought life, implacably. She would allow no doctors to come near her; she took almost no food and drink; she sat propped up in a chair, knowing that if she left it she might never sit there again. The great courtiers around her bade her do what the banished physicians recommended, and rest. At last Robert Cecil said boldly: 'Your Majesty, to content the people you must go to bed.'

Elizabeth turned her head, slowly. Movement racked her. She spoke in a whisper but it was the whisper of absolute authority. 'Little man, little man,' she answered, 'is *must* a word to be addressed to princes?' But as lutenists played softly and aged Whitgift, Archbishop of Canterbury, knelt and prayed and prayed until he almost fell over, she took at last to her cushions. What the whole court, what the whole of

Europe wanted to know was who would be her successor. James of Scotland?

It is possible, likely even, that she had other matters on her mind. There is that tale of how, during one of her happy periods with Essex, she had given him a ring with the promise that whenever he sent it back to her, he could be assured of her forgiveness. During those agonized last days in the Tower, Essex entrusted it to a boy with orders to take it to Lady Scrope and beg her present it to the Queen, at once. By mistake the boy gave the ring to Lady Scrope's sister, Lady Nottingham, wife of the Earl's enemy who kept it and said nothing until, on her death-bed, she confessed. Gloriana is reported to have said: 'God may forgive you, Madam, but I *never* can.'

The walker's way out of Richmond, south and then west around yet another one of those lazy loops, takes you past the landing-stage where the big pleasure boats chug up and down between Hampton Court and Westminster, never so popular as before and after closing time since, once aboard, the ever-thirsty are not subject to the licensing laws. A glance over your left shoulder upwards, and strangely decayed or curiously refurbished mansions appear on the skyline above the river park, some of them turned into expensive apartments or hotels. No other London borough has a greater wealth of palaces than Sheen (Old English for 'shelter') by which Richmond (*Richemounte*) was known until the early part of the sixteenth century. Medieval kings and the Tudors took to the place and the aristocracy, their master craftsmen, the literati and artists followed where today you may find only rich businessmen.

Close by Petersham under Richmond Hill are wet meadows where half a dozen Dutch cows can be seen lying on their udders in a field of cardamines or Lady's smocks, deep lilac in colour, curious flowers which are said to portend violent storms. From the Black Forest where they call those blushing blossoms *Donnerblumen* to Provence where they go under the name of *fleurs de tonerre*, the legend is the same. Even to touch

the flowers is dangerous. It's an invitation to be struck by lightning.

The cows looked contented enough but, come to think of it, their expressions never change. For better or for worse they look wholly resigned. This was noticed by William McGonagall, that much-neglected poet born in Edinburgh in 1830 of 'poor but honest Irish parents'. He has the edge, occasionally, on Burns and, like that poet, went oft a-chambering but, unlike Rabbie's girlfriends, his young women never seem to have had much fun on the road to ruin. They are all downright miserable. In his 'Invocation to a Cow', McGonagall wrote:

The hen is a noble animal
But the cow is much forlorner,
Standing in the rain
With a leg at each corner.

What I'm wondering is what does a cud-chewing cow *think* about? About a handsome farm lad's hands around her lacto-genic apparatus? No! No! *Click-clack-click.* Nowadays it's mechanical. Of a hefty bellowing bull? No! No! The same old story. Artificial insemination. *Bos ex machina.*

Like a loudly crowing hen, a cow sometimes acts in a distinctly mannish manner. This may be what physiologists describe as an expression of endocrinal imbalance or plain darned sexual frustration. I prefer the explanation of a Sussex farmer I knew who, when an embarrassed visitor asked why one of his cows tried repeatedly to mount the others, said, 'Well some women like to think they are men and as I see it cows ain't no different.'

Teddington Lock and weir, where boats of all shapes and sizes queue up to be raised I don't know how many feet, appeared to be infested with frustrated fishermen who sat in comfortable chairs beside keep nets big enough to have con-tained an immature porpoise although, as far as I could see, they all appeared to be empty. I wondered if they'd heard that sad story about how 200 St John's Ambulance men contested their annual championship on a stretch of the nearby Grand

Union canal and lined its banks for five solid hours without catching a single minnow between them. They might have sat there until midnight thrashing the water to desperate foam to avoid a double-century dead-heat had not a kindly local resident turned up and told them that the canal had been drained completely the previous week and all the resident fish removed to other waters.

I looked, fascinated, at their tins of multi-coloured maggots which cost them, they told me, about a quid a pint from that famous supplier, Mick the Maggot at Kingston. It seems that before the Customs officers rumbled what he was up to, Mick used regularly to ship a small truck-load of frozen maggots to Stockholm under the pretext that they were some form of pet food.

Unfortunately, unknown to him, the shipment was delayed at Hull; his refrigerating apparatus broke down. The maggots became very much alive and when a ship's officer, noticing the characteristic smell which is somewhat like ammonia, opened the rear door of his truck, about half a hundredweight of the multi-coloured larvae of the bluebottle cascaded down into his clean-swept hold.

I debated whether to cross the river by the footbridge and visit one of my old haunts, the National Physical Laboratory at Teddington, but Hampton Court still lay some six miles ahead and, the overdrive almost spent, I spooled back some dramatic incidents in that laboratory in the privacy of the skull cinema instead.

It began, as I remember, with the capture by spearheads of our forces near the Dutch frontier of a few specimens of those huge German V2 rockets which homed down on London in the summer of 1944. Two of them were shipped back to Britain for examination by ballisticians and on the grapevine I heard that one had been taken to pieces at the NPL. Could I see it? Not on your life, said Security. But later, carrying the passport of the *New York Times*, I struck up a friendly association with the Director who allowed the rocket (see page 24) and other fascinating pieces of technical hardware to be photographed.

For the benefit of *Picture Post,* the laboratory staff simulated flashes of lightning between the discharge points of Wellsian-looking storage chambers; they manufactured super-cooled liquids which, apparently defying laws of gravity, crept up and over the sides of beakers, and froze tomatoes to the near-absolute point of frigidity so that, when struck with a hammer, they shattered to a glass-like powder. In short I had a rare old time at the expense of the popular press.

But there was a serious side to these diversions. My note-booked list of scientific mandarins at the Royal Society contained the names of several who were not averse to seeing their exploits soberly reported in the columns of New York's largest and best-known newspaper. Unfortunately, what might have been the most dramatic experiment I have ever witnessed ended not in a bang but a splutter and a power-cut. The experiment was no less than slamming the brakes on the seemingly unstoppable vibrations of sub-molecular particles.

The man who was to become one of the leading physicists at Harwell telephoned to ask whether I could dine with him in college before we spent the night at the Clarendon Laboratory at Oxford. He would explain when I arrived. He did explain, in detail, but since I was bidden to write down nothing whatever until we could talk over what might be published, I now see those vaporized electric cables as through reinforced glass, darkly. At this point I shall take a deep breath and summon up some basic facts of physics, dimly remembered.

Atomic particles are constantly in motion. The kinetic energy of their motion is supplied by heat, even that scarcely imaginable heat near absolute zero which is *minus* 273.16° centigrade, a temperature which has never been achieved. The Clarendon physicists believed that if truly enormous power could be applied through truly enormous electro-magnets to a liquid gas at that point when, near absolute zero, it was down to its last feeble ticks, the motion of the particles, they hoped, could be stopped. Or did they really hope that? One of them didn't. Me. I thought I might have the dubious privilege of being present at what could have triggered off the end of the world.

They, those physicists, were a bit secretive about their

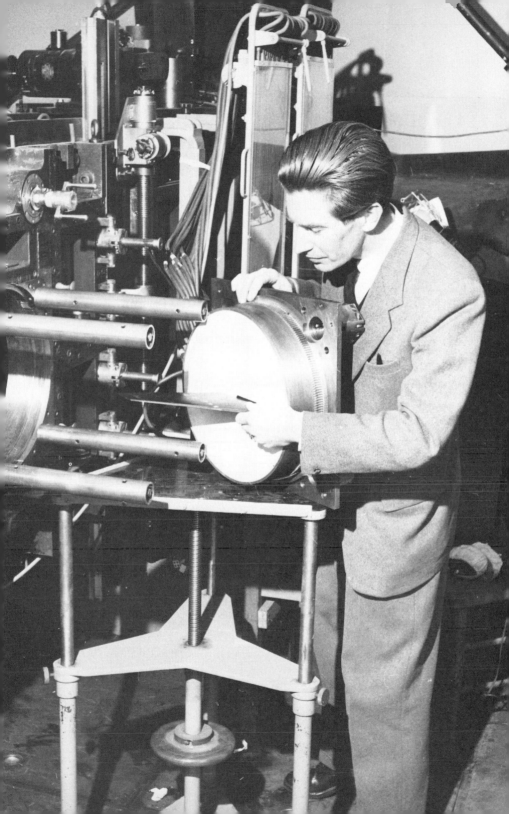

power supply. It came, I discovered, from drawing on every possible power source when supplies were at their highest, that is in the early hours of the morning, and passing it through some obsolete tramway generators bought from Manchester City Corporation, under God knows what pretext, by Lord Cherwell, Churchill's imaginative scientific adviser. The temperature, or, more exactly, the slowing-down movement of the super-cooled gas was monitored by Geiger counters which register the ticking of atomic particles.

As we started the countdown on the first run the cables sparked and spluttered until they turned the power off at a point nowhere near the critical one. When we got down pretty low on the second run, the heavily bandaged cables seemed to burst into flame and had to be re-spliced, which took about an hour. I literally held my breath when we seemed all set to achieve the atomic nadir on the last run, but everything blew including the mains outside. Parts of Oxfordshire were plunged into temporary darkness. We all went home and that's why, I like to imagine, we are all here today.

If it weren't that, despite trespass, the evening closed on a note of utter serenity in Hampton Court Park I should have had more to say about the mind-bewildering noise in that pub on the eastern shore of Kingston. A pleasant enough place, half filled with youngsters who clustered round the light-flashing gaming machines and kept an enormous disc-player at work. The repertoire ranged from the screaming stuff of the love-lorn to the *tiffty-tiffty-tiffty-tiffty* noise made by percussion, cymbals and guitars of the kind used to sustain periods of tension during TV drama, and was thrown at us so loudly that I couldn't make out what the barman said about the time the Park gates were locked. No matter. A quarter of an hour's rest gave me energy enough to shin over a wall partly breached by a fallen tree.

Knowing the place well, I took a roundabout path to avoid the Park Lodge near Hampton Wick pond and within minutes had entered another zone of noise that washed aside cares, the fatigue of near fifteen miles done and the possibility tinged with mild apprehension of encountering Authority in gum-boots.

Some ducks half seen were chuckling about something or other; blackbirds shrieked but, together with some conversational rooks in a faraway wood, they merged together as the continuo behind the nearby soloists. An insistent Mistle thrush called, a Tawny owl stuttered, slightly, between his sonorous *hoo-hoo* which echoed or was challenged in the gathering dark. Hedge sparrows were squeakily restive and pheasants put me in mind of old-fashioned klaxon horns.

Here, then, were various levels of parkland noise. What does it *mean*? Much, I know, has been written about the language of birds, but I've never been convinced it's because they're up to their necks in the real estate business. As Lewis Thomas once put it: 'Behind the glossaries of warning calls, alarms, mating messages, pronouncement of territory, calls for recruitment and demands for dispersal, there is redundant, elegant sound that is unaccountable as part of the working day,' and if to that mighty orchestration you add the contribution of invertebrates, remembering that even leeches and earthworms make faint tapping noises, I think we might conclude that light social conversation, designed to keep the party going, prevails. Nature abhors a long silence. As I whispered that phrase into my pocket recorder I reflected, ruefully, that those youngsters in the pub might have said much the same thing.

I moved fast, listening and peering through the gloom, encircling the brightly lit Stud House where I thought the estate agent lived. Pray God he had no dogs on the loose. Ahead, so far ahead I had to stop and cock my ears, I could just make out gentle squeaks and blabbering noises above the gradually diminishing clamour of birds. The deer were talking to each other. This posed a considerable problem. Deer have uncommon powers of hearing. By keeping fairly close to the walls of the Barge Walk I thought I might outflank the main herd which is normally to be found around the Long Water. No such luck.

A high-pitched whistle and a sustained crashing noise as I don't know how many animals swept towards the Palace

Gardens. At this I clung to the wall looking for some place to get out of where I had no right to be. All bird song had ceased except the alarm calls of robins and wrens. A long silence is Nature alerted.

This applies to us in a not dissimilar way. Auditory zero, like that abortive effort to attain absolute zero at the Clarendon is an impossibility. Lewis Thomas says given any new technology for transmitting information we seem bound to use it for greater quantities of small talk. Club secretaries deplore the progressive decline in intelligent conversation. In pubs in pre-eminently working-class districts it's reduced to the reiteration of platitudes where the word 'fuck' in a non-sexual sense is often used as an adjective, adverb and noun. The bonding mechanism is the juke-box with its amorous screamers or rhythmic *tiffty-tiffters*, probably of interest to psychologists and cardiac specialists. 'It makes you feel you're not alone,' said a hopeful teenage girl with her teenage girl-friend.

Almost any kind of communication that an animal can employ from sonar (bats and whales) to chest-beating (gorillas), head-banging (woodpeckers), duetting (toads and frogs) and buzzing and clicking (insects and crustacea) is in constant use. It has been so, unchanged, for millions of years. We don't know what the biggest animal in the world, the Blue whale, is saying except that even to us its rich vocabulary sounds sadly beautiful. Perhaps it's best not to talk of the fearful decline and possible extinction of some of the whales lest we join the march to oblivion.

How and where I got over the wall when the lights of the Palace appeared over that avenue of trim-cut yew trees is a matter for my own conscience – and I was only just in time since a frail soul with a little dog on a lead slowly walked towards my unorthodox point of exit. Many of the Hampton Court apartments are used 'by persons of good family in reduced circumstances'. Once on the towpath I blithely walked round to the main gates.

Reflecting light from the flaming west, the brick, described by Edith Sitwell as 'of the colour of strawberries or of the bullfinch's rosy feathers', had sunk to episcopal purple but viewed in silhouette the palace looked more royal than any other I have seen. In light or dark it breathes regality. Built for Cardinal Wolsey, son of an Ipswich butcher who had the audacity to write a book entitled *Ego et meus Rex* and entertain 400 guests at a single sitting. When he shrewdly foresaw his own downfall, the consequent attack on the Church and the triumph of the secular party, the Cardinal, of vast ability, vast greed and arrogance, hastily handed it over to Henry VIII.

In that palace, Cranmer told his royal master that young Catherine Howard had about her the attributes of a common whore. It may or may not have been true. What is certain is that much went on in Henry's bed, eleven feet square and set about in a canopy of woven gold and silver.

Of Wren's inspired rebuilding and the palace's occupation by asthmatic William and Mary to escape the smog of Westminster I have no space to tell. For me the spirit of the place is Gloriana, with those hauntingly beautiful eyes of her mother Anne Boleyn in the face of a Plantagenet. That high thin nose, those arched nostrils which look as if they were breathing fire from that Minotaur of a father. She reigned imperiously since in her heart she had always one great fear, the fear of fear.

There is a tale told about how, out hunting one day behind Hampton Court – or it could have been Nonsuch – her hounds bayed a huge stag that had been known by repute for years. And there it stood, panting, wild-eyed with but minutes to live before a bolt crashed into its heart. As she slowly raised her jewelled finger for the *coup de grâce*, Gloriana smiled, but a courtier whispered something in her ear. It may have been a saint's day or the anniversary perhaps of her own coronation, and the smile faded. On such an occasion the stag ought to be given his freedom. It lay in her charitable fee. It would be unseemly to act otherwise. So the stag bounded away, but not immediately and not wholly unhurt since, before it fled, she ordered both ears to be cut off, low.

More evidence of her lightly veiled sexuality comes out plain in one emotion-laden sentence of which her best-known playwright might have been proud. Some ambassador, possibly that Edward Dimmoke, Knight, her Champion at Large,

had grown tired of her dissimulation on the subject of marriage and wrote to her saying so, delicately. Gloriana sat upright for five minutes, thinking. Then calling for quills, sand and ink, she vented her passion on parchment, ending: 'Had I been crested and not cloven you would not have *dared* write me thus.'

Wolsey's place

When the living is easy

For years now, certainly within my generation, London cabbies of the older sort have been telling us that between the closure of the January sales in February and the opening of the Chelsea Flower Show, they are forced to make the best they can of the 'Kipper Season' – 'because it stinks'. But this is no longer true. The tourist season has been vastly extended. It so happens that I have learned a great deal about how cabbies go about their business from my good friend and neighbour Norman who for the last thirty years has been running a succession of diesel-powered Austin FX4s as all his fellow cabbies do. What makes Norman a pleasure to talk to is not only that he's unfailingly cheerful; like many good Jewish boys born in the East End he's an outstanding raconteur. Norman loves his job. Wouldn't swap it for a fortune. London for him is an endless pageant that changes from day to day.

'There's this classy bird I picked up at Kings Cross a couple of days back. Wanted to go to Buckingham Palace she did. When we gets there she tells me to park and hold on since she wants to see the Changing of the Guard. Can't do it, love, I says. I'll get nicked. But I pulls in for a moment to stash away some big notes in my secret hidey-hole. And then, blow me down, up clip-clops a mounted police woman on an 'oss that was sweating and blowing out froth like it had just won at Kempton Park.

'"Cabbie," she says. "You know damn well its illegal to park here." I'm not parking, says I. I'll be off in a tick and look what your sweating 'oss has done to me nice clean bonnet. She didn't smile. She looks me straight between the eyes and says, "Listen, ducky, if you'd been between *my* legs for three hours *you'd* sweat."'

From many talks with Norman I've put together a lexicon of cab-drivers' in-talk some of which, I suspect, came in with the Polish and Russian refugees after the pogroms. They refer, for example, to their taxis as 'droshkies' and the meter or clock as a 'zaiger' which is, I believe, a ghetto expression for a tally-stick. A 'butter-boy' is a newcomer to the trade; a 'single pin' means a solo passenger; 'a bowler', a City gent; a 'legal' an exact fare, no tip. 'Kipper Season'? No, it's not that it stinks, it's when you eke out a living on what used to be the cheapest food known to a poor East-Ender, a twopenny kipper. Cabbies who hang round stations are 'working the rails' whilst those who graft night and day, maybe to help pay for a new cab, are 'Cole Porters'.

To see London through the benevolent but ever-watchful eyes of a fare-seeker I have asked Norman to describe a dawn trip from, say, here to Paddington to meet the yawning passengers from the all-night Cornish Express. On the way he notes the rough sleepers, the furtive tramps that shuffle off the Heath to join their tattered fellow tipplers in the cellars of ruined buildings; the specialized bread vans that reek of garlic; the smell of coffee from the Greek places in Mornington Crescent and Somers Town; the Philippinos and Malaysians making for the kitchens of big hotels where no embarrassing questions about permits are asked.

There are the 'Mick-nobblers', the smart operators who cruise round Camden Town tube station at half-past six in the morning, slowly, whereupon, almost miraculously, hundreds of labourers, skilled and unskilled, by far the majority of them Irish, bundle into the converted vans and jalopies to be driven off to building sites within a sixty-mile radius of London, for work paid in cash every night and far from

253

uncharitable neighbours with thoughts about unemployment benefit.

Who are the best tippers? In his opinion probably Yankees who work out what fifteen per cent amounts to – the bill addition to a meal in Manhattan or a cab almost anywhere in New York. Who are the worst? Australians. They expect to be gypped and sit on the back seat poring over an open street map. What about the Japs? They don't take cabs unless they're businessmen. The teeming tourists go around in package-hired coaches, photographing each other at intervals. How about the Arabs? Unpredictable, generous unless they suspect you are Jewish.

He told of several cases of veiled Muslim women sitting back in his cab and solemnly clipping the label off goods bought in Marks and Spencers and putting them in C & A carrier bags before being driven back 'to those three-star pubs in Park Lane'. What were his no-go areas? His answer wouldn't get him a seat on the Race Relations Board. But after spending an hour, sipping tea and talking in that big cab-drivers' shelter, I can confirm that, to a man, they agreed with him. They fear particularly the pathetic-looking young white girl who flags them down at night. She opens the door and promptly disappears as three blacks step in. 'Then you know you've had it.' At best they won't pay the fare: they make a run for it. At worst . . . After a nasty dust-up Norman vowed that never again would he operate after dark and never in certain areas at any time. But it's a hard living if you don't enjoy it.

There used to be over 14,000 cabs in Greater London. They are commodious to the point of being downright archaic in design, mere boxes on wheels with the cabbie insulated from all sociability unless he speaks over his shoulder, keeping one eye on the road. Stomach ulcers are an occupational hazard. See how often they stop to buy a carton of milk. Old cabs make splendid family cars into which can be bundled the wife, three kids, a folded-up pram, chairs and a small table, a caged parrot and granny too, leaving ample luggage space beside the driver. Nubar Gulbenkian, the multi-millionaire, bought one and converted it into a luxury car. When asked why by a radio interviewer, he said in a sentence ripe for the *Oxford Dictionary*

255

of Quotations: 'The thing will turn on a sixpence,' pausing before adding, 'whatever *that* is.'

But what are the (visible) majority of commuters up to during that awful hour between eight and nine o'clock in the morning? To judge from our one-minute exposure to that north-west artery, the Finchley Road as we cross it on our way back from the Heath, they are blocking that wide road in their nose-to-tail wheelchairs with here and there a bus which can carry up to ninety passengers. Cars rarely hold more than one. The stench is terrific and the air blue, a sort of inverse aura to judge from the expression of the drivers. What percentage of daily commuters do they represent?

I put the question by phone to an efficient information officer at the London Regional Transport's head office within duck-quacking distance of St James's Park.

He'd obviously been asked it hundreds of times. 'Nineteen per cent,' he said and followed it up with a burst of statistics, delivered at such speed that I'd difficulty in jotting down the essentials. Over a million people travel into central London each working weekday morning between seven o'clock and ten; four out of five of these commuters travel by public transport. They are served by 450 Underground trains within a network of 250 miles, plus 5,000 buses which carry more than three million passengers each day.

When not walking, as I usually do in London, I have a deep and abiding affection for buses during off-peak hours and on one memorable occasion both walked and rode home from Fleet Street in a literally misguided effort to help the driver. A fog, one of the last of the classic pea-soupers, came down about seven o'clock during a freak temperature inversion in the early autumn with visibility down to a few feet. Figures loomed out of the murk. Cars were abandoned the length of the Strand. I walked to Trafalgar Square and up to Piccadilly where, seeing the gallant driver of a 159 bound for West Hampstead, I coughed myself aboard that packed bus. But he took the wrong turning at Oxford Circus where we all baled out and I walked on.

Providentially I found another heading in the right direction and by walking in front, I saw him round a roundabout on which two buses were on the pavement, their radiators bust in by lamp-posts. This self-appointed boy scout duly got off and on again at cross-roads, mistaking only that one on the verge of West Hampstead where I took a wrong turn and led him down to Kilburn where he couldn't turn round. He was rather nice about it when I left him there, and I walked home, coughing most of the way. Deaths that week from asthma and emphysema were phenomenal.

Late that night, the manager of a bank at Swiss Cottage, a man I knew who lived in that baroque building, somewhat like Rumpelstiltskin's *schloss*, phoned me up in some perturbation to say that he had been invaded by thousands of roosting starlings. They were whistling and twittering on every available ledge, nook and cranny. Half a dozen had got into the counting-house. What could he do? Apart from suggesting he banged tin trays, I said I didn't know. The next morning I inspected the grimy building which looked as if it had been badly sprayed with whitewash. On their evening flight back to Trafalgar Square, the birds like the buses had lost their way.

My father recalled the first petrol-driven motor bus when he arrived in London in 1899 as a young lad from Pontefract. He also recalled the first tube railway proper, the City and South London which ran from King William Street to Stockwell, close to where he worked. He often told us how the hansom cab drivers, foreseeing a threat to their business, gathered round the exits and shouted, 'Look at the bleedin' sewer rats.' It still seems to me incredible that, as late as 1930, not long before I first visited London myself, there were more horses than cars on the streets.

I have this from Benny Green, the author, bandsman, critical broadcaster and a pro to his fingertips, whose book, *The Streets of London*[1] is a veritable bonanza of old photographs of London's transport around the turn of the century when the carts, the horse-drawn buses, the hansom cabs and the growlers were being slowly replaced by the Iron Horse and the infernal combustion engine. He describes how but, like a skilful magician, not precisely how he came across a marvel-

[1] Pavilion/Michael Joseph, 1983.

lous collection of old photographs, collated, commented upon and grouped under geographic headings in the administrative office of London Transport by a strange man called Charles White (1876–1968), a Londoner born and, as he described himself, 'ill bred'.

Surprise follows surprise. Who took the photographs? I can neither compress nor better Benny Green's explanation: 'Whenever it became apparent to the executives of London Transport that nothing short of a new bus route would meet the requirements of some newly flourishing corner of the town, or the growing tendency of its inhabitants to move regularly from one specific spot to another, meetings were convened, discussions mounted, debates entered upon to determine the route and the frequency of the new service.

'Advance scouts were sent out to examine the lie of the land, and it became the practice of the authorities, once the proposed route had been settled upon, to send out a second group of investigators, a team of photographic outriders who would cover the ground so thoroughly that the drivers pioneering the new route could become familiar with its contours without leaving the garage.'

The discovery of the photographs is hugely to Benny's credit, but those lively pictures (almost) pale beside the ferocious commentaries imposed both on them and almost everything else that concerned London's 'hideous development' by the mysterious Mr White, the hitherto unknown London Transport clerk who fumed, railed and ranted against the New Movement, the destruction of the picturesque and the crushing of the luxuries of the poor. The photographs show airy hansoms cruising about like gondolas and carts piled high with spuds and brussels sprouts. Young bucks in boaters skip out of the way of open-decked buses and honking taxis. Moustachioed soldiers in pillbox hats lounge about waiting for the boozers to open. The newspaper-sellers' bills proclaim not only the decade but also the exact date.

Everybody seems to be advertising something: Sunlight soap, Nestlé's milk, Cerebos salt and Sunmaid raisins, that new store in Holborn called Gamages and Maud Allan's matinées at the Palace Theatre. We learn that to the very end

258

that 'artistic' dancer (1879–1956) attracted 'a sharp intake of watch committees' and was remembered chiefly as the lady who displayed her colonial loyalty by dancing before Edward VII wearing two oyster shells and a five-franc piece.

The Kipper Season has come and gone with the Flower Show. The school holidays are upon us. We have got through what Julian the Apostate called in his own precise lingo *Caniculares*, the Dog Days, that period of acute disquiet between the third and the eleventh of July when Sirius rising with the sun was thought to combine the heat of both stars. But no matter. Recalling what Ian Mackay did thirty years ago I calculated that on 24 July 1987 I had been writhing about on the battered crust of this planet for 25,567 days and nights or, in simple Julian terms, for the awesome total of 36,816,840 minutes. In short my allotted span has extended beyond Orwell's doom start and if you ask what I have done during that time I will give you the answer Emmanuel-Joseph Sièyes did to a similar question at the end of the French Revolution – 'I survived.' Caesar, according to a chap called Shaw, a playwright, said to Rufio: 'We may grow old and die but the crowd upon the Appian Way is always much the same.'

London, the Great Wen, has no Appian Way but, at this torrid time, millions upon millions pour in from the northern motorways that converge on the thromboses of the Finchley and the Edgware Road known to the Saxons as Wætlingastraet. The East India Dock and the Old Kent Roads carry human cargo from Harwich and points south and northeast whilst, in addition to trains from almost everywhere, the Bayswater and the Great West Roads thunder with traffic from Wales, the southern harbours and the airports.

How many tourists, in good round numbers? Over three and a half million annually from the USA and Canada and a little more than half that number each from France and West Germany. Belgium and Luxembourg, Italy and Australia are notable runners-up. They represent nearly six per cent of a thing I don't really understand called London's Gross Domestic Product.

When the living is easy

To see them at their laborious play ('Oh shit, Henry, I jest feel Gar-damned clapped out. Lead me to a drink.'), I suggested to Madam that we took a birthday off in that most luxurious of byways, Jermyn Street. She demurred, politely, and suggested we operated between two well-known pubs, the Savoy and the Ritz, with the thought, no doubt, that we might nibble something at the latter, a place to which we resort as often as to the Mormon headquarters in Balham or the Dogs' Home, Battersea.

Whilst the Ritz may be Ritzier and Claridges, Browns and the Connaught more for the ten top transatlantic tribes, the Savoy is heavily pickled in history on which identity-seeking Americanos are prepared to spend a fortune. Froissart, that fourteenth-century reporter, described it as a 'handsome building on the road to Westminster'. A notice outside the present Grill Room (one of the most famous eating-spots in Europe) describes how Peter, Earl of Savoy and uncle of Henry III's wife, used the place as a marriage agency to fob off his beautiful but impoverished wards on to the prosperous English nobility.

There is much more to the place than I intend to relate. Enough to know that the present building was built by the enterprising Richard D'Oyly Carte who was also responsible for the old theatre next door, and that by a special Act of Parliament the Americans who swarm around the place can legitimately drive in on the right from that narrow covered-in passage just off the Strand.

Notabilities, famous actors, film stars and directors like to be seen there and some like the Chaplins, the late Sir Charlie and now his sad-faced wife Oona, have suites reserved on the upper floors from which a great arc of the Thames can be viewed as if from the lower slopes of Mount Olympus. With a modest safari ahead of us, Katie and I sipped a refresher and surveyed the well-heeled human traffic. Safari is the appropriate word since at the end of one of my own in Lightest Africa, I recalled meeting a generous man, a well-known New Yorker who gave me a tremendous shove in the direction of authorship.

The scene: the Norfolk Hotel in Nairobi where some two

Conker flower-show

days earlier I had turned up after a foot safari to and from the border of Ethiopia, bronzed like a Cherokee chief.[1] Would I appear on KB Television that night? I would, I could and I did, and said God knows what. I was still a bit bushed. What made the evening memorable for me was the appearance of the ghost of 'none other than' (burst of recorded applause) Sid J. Perelman in a studio barely capable of containing an amiable Masai, Sid, me, the interviewer and two technicians behind an early Baird camera.

I say 'ghost' since, under mild sedation (Courvoisier) Sid told me afterwards that for three days he had been living on drugs and kaolin and hadn't stirred more than twelve feet from a john where, as he put it, he had discovered the fundamental principles of the hovercraft. On an assignment for the *New Yorker* – which subsequently became 'Small Bore in East Africa' – he had gone down with dysentery and hoped only that they would cancel his trip on a hired dhow before wheeling him to the waiting Pan-Am under lowered American flags.

Whilst I hung about for a cheap flight home, I spent three days in the Norfolk that still flicker in what's left of my memory cells like a film by the Marx Brothers, for whom Sid had a deep and abiding disrespect. On the second day he came through on the interphone to ask if I could keep the 'Artimisses' at bay. It seems that sixteen ladies from New York had turned up the previous night for a widely publicized All-Girl hunting safari largely made up of divorcees from the age of forty 'and far onwards' as he glumly put it.

Lightly disguised as Sid's agent, I tried to get in a word with an uninhibited shikari anxious to put on her jodhpurs and solar topee, two bits of gear unseen in Nairobi for many a year, ready for a Land-Rover trip up to the Thompson Falls. Apparently they had hoped to lionize Hemingway but his plane had crashed somewhere out in the bush, and they had fallen back on Sid as first reserve. Entering into the spirit of the thing I said it was questionable whether he would see the week out and tiptoed back upstairs. Sid, who

---

[1] *Journey to the Jade Sea*, Constable, 1964.

had been surveying the whole scene through field-glasses normally used by submarine commanders, squeezed my hand weakly.

In between drinks for about two or three hours each day I answered his questions about the habits of the 'big three' (elephant, rhino and buffalo), the easy-to-hit stuff (Grant's gazelle), light and heavy slugs and artillery, the cost of formal derring-do, who not to take on safari, the sheer damned idiocy of it all and how, in my view, there wouldn't be anything left for the Fauna Preservation Society and what was then Peter Scott's ever-increasing empire, the World Wildlife Fund, but for the utter incorruptibility of British game wardens. Some of this came out with embarrassing gratitude under the title of 'The Importance of Healing Ernest'.

With his lower guts blocked like an old church crypt Sid walked, stiffly, towards the hired plane for Zanzibar ('Go now, Splendid Wayfarer') and the assurance that he'd spoken on my behalf both to an American publisher and the editor of the *New Yorker* about this disenchanted science writer ('Revolt in the Desert'). He did just that and we met again in that lounge at the Savoy where years later Katie bade me not bring up disputatious subjects in the presence of Americans.

Sid had not been staying there. He had favoured Brown's which he described as populated in the main by 'over-affluent scriptwriters, dehydrated colonials with saffron faces and elderly spinsters who still clung to ruching and avian headgear'. With a deep disregard for precedence at the Savoy he introduced me to a bell-hop who spoke Kiswahili, a Vanderbilt, and a publisher's pimp.

His suggestion on that occasion was that, after we'd exorcized the spirits of the night before, I should guide him back to Brown's by way of unfamiliar streets but, if possible, taking in Trumpers, the Gentlemen's Perfumier from which he had an irrepressible urge to buy a bottle of bath essence favoured by the Duke of Wellington. With that route in mind I fished Katie out of the powder-room and we set off from where, in that public palace years and years ago, Sid had warned me that, in dealing with publishers 'a soft answer turneth away royalties'.

The street almost opposite the Savoy leads direct to the national home of opera and ballet, Covent Garden and behind it the former market-place where Nell Gwynn sold oranges before she became an actress, the mistress of Charles II and the mother of dukes. To make room for what is now an elegant centre for food, shopping and entertainment of a boisterous kind, the marketeers were obliged to exchange their over-crowded iron and glass halls for the spacious wastes of Battersea.

Katie and I watched in mild amazement as a fire-eater swallowed what appeared to be two flaming ice-cream cornets; a Nigerian acrobat did half a dozen back flips before he danced standing on his hands. Three trombonists blew their heads off in perfect harmony and an aquarist, seeing me admiring his Guppies and Angels asked me if I wanted gladiators 'or something for the social tank'. Apparently the local Chinese are much given to betting on bouts between fighting fish.

In the old days Covent Garden would come to life shortly before midnight and, if they wanted to, the truckers could then legitimately drink until six o'clock in the morning. When Sid and I inspected the original arcades of Inigo Jones's seventeenth-century masterpiece, the place had been as dead as a churchyard so we tramped off ankle-deep in husks, straw and over-ripe fruit to the nearby Bow Street Police Station where he interrogated the polite desk sergeant at some length on the habits and treatment of violent internees.

Katie and I wove our way through King Street to St Martin's Lane where Sid had twice raised his natty fedora, once outside Moss Bros and the second time almost as if in prayer at the doors of the Garrick Club. Nothing much had then happened until we reached Berwick Street market in Soho, a place now entirely surrounded by dirty cinemas and peepshows where, to our enormous surprise, he was mildly assaulted.

As we edged our way between the lines of fruit stalls, an old lady had waddled up and paused to fumble in her capacious basket. In the process she dropped her purse whereupon Sid, as polite as ever, again raised his hat and bent down to pick it

up. In reward for his gallantry, she bonked him over the head
with her brolly.

I doubt deeply whether in the intervening years Jermyn Street
has changed much except in the matter of doubling its prices.
Whilst Katie went off to admire some frippery or other I
sauntered into the premises of George F. Trumper, Gentlemen's Perfumier to fondle their badger-hair shaving brushes.
A fine ivory-handled specimen with which you could have
mopped the floor cost, I was told, a shade over five hundred
quid. Did he still sell the Duke's favourite bath essence? 'Yes,
sir, and in fair demand by connoisseurs if I may say so.
Though, of course, we sell much more in the way of after-
shave lotions nowadays.'

Our joint inspection of the street 'which hugely enlarges
covetousness' brought us to Paxton and Whitfield's where the
combined aroma of just about every cheese in the world put
me in mind of something it would be libellous to record:
Wensleydales the size of cartwheels, Swiss Vacherin, Cornish
Yarg originally fermented, some believe, by Merlin and an
Alsatian Munster which, cautiously sampled, made my eyes
water. Sid, I remember, had bought a quarter and said that
when he nibbled it in the privacy of one of Brown's bedrooms,
his toupee hit the ceiling. I was all for buying some but she
who must be obeyed said it might get us chucked out of the
Ritz.

That French urban chateau (1906) with an iron frame for-
midably fronted by pink Norwegian granite is graced to the
west by a line of ancient planes as old as any in London. Rich
tourists, regular visitors and the curious drift in and out of that
arcaded Piccadilly frontage like jellyfish under a Tiberian
bridge. Madam sauntered off to inspect the adjacent boutiques
leaving me to take a stiff one in that bar near the door
dominated by an immense but modest gilded nude in the guise
of Artemis.

How I got into mild argument with a citizen of Florida who
imported Brazilian rubber and cocoa I am rather unclear but it
had something to do with Artemis and hunting, the destruc-

tion of huge forests and their inhabitants. Incautiously, perhaps, I paraphrased Carlyle's remark that the American Civil War was being fought out between one set of people who preferred to keep their servants for life and the other half who hired them by the hour. But I didn't get very far and, to the relief of the waiter, Madam turned up and hauled me off. She had seen the price of the lunch.

The stylized diagram of the Underground system outside Green Park Station, an ingenious thing which reduces complexity to verticals, horizontals and diagonals, appears to be simple, almost Euclidic. It isn't. After doodling for three years Henry Beck put it to paper in 1933. An actual map of the wavy lines that undulate outwards from Piccadilly Circus looks like the head of Medusa the morning after she lost her hairbrush.

After lunching in a little Cypriot place in Shepherd Market we've known for years we returned to the station to find that in one of the underground corridors with superb acoustics, Rachel, an attractive lass from St John's Wood, was already deep into the first movement (*Allegro ma non troppo*) of Beethoven's Violin Concerto in D Major with its superb octaval leaps and G-string twiddly bits, *staccatissimo*. She looked up and smiled gratefully as we dropped tribute into her empty violin case which, I noticed, contained no shrapnel, the buskers' word for copper coins. She was accompanied by a taped orchestral backing known to subterranean maestros as a 'one out', that is with the solo parts professionally erased.

I have talked to Rachel once or twice on the way to the Club. The money she deservedly earns – between five and ten pounds an hour if she's lucky – helps to pay for her advanced classes at the Royal College. She's getting near the top of a steep ladder with a lot of formidable executants on the way up. Her violin's a beauty, too. A Sebastian Klotz. Her father – who doesn't play – gave it to her. A neighbour in Potsdam had looked after the instrument when they dragged off his father, a concert violinist, to a place called Dachau.

I am on nodding terms, too, with Gonzo Gonzales who plays a Paraguayan harp, Phil the fluter (real name Phineas), El

Greco on the bouzouki forever strumming out Mikis Theodorakis, one or two sax players and the irrepressible Tim the tap-dancer, all members of a self-appointed buskers' union with rules as strict as Boodle's or the Beefsteak and far more entertaining.

They play for an hour timed to the minute. Names in strict chronological order are scrawled on a poster near the pitch or passed round on a sheet of paper which is handed from player to player and, towards the evening rush-hour, looks pretty tattered. Although it is strictly illegal, benevolent cops take as much notice of them as they do of elderly winos sleeping it off under the trees in the park. Buskers brighten up tired commuters no end and are tuneful examples of London's unique and tolerant autonomy.

With the coming of the Horsemen's Sunday at the Church of St John the Evangelist near Hyde Park, the Pearly Harvest Festival and the Trafalgar Day parade a fortnight later, the zodiacal Balance has yielded to the Scorpion which in turn been pierced by the Archer. Leaves yellow and blush as late October rains wash out their oxidized pigments, so evident at Burnham in Bucks where the beeches are at their flaming best.

No late autumn within our calendar is complete without a forest walk and, since our good friend the Apothecary can hear the owls hooting from the famous hornbeams of Epping almost at the bottom of his garden, we joined him there for a fungus foray. Mushrooms, if you prefer the vernacular – but as might be expected he takes a purely clinical interest in those very few native species which are downright deadly. But first to the succulents in the gastronomic sense of the word.

Frank, though of different shape, has the ability of a truffle-hound to locate one of his favourites, the Oyster mushroom, found at the base of fallen trees in clustered, overlapping masses. He filled a carrier bag full in less than an hour and recommended them for stewing, especially in a *blanquette de veau*. They also dry well for storage 'and keep no toxic company'. The squat Boletus, the renowned cèpe of French cooking adds grace to fried kidneys and bacon whilst the yellow, trumpet-shaped chanterelle is another culinary beauty and smells of squashed apricots. The Beefsteak fungus, looking somewhat like an ox-tongue is, in his view, disappointing with a flavour like unripe tomatoes.

The Apothecary has a keen eye and a keen nose but knowing a great deal about toxicology he is gun-shy of anything dimly resembling the killers. The Amanitas, especially *phalloides*, the Death Cap, are responsible for almost all the deaths of incautious fungus-eaters. They kill and they kill mercilessly. The Death Cap might be mistaken for a field mushroom but when in doubt try one on your tax inspector.

The Romans recognized fungi as a convenient way of administering poison (*venenis accommodatissimi*) and we have it from a number of classical authorities, notably Suetonius, that the last thing Claudius ate on this side of the Styx was a *catillus* of mushrooms lightly garnished with Amanitas. The Emperor, the invader of Britain (AD 43), the man who had received over a score of imperial *salutationes*, was going off his chump at the time and Agrippina, his fourth wife, possibly aided and abetted by that little swine her son, Nero, already 'an angler in the lake of darkness', merely hastened his ascent into heaven. As he had been having a quiet meal at home that night, some think that Halotus the eunuch, his taster, had been given the evening off, leaving the kitchen to Agrippina and that awful child. The toxicological dynamite is amanitine.

In October our open pastures are flooded by a river of redwings and fieldfares. In November the robin's song seems to embody all the sadness in the world. We have put the clocks back and made our peace with All Saints and All Souls. But winter is not here until there is a frosty rime on the grass and the Mistle thrush conducts a clarinet concerto from the crowns of tall bare trees.

The Iceman cometh

You rarely see snow in London nowadays. Before some dry-brained barometer-watcher baffles me with comparative statistics I shall qualify what I've just written by saying you rarely see snow in *central* London. Up here on the fringe of the Heath, and no doubt in Wimbledon and wilder places south and west where they regularly dig out their Mercs and Minis from huge drifts, I must presume they see it almost as often as we do in the more snow-favoured parts of this island. It's within the radius of a mile of Nelson's column that I assert — and I assert with authority — that you rarely see a *good* snow-fall, the sort of thing that looks as if flock after flock of Brünnhilde's geese were being plucked away up in the dark sheds of the night. The corporations of Westminster and the City whip the stuff up almost before it's decently settled.

Nevertheless it happened that we not only saw virgin snow in London, we left our visible mark on the diameter of Trafalgar Square as we looked for a cab at two o'clock in the morning after leaving a party at Leslie Randall's place in Soho.

Somebody, probably James Bone, wrote a superb essay about a fall of snow in the gardens of the Temple where he lived in an attic, describing how the long vista in lamplight

seemed as if he were looking through gauze but in the vicinity of each lamp the flakes fluttered suddenly bright, like birds flying into the glare of a lighthouse.

In that famous square we looked up in wonder to see that, under each lamp, the flakes were dancing with their own shadows which flickered up and down as if they had found a new game which couldn't be played in the country where they fly only in darkness.

It took me twenty minutes to find a cab which, I suppose, isn't bad for somebody who has been waiting all his life. But since we were to be out again at first light, it led to some debate about whether it'd be worthwhile going to bed at all. Katie, a Yorkshire lass, is essentially practical.

I have made a brave attempt at trying to describe the indescribable and have failed and shall probably fail again when I say that the dozen or more ponds on the Heath were frozen but the one we were heading for, that one under the Russians' spy-shop in Highgate, was curiously misted over so that there was no visible distinction between water and sky. Along where we knew the rim of that pond to be flew a solitary white gull which is one of the Zen Buddhists' symbols for infinity.

My attitude towards snow is more than somewhat ambivalent. In Trafalgar Square in the early hours of the morning it looks fine, almost inspirational. London comes close to silence. On the Heath it adds another dimension to our daily walk. Yet walking alone above the Bonnette, that great pass on the fringe of the Maritime Alps, I narrowly escaped the downfall of a thunderous avalanche and vowed that never again would I walk alone in mountains when the snow is incoherent. But in the Canadian Arctic several years earlier I had seen the grandeur of snow in all the forms known to the Eskimos.

What was left of the three local Indian tribes, the Hares, the Dogribs and the Chipewyans were, in order of importance, wholly dependent on the caribou, the half-cousin of the Euro-Asian reindeer, the salmon which they fed to their half-starved huskies, the wolves and the snow. Caribou migrate south in the fall to avoid the Iceman and north again in the spring to avoid the terrible flies of the tundra. If it weren't for the wolves the stupid caribou would hang about. They would 'yard' as Scottish ghillies call it and they would be trapped by deep snow which, with their ungulate feet, they can test with the sensitivity of sonar equipment. The question, therefore, for the zoologists at Saskatoon and Manitoba concerned the minimum wolf population necessary to keep the caribou constantly on the move.

For ten days we flew the length of the most spectacular peaks on the Yukon border, the Mackenzies, cautiously skimming down on to ice-free lengths of Great Bear and Great Slave lakes in a float-plane, counting wolves and caribou all the way. Wise in these matters, the Eskimos can distinguish between eight kinds of snow which correspond to different physical conditions such as sudden freeze or melt or the impact of sustained blizzards. Written down phonetically, there is, for instance, *khali* for feathery snow on trees; *appi* for snow on the ground; *pukkak*, the layer below in which small animals live in a labyrinth of corridors permeated by a pale blue light; and *sikok-toack*, that hard crusty stuff which is like walking on puff pastry.

With our heavily treaded boots making flatulent noises, Katie and I walked back for breakfast through a less spectacular snowscape, but one that could be deciphered. The Heath is a haven for I don't know how many pairs of foxes, certainly a dozen or more. By comparison with the tracks of dogs which are characteristically 'paired', the fox leaves behind delicate, evenly spaced tracks in an almost straight line. Usually you could see the trail of his snow-laden brush. No badgers have been seen on the Heath since that day, recorded in my first notebook when an RAF trainee on his first solo in a Moth pancaked down at dawn under Mouldy Maudie's Wood and later told the police he had seen one on his way to a telephone-box. To judge from the snow-prints we see in the north, badgers seem to walk on their claws. But on the Heath we have an abundance of rabbits and moles which, when the ground is snow-clad, appear to move on the surface of the ground, wobbling about, burrowing only through their own heaps of upturned soil. But at that party at Leslie Randall's place in Soho the previous night we had been talking about other forms of local life.

Soho is tucked away between Regent Street and the Charing Cross Road. In *The Forsyte Saga* Galsworthy considered it 'untidy, full of Greeks, Ishmaelites, Italians, tomatoes, restaurants, organs, coloured stuffs, queer names and people leering out of upper windows; it dwells remote from the British Body Politic.'

The present owners of a score or more of top grade nightspots and restaurants such as Quo Vadis and Kettners shrug their shoulders when they hear the tourist guides describe the district as London's Black Mile and Sin City. After all business is business, and, as they put it, visitors come for what they want and what they can afford to pay for. Their business is with three-star entertainment and good food and drink for those with well-lined pockets.

But what of the fluorescent-lit peep and wank shops and the dirty cinemas? The answer seems to be that they are being slowly but inexorably driven out of business by indignant residents and Westminster City Council which has drawn up a strict and expensive licensing system: £13,000 and subject to regular inspection. Nothing really happens in the clip shops where the operators charge those with a fourth-form approach to suggestive goings-on a stiff entrance fee and a minimum of £10 for a non-alcoholic drink. They are rarely in business for long.

This view is reinforced by several good friends, mostly entertainers, who either live there ('there's always something going on') or work within half a mile of Gaston's French House in Dean Street when there's nothing more lucrative in the immediate offing. Leslie Randall is one of the dedicated residents. In between out-of-town shows he tenants what he calls his eyrie, a cosy apartment above the Phoenix Theatre in the Charing Cross Road, a thoroughfare known in the old days, when some men favoured virility pills, as the Damaroidstrasse. 'When somebody tells me their old man is playing at the Phoenix I say well tell him to keep his voice down as I shall probably be on the phone.'

He firmly believes that sleaze is now on the slide in Soho. He sees it as being like *La Ronde*, the spinning round of a series of inter-related situations. Up to the mid-seventeenth century, Soho – so-called from an old hunting cry – was a hunting-ground for hooligans. Then the Protestants arrived in considerable numbers when they were forced out of France after the fearful Revocation of 1685. Foreigners, speaking their own languages, have been settling down around Old Compton Street and Gerrard Street where, as Leslie puts it, 'they serve damn good chop suey and gamble with small stones which only the Chinese understand. Then came the tarts and a lot of good cheap food, and now we're back to square two.'

Leslie gets up at half-past eight and if his agent hasn't got something on the nail he sits in a dressing-gown, writing one-man shows until somewhere around one o'clock when he gets down to food and 'light diversions'. His passions include golf and poker 'where you don't play against odds, you play against people'. All his activities are fundamentally one-man shows.

In what other ways does he see the pattern of Soho changing? He believes the sweat-shops are back. 'Cheap labour in the kitchens; tailors who will carry out instant alterations; mechanics "of a kind" able to repair duplicating machines, typewriters and cameras. Soho is a paradise for impresarios and swift-buck operators.' But he can't think of anywhere else he'd rather live.

The Iceman, O'Neill's dread symbol of death, has slunk off, leaving slush in the gutters of Gower Street where, on my way to Leicester Square, I walked, glancing up at London's most outstanding priapic emblem, the Post Office Tower.

Gower Street is where, not so long ago, I first met Eric the Geologist in nearby University College. Gower Street is where I took my copy down to what were then the splendid offices of *The Spectator* at Number 99. Gower Street, spiritual home of the Godless Whigs, the Genes of Gloomsbury: the

Bells, the Stracheys, the Keyneses, the Nicolsons, Roger Fry and Ottoline Morrell – names that punctuate Virginia Woolf's seemingly endless flow of published letters and diaries.

I paused, mentally, at the thought of Virginia whose series of essays, *The Common Reader*, opened the eyes of my generation to a whole galaxy of literary figures from the Greeks to George Gissing. I read her in the back of my wireless truck when, during manœuvres in the army, she did much to assuage stark boredom. Imagine then how much I made of seeing her twice at a distance as we fought a mock-battle around Rodmell in Sussex where, until her suicide, she lived with her husband Leonard. A sort of ghost figure in either mauve or grey, always, the villagers told me, long-skirted and usually in a floppy picture hat. The suicide, one must assume, of a chronic depressive. A tortured soul, who strove too hard for literary perfection.

Yet after spending hours and hours in that room of her own, striving for the exact phrase, the exotically arresting simile – Edith Sitwell, she said, 'resembled the whitened bones of a hare encrusted with emeralds' – Virginia consorted oddly. She was in and out of bed with the snobbish, the supremely anti-vulgarian Vita (Mrs Harold Nicolson). She hobnobbed rather more than casually with her beloved Lytton Strachey, a notorious homosexual, at the time when he was pursuing Dora Carrington who, before she shot herself, was living at one and the same time with Mark Gertler and Ralph Partridge. Her marriage to that 'poor Jew', the gentle, the ever-attentive Leonard who seems by far the best, the most charitable of the lot was, by almost any standards, disastrous. It may never have been consummated.

The thought-stream disappeared abruptly as Shaftesbury Avenue shattered the calm of Bloomsbury until, taking refuge from the spattering of countless thousands of birds in Leicester Square, I gazed upwards for evidence of yet another theory about what makes those out-and-out pests, the starlings, fly in their own curious fashion.

The ledge theory I have mentioned before: the birds fly into cities at dusk possibly to find something like their aboriginal homes on cliffs and high rocks. But on arrival at their night roosts they wheel round in the air in different kinds of spirals, like smoke, before plunging down on to their ledges or, if they find them occupied, flying off somewhere else.

Some incoming flights ignore the mêlée, the dive-bombing, the whirlabouts, the aerial combat. Arriving rapidly, purposively, at various heights but almost always much higher than the buildings, they fly on directly, perhaps to Whitehall or the island in St James's Park lake. How can these behavioural patterns be interpreted?

The answer, I suggest, lies in those two words 'like smoke'. The spirals are the avian equivalent of the Red Indians' smoke-signals. Knowing they are going to get a night's wind-free lodgings, the starlings that arrive early are putting out 'house full' notices which can be 'read' at a distance by latecomers who must make the best they can of it. Starlings are darn smart birds.

As for myself I made for the Club and a sun-downer since it had been a long and busy day. Up an hour before the starlings stirred in Kenwood I had driven down towards the clamour of new Covent Garden near the Dogs' Home to watch the wholesalers of Christmas trees, mistletoe and holly make a packet before Christ-tide. The selling season seems to start earlier each year.

Few of the buyers, I was glad to find, thought much of the Forestry Commission's trees. Too expensive after being trucked down from our National Parks and you can get a nasty jab from spiky Sitka spruce, whereas, if you've a mind to, you can all but roll about on some of the other firs, especially the aromatic balsam species. In these days of lunatic squandering even the wholesale prices were ferocious at over £1.50 a foot plus tax.

Probably because it is winter-green and its roots don't touch the ground, mistletoe has been revered right across Europe for thousands of years as proof against Dark Night, demons, hob-thrusts and the like. And pretty costly, too. Under the old dispensation it worked out, wholesale, at about five bob a bunch. Despite the fact that it had been a wonderful year for the stuff, holly was no cheaper but it's an old favourite of mine. And birds love it.

Holly berith berries,
Berries rede enow;
The thistlecok, the popinjay,
Daunce in every bough.

There is a bit of a mystery in the distribution of its foliage for whereas browsing beasts are kept at bay by the prickles on the lower leaves, those higher up are often entirely devoid of protection. A case, surely, of double-locking the ground floor whilst leaving the fanlight open to the sky. Because of its blood-red berries and thorns, the Medieval Fathers of the Church had no difficulty in working it into the Christian tradition, which has stuck to this day. Thus do we flout Old Winter with Green Tree and Old Mortality with Child Worship.

At ten o'clock that night or maybe a little earlier our steward shook me by the shoulder, gently, to say that a fellow club-man, an old friend of mine, wanted me on the phone. Sleepily I answered it to recall, almost too late, that I had a date at Gaston's French House in Dean Street with John the Magician. A cab took me there within half an hour.

John Wade had been giving a private show just around the corner and said he felt pretty well shagged out. An agent's call for a casting session at eleven o'clock: he'd got the job. Then a so-called working lunch about how and where the commercial could be filmed. 'And dammit,' he said, 'I couldn't drink.' He'd had a children's party for Japanese restaurateurs at half-past two. Delicate close-up stuff with youngsters. Then back home for props, a last-minute request, a tricky one for his engagement at Kettners that night.

We had Club business to discuss then and there since he was booked for Rotterdam the next morning. 'Doesn't always come as easy as this,' he admitted. 'I'll be back sawing young ladies in half next week.'

What intrigues me about these professional entertainers is their seemingly unquenchable optimism and adaptability. To me, an outsider bound to entirely different routines, their lives, often precarious, seem to be part of a variety show. Maybe this is part of the player's mask. The *Pagliacci* syndrome. What's certain is that children love them. 'Tell me about your Japanese kids,' I said.

With little Kioto, Mariko, Yuko, Yoshi, Miyoko, Yumi and several others sitting round him – names he'd carefully memorized – he felt 'it was like taking part in a miniature *Mikado*. With their shiny black hair and pearly skins they looked almost edible,' he said, 'and of course they were wearing their little kimonos and obis.

'What makes it so good for me is that I've got a *pretty* audience. An odd thing about Japanese parties – and I've done many in my time – is that the parents all turn up with cameras and seem as interested in what can be photographed, especially themselves, as what can be seen.'

What sort of tricks did he put over? I asked. John smiled. He leaned over and delicately extracted a thimble from my breast-pocket using only his forefinger and thumb. He squeezed it in his clenched fist whereupon it became five thimbles, one on each finger with a big one on his thumb. 'Mind you, I did some special ones,' he said. 'Like the big castle made out of cards that appears from under a sheet of paper pressed flat. And then I pour out a glass of milk, slowly, and look round for some little chap who looks particularly apprehensive when I say I'm going to pour it over his head. Oddly enough, out falls a glass full of confetti.'

Did he find Oriental audiences easy to work with? He said he thought them 'absolutely marvellous. They believe what they see. They have a sense of magic, especially the children. They are wide-eyed and open-mouthed all the time. By contrast, some parties for British kids can be absolute hell. They've seen it all.'

Sawing girls in half is an operation John has given much thought to. Apparently it gets more and more sophisticated. In 1912 or thereabouts, he said, you couldn't see your trained apprentice when she'd disappeared into the coffin-like box. Nowadays he selects 'victims' at random from the audience and you can see them with head dangling over the latest in trade guillotines. But usually, as he put it, 'they walk up with a degree of reluctance when they hear the shriek of the power-saw which, you can take it from me, is the real thing. "How do you feel about joining my Fifty-Fifty Club?" I ask. Many of them want to know if the trick can go wrong and of course I tell them I don't know as I've never done it before.'

For many years John 'worked the boats', that is he shuttled between Southampton and New York on the QE2 more than twenty times in the dual role of licensed Court Jester and benign watch-dog. Every night there were big shows which he compère'd, 'with Joe Loss and his band for some background music' whilst his carefully thought-out card tricks and patter on the first morning out carried a clear message to card-sharpers and their potential victims. As he glanced at his watch and rose to go I asked him if he looked back on those commissioned trips as his finest hour? With that in-built modesty I've come to expect from him, he shrugged his shoulders and said, 'No, that would be when I was on the finest variety stage in the world, the Palladium.'

A cold uncharitable rain had begun to fall as I stepped out of that warm pub. Not a cab in sight so I strode through London's Black Mile towards the nearest Underground with touts beckoning towards dim-lit interiors.

In his first, second and third league grading of districts where a woman can be picked up easily, my friend Norman the cab driver ranked Shepherd Market at the top and Kings Cross at the bottom of the table. His opinion of Soho was almost unprintable. His passengers, rich and poor, often asked him where they 'might go for a bird', he told me. His reply always was that it depended on how much they could afford to pay and what they really wanted: European, Oriental, black, white, straight sex 'or kinky stuff'?

He related a rather touching story of a middle-aged provincial who had in mind a short brunette with large breasts and quite a big belly. 'Sounded a bit odd,' said Norman, 'so I asked him why. And do you know what he told me? He sighed and said he felt homesick.'

Sex is older than Olduvai Gorge; not even the Russians

claim to have invented it. The roots of the language of sex in all its forms, pure and impure, are also extremely old; pre-biblical if we are to believe that archaeologist who claimed to have deciphered some hieratic script in the chamber for the Royal Concubines in the great pyramid of Cheops. In what appeared to be a fragment of a Middle Kingdom limerick, it came out as:

> She had for her clients
> Both pygmies and giants

In one of my notebooks – and you may take my word for this – I have an account of a long session with Eric Partridge, lexicographer extraordinary who had just revised another edition of his famous *Dictionary of Slang and Unconventional English*. We met in one of Dylan Thomas's favourite taverns, the Fitzroy in what Partridge called Alsatia, that is Charlotte Street to the north of Soho. What I wanted to know was how he managed to collect his extraordinary words, but as he was talking to someone else at the time, I stood by the bar and watched him.

He looked uncommonly like my notion of Edgar Wallace's Mr Reader, the short and rather tubby gentleman-detective who regularly associated with the lower rungs of the social ladder. Eric Partridge did much the same. He took a slip of paper from a man in a cloth cap, glanced at it, smiled and shook his head. Somebody else promptly approached with another slip, and he nodded and pointed towards the bar. At this point I introduced myself.

Eric Partridge said that most new words cost him a drink in proportion to their value to him. He made a round of pubs and markets and must have been known to hundreds of people. He pounced on absolutely new etymological oddities like a kestrel on a fieldmouse, especially vulgarisms though he confessed in the preface to his Dictionary that 'in a few instances I had to overcome an instinctive repugnance'. In the copy he signed for me, really *rude* words are punctuated with asterisks.

No such reluctance encumbered that American word-master, Willard R. Espy whom I got to know through the

New York Times. He revelled in ribaldry, notably in the rich fields of the proper and improper noun. 'Ribald' for example. From the written works of Jean Ribaut who claimed the territory of Florida for the French? Not so, he thought; they were as clean as a whistle. The Old High German for whore (*Hriba*) is the probable origin.

Between those two wholly dissimilar lexicographers, Partridge and Espy, I assembled a lexicon of lust not inappropriate to the Black Mile. We might start, alphabetically with Athanasian goings-on – strumpetry, of course, from the beginning of the Creed of that name: '*Whosoever shall desire* . . .' And now, to get it over with quickly, a bugger. Espy pointed to the Volga River from which the allegedly androgynous Bulgars took their name: a case of etymological river pollution? A catamite, defined in our down-to-earth *OED* as 'a boy employed for unnatural purposes', is also a nice example of corruption. It comes from Ganymede, that beautiful Trojan youth who, among other things, served up liquor. Zeus, up to his usual tricks, carried him off in the guise of an eagle. That much over-used vulgarism for the female pudendum – which itself is literally Latin for 'that of which one ought to be ashamed' – is cognate with wedge-shaped and the Hittite form of writing.

As this is liable to lead me astray, I shall drop several letters, English and French such as C for condom (roots multifarious), and mention only that 'concubine' contains verbal elements of both of those seducers of the somnolent, *incubi* and *succubae*. 'Erotic', it should be obvious, is amatory, passionate rather than pornographic; the difference in short between the names of that foam-born three-in-one, Aphrodite Urania (symbolizing spiritual love), Aphrodite Genetrix (marriage) and Aphrodite Porne, the patron of lust and prostitution.

The Iceman slunk back. First in mid-January when the Portland-stone whiteness of the West End was lost against a whiter London and then again in early March when six o'clock dusk on the Heath didn't seem asleep so much as dead – dead, shrouded and shriven in the corpse-light of a last moon.

I had heard of the Iceman in boreal Canada where among the Athabaskan red-men he is *ka-utcha*, the famine-bringer who drives the caribou south. In Africa, that graveyard of colonies, he is *Masungu*, the one who beckons and cannot be gainsaid by those who live in the high Ruwenzori. In the Himalayas, the roof of the world, he is of the *Yeti* sect, a Tibetan word grossly mistranslated as the Abominable Snowmen, for they are mystics who, after practising almost unimaginable austerities, are able to glide, sun-blackened and stark naked from one lamasery to another, leaving behind in the snow those notorious footprints.

In the Hell Hole, a ramshackle saloon-hotel on the corner of Sixth Avenue and Fourth Street in Greenwich Village, New York, the Iceman achieved something close to immortality where among the customers, the truckers, teamsters, gangsters, pimps, whores and almost hopeless alcoholics, Eugene O'Neill drank himself silly while making spidery notes about prototypes for the characters in *The Iceman Cometh*, one of the greatest plays written by that enormously gifted playwright.

The sinister title with its verb which is both archaic and sexual suggests the inevitability of death and, according to two of his biographers,[1] O'Neill considered drinking to be his rehearsal for death. He drank his five-cent shots of whisky straight, not to get drunk but to keep going. This took place in the 'twenties and the marvel is that he managed to survive days and nights in that saloon (real name the Golden Swan) and others to write *The Iceman* twenty-four years later.

At times he became insensible, almost paralysed, on bootleg Tiger-piss made from old raisins. Contemporaries recall that when he was in the grip of staggering hangovers, unable to speak coherently, unable even to pick up a double shot without splashing it down his shirt, the barman would casually drop a towel within his quavering grasp. Gene would drape it round his neck and tie one end to his wrist so that, by using it as a hoist, ten cents' worth of near-pure alcohol could be hauled up with his left hand and gulped down. 'Bartenders are the

[1] Arthur and Barbara Gelb, *O'Neill*, Jonathan Cape, 1962.

most sympathetic people in the world,' O'Neill often told friends when, from time to time, he went on the wagon. Rarely for long except towards the end.

One day he squandered a hundred dollars on a case of good whisky and sent it round to the home of his friend Frank Shay together with a phonograph and an invitation to five or six cronies to join him in a Bacchanalia. According to Arthur Gelb it went on for two days, with emptied bottles tossed into the fireplace. Finally there was no one left except O'Neill and Shay who found the sound of breaking glass so entertaining that they threw in glasses, plates and cups and started on the lamps before they both passed out.

On another occasion Wallace, the boss of the Hell Hole, bought a pig and fed it on garbage in the cellar with a Christmas dinner for the regulars in mind. As the season approached, O'Neill and one or two others brought the pig up into the bar and offered it whisky. It was a strong pig and when drunk became unmanageable, rushing about as O'Neill did when he had exceeded his limit. The only man who could subdue it was a large negro who pinned it down and crooned into its ear. 'You got to reason with him,' he explained.

In addition to his Irish ancestry, O'Neill had in him all the elements of drama. Deckhand on cattle-boats and beach-comber where, in between bouts, he devoured literature, especially Greek tragedies, Ibsen and Strindberg. His father, a mean man by all accounts but a notable actor, married a drug addict. Gene, fundamentally a manic-depressive, married three times 'to women better than he deserved' and plunged up and down on an emotional roller-coaster. Like Poe he seemed to be surrounded by an aura of mysterious and self-induced misery or, as he put it himself, 'Man is born broken. He lives by mending. The grace of God is the glue.' His emotions boiled over into thirty plays which gained him a Nobel prize. In my view *The Iceman* is the greatest of them all.

Philip Hope-Wallace took me to see all four hours of that rigadoon of death at the Arts Theatre Club in 1958 and, since we drank treble gins during the intervals, I walked out into Great Newport Street slightly drunk and overwhelmed by the understated passion of every act. It was as if I had read the

Gospel of St John for the first time. 'In the beginning was the Word . . .'

Behind a bottle of his usual Bollinger, Philip, sympathetic as ever, sensing my mood and knowing much of my domestic discomfort, sought to unravel some of the complexities of the wholly amorphous plot staged in one eternity-long bar with its fearful Greek-chorus-like repetitions, with a few nicely phrased sub-epigrams of his own. I notebooked one: 'No happy person lives on good terms with reality. We don't know what it is.'

A bad period that, and one over which I intend merely to skate. Long months in Congo the previous year had flung open exotic casements that were slammed shut when I returned to the ruins of a marriage and jobs that amounted to little more than money-raising for the camel safari to Lake Rudolf. My notebooks reeked of drink, gloom and good intentions.

I doubt deeply whether a curious obsession with the works of O'Neill especially *Long Day's Journey into Night* and *Mourning Becomes Electra* did much more than exacerbate my own condition but with hindsight I see that I absorbed a little of his sense of fate, the way in which he stressed man's constant need for illusions. My own need for them evaporated not long afterwards when I returned to reality after a splendid affair with a lake. I came back to England and met Tilly, that compassionate woman to whom three of my books are dedicated. *Journey Through Love* relates, obliquely, badly I think now, how after ten years she died tragically. The wheel swung round again. *Ritornello*. Let it turn. The past cannot be recaptured.

Because, significantly, I kept no record of that journey into another long night I can't remember even which year it was when the phone rang incessantly in the early hours of the morning. 'New York,' said the operator. A friend, an editor introduced to me by Perelman, said she'd been trying to reach me for hours. Did I, she asked, recall Oona? Oona O'Neill, the daughter of the Iceman, now the widow of the late Sir Charles Chaplin? Would I phone her? And she gave me the number of a mansion that looks down on Lake Geneva.

I didn't know that I had walked very close to the gates of the Manoir de Ban at Courcier on my trans-Alpine walk, but apparently Oona did. She had read the book and she may have known, possibly from Sid who met me whenever he came to London, that for a period I had been obsessed by Eugene.

After turning over that suggestion (from New York) that if I cared to visit Oona she'd be glad to see me, I wrote or phoned or did both within a week. I cannot remember. There is a great deal about what became a luxurious if somewhat embarrassing weekend which, in retrospect, has less clarity than a heavily watered Pernod.

The Rolls met me at Geneva airport. The lakeside drive. The telephone that rang behind my ear. Oona speaking from home. Apologies for not meeting me herself. The children had arrived, unexpectedly. Grandchildren too. How many? What were their names? I can't remember. In the light of flambeaux perhaps a dozen of us dined on the *terrasse*. Gifted children. Conversation largely in French, mine atrocious. Two elegant Parisians who were all gestures and raised eyebrows. Mimes. Subtle, rapidly delivered in-stories, family references I could make little or nothing of. Oona shy, wan, maternal. The whole place heavily guarded by high railings and huge dogs since there had been that dreadful business of Charlie's body exhumed for an abortive attempt at ransom.

Much the same the next morning. Nobody about except impatient grandchildren whom I drilled with broomsticks, parade-ground fashion, marching them round the swimming pool with stentorian commands. I needed some identity with the place.

A novelist might make much of a relationship between a multi-millionairess, the deb of her coming-out year in New York, the lifelong friend of Gloria Vanderbilt and me, a jobbing writer for the carriage trade. But I can't. She took me up to her bedroom, apologetically, where she was concerned about an *éclosion massive*, an infestation of lake flies – and on firm ground at last I talked, probably over-volubly, on the biology of aquatic insects.

In their huge library with its uniformly bound leather volumes with too many uncut leaves she told me that Charlie had had a bit of trouble with his reading. As for Eugene, her father, he had not spoken to her after he read in the papers that she, eighteen, had married Charlie, a man of fifty-four with political and sexual complications. Dead ends which for the Chaplins had ended – against all press predictions – very happily together in Switzerland.

There seemed only one way out. Cutting the long weekend short I asked for the Rolls to Geneva and kissed the daughter of the Iceman on both cheeks, warmly.

Evensong

On trips to and from our Yorkshire cottage we usually drive for the excellent reason that, when we get there, Katie has grandchildren to fondle in a market town beyond Castle Howard on the plain of York, but when I yearn for the London Library or other sources of refreshment, if only for a long weekend, I take the Inter-City back to Kings Cross. There is about those two great arches of simplicity a sense of homecoming. In modern life the great railway stations are the city gates.

For some unfathomable reason that district between Kings Cross and Euston including the Blessed St Pancras (martyr) is a sort of Debatable Land, neither residential, commercial, industrial, trading nor theatrical. It abounds in lodging-houses, cheap caffs, pubs, pawnbrokers and parade-grounds for whores. Hope-Wallace and I once found ourselves in the unenviable position of occupying seats in a slow and dry train south which for the better part of four hours left us not high but very dry. It followed that we made for the first available tavern in the Euston Road with considerable haste.

Standing there facing the bar, Philip was nudged between the shoulder-blades by the bosom of an old tart who courteously offered her services. Philip shook his head benevolently and, not to be outdone in civilities, admired some bauble in her cavernous cleavage and suggested she might care to take a drink with him. Scarcely had the port and lemon touched her lips when it was knocked out of her hand by an even older tart who called her a bleeding shit-house who'd nicked her pitch.

Tart Number One scratched her face ferociously, Tart Two dragged her rival to the floor by her hair, and before two bouncers could chuck them out through separate doors, one had lost part of her blouse and the other was unquestionably bleeding. They resumed battle in the Euston Road. Philip sighed and muttered something about *hors de combat*. Never again have I dallied thereabouts.

Not long ago I arrived at that south-bound terminal alone and idly loitering, and recalling the past and something Leslie Randall had said about affairs when Soho was covered in snow as soft and light as kittens' fur, I made for his eyrie by way of Gower Street and Leicester Square on foot, touching not a drop on the way. His phone was engaged and he wasn't at home when I got there so I had a large one, my first of the day, in the French House. I am inclined to think that the first whispers of senescence (I didn't say senility) can be gauged, not so much by one's capacity or incapacity to put it away, but by an inability to burn it up quickly. In our salad days we could knock back several at midday, think nothing of it and start another session at night as 't were the first of the day. But over a certain age you tend to bank the stuff and, at worst, take Heminevrin as substitute for the sweaty scrum or an hour's benign siesta. I drank the gin and in Katie's absence made for a hell-hot goulash in a nearby Hungarian place.

Because I have an impaired sense of both taste and smell due to dabbling with formaldehyde when I dissected beetles, as far as food is concerned nowadays I like foods that know their own minds. People who don't much care for fish often tolerate sole, the reason being, given their debased taste-buds, that sole doesn't taste much like fish and even that degree of resemblance disappears when it is submerged in the kind of sauces that restaurateurs imagine to be characteristically French. Likewise, they go in for meat and vegetables frozen as deep as Siberian mammoths. They prefer processed cheese because it isn't cheesy and synthetic vanilla because it's more vanillary. The relatively new habit of asking for a pint and a dash of lime stems from the fact that inert beers and lagers taste of almost nothing. And as for vodka (no colour, no taste, no smell) it needs to be laced with the reassuring juices of infancy such as orange and tomato. It is the ideal intoxicant for the drinker who wants no reminder of how hurt mother would be if she knew what he was up to.

At that point where I all but took up with the suggestion of a couple of villains known to me slightly, I shook my head righteously, paid the bill and made for the Underground, back to an empty apartment in West Hampstead, where I hoped to bring this itinerant narrative to a close the following day.

A glorious morning. To reach what we call our estate with its cheerful bunch of brown-coated gamekeepers one is obliged, as I have mentioned before, to endure a brief brush with a length of the Finchley Road chiefly remarkable for its vendors of onyx-topped tables, rather awful gilded reproductions of classical statuettes and electric log-fires in mahogany fire-places. And then all is peace, either along Shrinkville, a tree-lined avenue which is the home of half a dozen well-known psychoanalysts, or Via Accademia, the narrow path alongside the campus of Westfield College. I prefer the villas of the shrinks, for you can speculate on the mental state of those coming out and those going in. It's here too that we often bow gravely to the prototype of Beachcomber's Mr Tinkleberry Snapdriver QC who raises his black homburg with uncommon courtesy.

Not far from where Ruth Ellis, the last woman to be hanged, shot her lover down I encountered Michael Foot, not fortuitously, for together with other regular Heath-walkers we often meet as ships that pass. This time I phoned him. We have never discussed politics in all the years I have known him but instead of a couple of minutes of casual chat about how our books are coming along (he's currently grappling with Byron) or why our common estate is looking more dilapidated I wanted to know what a man of his stature thought about as he

ambled along with his dog, Dizzie (Disraeli). Did he go out purposively to compose a great speech or think about his party's policies or sort out a tricky literary problem at his work desk? Or did ideas emerge spontaneously?

'I suppose it's a matter of all these things,' he said. 'Very occasionally I try to concentrate most of the time, like solving a chess problem or in my case writing the all-important first paragraph of a review. But one thing I'm certain about is that I come home in a much better temper than when I went out.'

I hadn't the nerve to ask him about the spiritual state of Foot in the bath or over his first cup of tea in the kitchen so I shifted attention to an exuberant greenfinch in a pond-side larch which seemed to be proclaiming its close relationship with the domesticated canary. Did he know what it was? 'Some sort of bird,' he said and then, apologetically, 'I'm wholly ignorant about these sort of things although my father was pretty good at natural history.'

We walked for about an hour, talking about a number of matters which fortified my belief that he is a generous, warm-hearted but essentially shy person who takes time to disclose what he really thinks. Too good, in my opinion, to have been the leader of the Labour Party. I left him talking to his beloved Dizzie which, when a young pup, I rudely referred to in some piece or other as a rather noisy, hairy Mars Bar.

Shyness can't be levelled against Hunter Davies, the author, broadcaster, columnist and professional funny man who has interviewed me on several occasions. To quote his wife, the author, Margaret Forster: 'He walks on the Heath mainly for exercise and often talks to himself, reasoning out work problems. In fact he talks to anybody who seems interesting, like an inquisitive dog nosing around. It clears his headaches which he is obliged to admit are tension-induced. If we walk together it's a darned waste of the Heath since we argue and by the time we get home I feel I haven't really walked anywhere. Hunter knows nowt about nature but I *love* it; I am soothed by it and almost jump out of my skin if anyone speaks to me.'

When he is not in wind-swept Cornwall or unravelling webs of espionage from a hide-out in Central Europe, John le Carré (David Cornwell) admits that 'almost anything' drives him out on to the Heath such as 'the Hoover going, a bad paragraph or the excitement of a good one; or the bloody radios that builders play specially in order to obstruct the course of literature.' And of course his whippets 'whose predictable time for asking for a walk is just after they've been out for one.'

'I have a walking appetite just as I have other appetites, and am quite frustrated if it can't be answered on demand. Moving gets me unclogged in my head. I almost never make a note when I'm walking and usually forget the great lines I have composed, which is probably just as well. But I come home knowing that life is possible and even, sometimes, beautiful especially when I have the whole Heath to myself on a perfect mid-week afternoon, particularly in the autumn.'

Smiley's People appear in South End Green. So do John Wyndham's *Triffids* and, years ago, *The Outsider* was written by Colin Wilson who slept on the Heath. Nearby Gospel Oak is featured in John Buchan's *Thirty-nine Steps*. The police had to be called out to find Chris Bonington, a native, who got lost at the age of five exploring Mouldy Maudie's Wood. The Heath is therapeutic. To calm herself down after her marriage Elizabeth Barrett Browning made for its rolling contours, alone, almost straight from the church.

What I feel about the maintenance of the Heath I don't intend to repeat and am primarily concerned about what will happen if it comes under the sway of the City of London. What did that quiet dynamo, Gerry Isaaman, the editor and revivifier of the *Ham an' High,* the *Hampstead and Highgate Express,* think about the latest developments? We talked, as we so often do, over a drink and sandwich in the Flask at lunchtime.

Gerry and his wife Delphine – who comes from Whitby on the Yorkshire coast – have been close friends of ours since he joined the paper as a junior reporter over thirty years ago. With a camera and notebook he has seen me off on most of my trips and on regular dining-table terms he is as fond of my wife as I am of his. Under his editorship the weekly *Ham an' High* has soared to a regular circulation of 22,000 with at least double that number who buy and read its durable hundred and more pages irregularly, like a magazine.

Whilst most local papers are parochial editions of the *Bazaar Exchange and Mart*, that is, the emphasis is on advertising, the *Aitch and Aitch* as it used to be called concentrates on news and features which the staff of twenty-two writers and distinguished outsiders present with the superficially simple wit, clarity and homogeneity of the *New Yorker*. No national daily or Sunday 'heavy' presents such a swag of arts as befits arty-tarty Hampstead. But it hits and hits hard, as our lefty-nutty Camden Council, hospitals and other social services including that much harassed super-Thatcherite MP, Sir Geoffrey Finsberg know to their nail-biting cost. Gerry implies both politely and not so politely that Sir G. used to be a good fellow who somehow stopped growing and fossilized. He's not really part of the world today. The editor's fed up with Dick Whittingtons.

Among the paper's regular targets is the management of the Heath. Gerry thinks that the City of London goes in for benevolent and liveried feudalism. He abhors, he fulminates against the traffic thromboses between the Archway and Finchley Roads with the Village between them in danger of becoming an expensive Montmartre of restaurants and glitter-parlours with increasingly few shops selling the residents' weekly wants. In terms of prices one Main Street foodstore is more expensive than Harrods. And he says so. Splendid stuff this, but Gerry's up against 'progress' which two centuries ago fortified the medicinal waters of Well Walk with Mother Huff's knocking-shops, patronized by princes and paupers and known the length of Europe. We argue, Gerry and I, and with God's help – for I have a Jewish mother-in-law – we'll argue until we drop.

As I write these last remaining lines late into the night I can see below a quadrant of blind Milton's 'beloved City' which would have astonished that imaginative poet-secretary to the Protector: a chain of static lights given movement only by the caterpillars of the last trains to Stanmore and outermost

suburbs. It happened that John Jacob, curator of the splendid Kenwood House art collection had looked into the Flask when Gerry and I were still arguing about how best to deal with Camden Council's perverse obsession with black culture, the (sic) rights of gays and lesbians and the implied inferiority of white heterosexuals. Would I, Jacob suggested, care to drop in later for a drink as he had something to show me. Up there I went, up on to the roof of his treasure-house, his own apartments where he has Adam fireplaces even in the kitchen and much else to be proud of.

After refreshment we looked at some of the pictures in the galleries below and in silence and subdued light I saw as if for the first time Rembrandt's great self-portrait, humanity in every line of his face. The luminous Vermeer outshone Frans Hals's whiskery he-man, up to no good one could be sure. There were the two Guardis which look as if one big picture had been carefully cut in half. In her web of lace which looks lacier than the real stuff, Gainsborough's Mary, Countess Howe literally looked down on us, beautiful, lightly tinged with eroticism but wholly untouchable.

Claude de Jongh's 'Old London Bridge' shows houses sandwiched together high over the arches but painted in such detail that it might be an assemblage of miniatures, some of them gruesome. Those traitors' heads on spikes for example. Before being impaled they were pickled in brine, like herrings and for the same reason. It prolonged their shelf life. But John Jacob was a bit impatient. He wanted to introduce me to his new mistress who, as they say nowadays, had been sharing house with him for the last two months.

Mrs Sandilands, a lady of uncertain years, sister and hostess to a fashionable eighteenth-century cicerone in Rome, posed for Pompeo Batoni who though he painted few women must have been fascinated, as John was, by her enigmatic expression. With her hand lightly touching her hair she is gazing to the right. A blue-stocking with something and perhaps somebody on her mind. Quite a small picture, a bust portrait as they call them at Christie's, but a lady to whom you feel you should incline your head respectfully as you pass her by, wondering always if she might have noticed you.

Evensong

We went back, up to his apartment and gazed out where the owner, William Murray, first Earl of Mansfield and Lord Chief Justice related how he had acquired sumptuous interiors and one of the finest prospects in London. With its Adam library and Adam swags on the exterior and the bridge at the end of the lake by Repton from whom John Nash had learnt a great deal, I recalled my talks with Sir John Summerson. In spirit I had gone back in time.

John unlocked one of the heavily barred doors. We shook hands in the garden where honeysuckle filled the air. Owls called from Kenwood. I walked out and as the evening opened the Morning Glory closed.